"This book addresses a critical niche in promoting the hope and truth of a biblical worldview to the process of research and practice in clinical counseling. Because everything exists within a worldview, and because research provides a necessary foundation for exploring, expressing, and treating concerns in counseling, applying a kingdom lens to this topic acknowledges the truth and purpose for cultivating a gospel mindset to our counseling process and practice."

Seth L. Scott, assistant dean of the School of Counseling at Columbia International University

"This book is a gift to students who feel intimidated by research. With warmth, theological depth, and psychological insight, Kristen Kansiewicz and Paul Loosemore reframe research as an act of curiosity rooted in faith. Rather than a technical hurdle, research becomes a spiritual journey—one that honors the image of God in each of us and invites us to play in the sandbox of discovery. Students are encouraged to engage their spiritual, emotional, and intellectual selves in the service of loving God and neighbor. This text offers companionship for students learning to do research as worship."

Jennifer Ripley, professor and endowed chair of Christian integration at Regent University

"Kristen Kansiewicz and Paul Loosemore have done an excellent job capturing the heart of research, offering insights that resonate with both graduate students and anyone curious about the topic. Their approachable style makes complex ideas accessible, encouraging individuals to engage academically and spiritually. This book is a must-have for graduate programs, especially those focused on Christian integration, as it helps students see research not just as an academic task but as an act of faith and service."

Chase C. McKinney, assistant professor of clinical mental health counseling at Huntington University

"Given the nature of their subject matter, most books on research are as dry as dust and as boring as a math formula. But not this book! Its style is far more personal and literary than we've come to expect in the genre, as the authors use personal testimony, stories, and metaphors to engage the reader. Throughout, research has been chosen to illustrate points that would have special interest to Christian students, for example, flourishing, meaningfulness, virtue, and one's relationship with God. The authors, I think, persuasively demonstrate that research can be personally rewarding and objectively important. There is simply no book like it, and I suspect that Christian professors of research courses will be very happy to discover this new option for a textbook."

Eric L. Johnson, director of training at the Christian Psychology Institute

"Kristen Kansiewicz and Paul Loosemore invite us to approach research with fresh imagination. Their approach engenders curiosity and interest in research and is supported with biblical wisdom and faithfulness. A great companion volume for faith-based research classes."

Jeremy Ruckstaetter, associate professor of counseling and director of the counseling department and counseling center at Covenant Theological Seminary

Engaging in Counseling Research *with* Curiosity *and* Wisdom

A CHRISTIAN INTEGRATIVE APPROACH

Kristen Kansiewicz *and* Paul Loosemore

An imprint of InterVarsity Press
Downers Grove, Illinois

InterVarsity Press
P.O. Box 1400 | Downers Grove, IL 60515-1426
ivpress.com | email@ivpress.com

©2026 by Kristen Michelle Kansiewicz and Paul William Loosemore

All rights reserved. No part of this book may be reproduced in any form without written permission from InterVarsity Press.

InterVarsity Press® is the publishing division of InterVarsity Christian Fellowship/USA®. For more information, visit intervarsity.org.

Scripture quotations, unless otherwise noted, are from The Holy Bible, English Standard Version. ESV© Text Edition: 2016. Copyright © 2001 by Crossway Bibles, a publishing ministry of Good News Publishers. Used by permission. All rights reserved.

While any stories in this book are true, some names and identifying information may have been changed to protect the privacy of individuals.

Figure 4.1. Barna survey of pastors. *Source*: "New Data Shows Hopeful Increases in Pastors' Confidence & Satisfaction," Barna Group, March 6, 2024, www.barna.com/research/hopeful-increases-pastors/. Used by permission.

Journal entry by Brian Fidler, PhD, LPC, 2019. Used by permission.

The publisher cannot verify the accuracy or functionality of website URLs used in this book beyond the date of publication.

Cover design: Faceout Studio, Spencer Fuller
Interior design: Daniel van Loon
Images: Getty Images: © olaser / E+; © filo / DigitalVision Vectors

ISBN 978-1-5140-1202-4 (print) | ISBN 978-1-5140-1203-1 (digital)

Printed in the United States of America ∞

Library of Congress Cataloging-in-Publication Data
A catalog record for this book is available from the Library of Congress.

To our students and readers:

May a love of research expand your sense of self and bring joy to your spiritual journey.

Contents

Introduction 1

1 The Heart of a Researcher 9

2 Moving from Curiosity to Truth 37

3 Honoring Diversity in the Kingdom 75

4 Measuring God's World 115

5 Sitting with Stories and Meaning-Making 159

6 Applying Research Through Wise Clinical Practice 204

Index 245

Introduction

THIS BOOK WAS A LABOR OF LOVE that reflects our passion for social sciences research. We are both licensed counselors by training, and we each hold a PhD in counselor education and supervision. We write to both a narrow audience of counseling students in CACREP-accredited programs and a wider audience of students and professors within social science programs. This book was designed to assist students as a secondary textbook in undergraduate psychology research courses, master's-level counseling research courses, or doctoral-level dissertation or research courses within helping-profession programs. This volume will not replace the primary textbooks that teach foundational course content, but it will enrich the learning researcher's experience and preparation by inspiring an enlivened approach to these courses.[1]

We will often default to the use of the word *counselor* as we describe the developing researcher, yet we also use psychology-related language and the terms "mental health provider" or "mental health clinician" (particularly in chap. 6, which describes clinical practice within counseling-related fields). There may be some of you whom we do not directly address—those in sociology,

---

[1] Examples of primary textbooks for counseling programs include Richard Balkin and David Kleist's *Counseling Research: A Practitioner-Scholar Approach* (American Counseling Association, 2022), and Richard Parsons, Eric Owens, and Cheryl Neale-McFall's *The Counselor as Practitioner-Researcher: A Practical Guide to Research Methods* (Cognella Academic, 2020). We both typically adopt the former for the research courses we teach.

anthropology, ministry, education, or other fields. We are confident that the interplay of faith and research is relevant to anyone who is intrigued by our title. May you find yourself within these pages and extract application to your calling.

We hope this text might begin an awakening of sorts—a reconnection with your inner child. Each of us begins life with an innate curiosity, as if we were natural-born researchers at heart. For many of us, formal education gradually strips away this way of engaging with the world as we are called on to memorize facts and figures rather than dig in the dirt just for the fun of it. What was once equivalent to play becomes work—a direct result of the entrance of sin into the world that we read about in Genesis 3. We'll expand on this theme in chapter one. We believe that God's design is for us to be explorers, filled with awe as we uncover God's truths all around. We'll talk more in chapter two about the discovery of truth versus the creation of truth, but we believe both are inherent in the research process. Yes, we were made to discover truth, and we were created to create as we reflect the image of God.

Those entering mental health professions may not see themselves as natural researchers because the word *research* (and the anxiety it can bring) often has been connected to interests in math or hard sciences. We would argue that those in counseling and psychology (and related disciplines) are regularly engaged in research as they sit across from others, curious about who they are and what makes them tick. The mandates of our profession, such as cultural humility and maintaining a nonjudgmental stance, are very useful for researchers. Throughout this text we encourage you to lean in to all the parts of you that are perfectly prepared for the process of research.

We chose to write this book because we have been in your shoes. Both of us now have a passion for conducting and teaching research, and we will share some of the stories that have led us into this passion. You'll find sidebars throughout the book that will give you an inside look at our process of development, from our childhood experiences of exploration, to our dissertation writing, and much in between and since. By means of introduction, let us share with you how we authors truly see ourselves: as fellow classmates.

Although we are now doctoral graduates and faculty members, we met in our doctoral program in counselor education and completed a group project in a first-semester course: Quantitative Research Methods. We were handed a data set by our professor and let loose—but we had no idea what we were doing! Just to give you an indication of how incredibly cool we were, we named ourselves "The Supreme Team." Our abstract must have had a 250-word limit because it was precisely 249 words, and on our first page of content we used "Introduction" as a heading (which APA style strictly forbids). Our literature review was long and fairly terrible, and our tables were unclear and nowhere close to APA format. As I (Kristen) write this and comb through our old files, I smile at the fact that the best part of the project was Paul's notes for the discussion section. His making sense of the data is inspirational even now—and it is just one of many examples of how we have made mistakes together, learned from each other, and come out stronger.

In the remaining years of our doctoral program, we chose to be in the same working group on every single project. The book in your hands now is no exception. Our experiences together illustrate two key lessons on the journey toward completing a research class and becoming a researcher: Don't research alone; find your people. So much of the research process is shaped and strengthened by others. If you attempt to conduct research by yourself, you will inevitably miss valuable insights that others could have noticed.

Your singular viewpoint is not adequate for thorough exploration. And because research happens best in community, it is important to find peers and mentors who inspire you, drive you, correct you, and complement you. If you have a group project for the course you are in right now, consider which classmates might be your best companions in your journey to become a researcher.

Let's walk through what you can expect from this book. Chapter one begins with a dive into the themes of curiosity and flourishing as well as connecting to biblical concepts of order and disorder. We explore the kingdom of God and the world he established in creation, noting in more depth how we are the *imago Dei* (imagers of God) and exploring the impact of the fall on our engagement with the world as work versus play. In this view of research as play, we take a walk through a garden of shalom that creates an environment in which we can flourish as researchers.

After introducing these concepts, we discuss the integration of the personal, professional, and spiritual selves and the relational nature of research. If God has created us to be curious explorers, how can we pull together all the pieces of ourselves to provide an impetus for a robust research agenda? We talk about honoring the Father, imitating the Son, and partnering with the Holy Spirit in the research process as a means of loving our neighbors. Might God invite us to collaborate with him on bringing new knowledge into the world? We will ask readers to consider what *you* want to know and offer discussion questions and learning activities for use in the classroom.

In chapter two we tackle the thorny issue of *how we know things*. We provide you with a rich framework for seeing truth as a part of God's good gift to us and invite you to partake in discovery. We explore how neuroscience facilitates our learning and how social contexts organize our understanding of the world and the questions we ask. We then help you reconcile how ordered, controlled, and statistical learning sits alongside emerging, constructed, and interpreted meaning-making.

Chapter three prepares the reader and researcher to see human and cultural diversity as a part of God's beautiful design and to see how a Christian view of research creates an ethical mandate to honor this diversity. We grapple with the effects of sin on our individual hearts, our cultural contexts, and the professional process. We offer a call to personal, cultural, and professional humility to help readers continue developing in their identity as researchers who are heirs of a wonderful and diverse kingdom. We lay out a practical map for curious, joyful, and humble research that ethically accounts for the person of the researcher amid the influence of cultural pressure. Our hope is to help you expand your vision for the needs and well-being of all people and to provide you tools to develop exciting research as a result.

Chapter four pairs with the quantitative and statistical portions of the research course. Because the primary textbook will teach the details, we will not repeat them here. Rather, we help readers identify and cope with feelings of boredom or anxiety that might arise as they enter the math phase of their learning. We will guide you through some inner work that can help you reengage in logical and mathematical thinking. For those who are enthusiastic about quantitative concepts, we describe the fascinating journey of uncovering these parts of self and how to nurture this with supplemental research challenges beyond the average student.

The meat of the chapter talks through each type of basic statistical analysis (descriptive statistics, correlation, between-group comparisons, within-group designs, and regression/prediction) and connects each in turn with God's established systems of order. We describe each of these categories as a unique pathway to the answers we seek. For each we provide biblical examples and demonstrate its clinical relevance.

Chapter five illuminates how qualitative research is a rich relational collaboration that honors the sacred space of personal disclosure. We consider qualitative research within the Christian imaginary and demonstrate how this way of thinking makes a difference to our approach. We move on to explore how Jesus demonstrated mature virtues and used careful questions to understand and bless those around him. Then we consider how the different schools of qualitative inquiry have sought meaning, and we consider practical research examples alongside biblical examples. We also help the reader understand how meaning-making is a product of synthesizing new discoveries and show how this was done historically and Christianly using oral traditions. The biblical, clinical, and research examples are intended to illuminate the clinical impact of qualitative research.

In our final chapter, we weave together the themes of the book, including curiosity, flourishing, engaging with truth, diversity, quantifying, and making-meaning, and applying them through wise clinical practice. We will explore the biblical concept of wisdom as a unifying thread and explore wisdom as an application of knowledge that is congruent with the kingdom of God. We use this framework to understand how ideas affect our work when we are sitting across from another human being trying to help them on a healing journey. Returning full circle to the ideas of chapter one, we will look at the character, virtue, and whole self of the counselor who seeks to use evidence-based practices. We will conclude by highlighting examples of well-researched integrative practices and point to additional resources in which future clinicians can find quality research.

A NOTE TO PROFESSORS AND INSTRUCTORS

Professors and instructors, a special note for you: Through whatever processes that exist in your context, you find yourself assigned to teach a research course for your students. Whether you volunteered for that job or simply drew the shortest straw, you are on our minds as we write this text. While we don't want to presume that you dread research, neither do we presume that you love it or feel confident teaching it. You've most certainly selected or been handed a primary textbook to teach your students the subject matter, and in one way or another that will be accomplished to some degree. Our hope is that this text may accompany you and your students on the journey of your course to bring the passion and zeal that can turn the class into a well-loved experience for you and your students. We hope you find yourself somewhere in these pages and that you feel excited about new ideas for teaching and engaging with research. Both of us authors are research enthusiasts, and we've both been told that we are unusual in this regard (and perhaps in other ways as well . . .). We will freely give our pedagogical ideas to you in each chapter so that you have both discussion questions and hands-on teaching activities.

If you are curious how we plan to incorporate this book into the research courses we teach, we offer the following insights for your consideration. Our syllabi front-load much of the reading since research projects will consume more of the second half of the course. For a fifteen-week semester, we suggest assigning the introduction and the first chapter in week one, followed by chapter two in the second week and chapter three in week three. These chapters align with the standard textbook material that introduces the concepts of research and ethics. By week four, you will likely begin to dive into quantitative research concepts, which pairs well with our fourth chapter. This chapter could be broken into chunks and assigned across multiple weeks. In the courses we teach, we arrive at qualitative research around week nine, which is when we recommend assigning chapter five. The final chapter could be assigned anytime between weeks twelve and fifteen depending on how you conclude your course. In a more compact seven-week course, students can read chapters one and two in the first week, three and four in the second week, and then five and six as determined by the remainder of your course progression (possibly in weeks four and six).

A final note: Our discussion questions at the end of each chapter can be used as in-class conversation starters for seated classes or turned into discussion boards for online courses. Your context and content may vary, but we have tried to make this textbook as user-friendly as possible for both you and the student reader.

ONE

The Heart *of a* Researcher

BEFORE WE CAN BEGIN OUR JOURNEY together as fellow researchers, we must first pause and examine God and ourselves. Think of it as checking to be sure your water bottle is filled and your emergency food supplies are packed before starting up an advanced hiking trail. Perhaps, like good researchers, we start with questions: Who is God, and who are we as humans? How might our relationship with God influence our approach to research? What is God's intention for you even in this first step of your research path? While parts of ourselves may feel trepidation about a research course, other parts may be excited or at least curious. Leaning into both of those internal places is a wonderful way to explore further questions. In this chapter, we are going to tap into that God-given curiosity and discover what it might mean to flourish as a part of God's design for us. We'll explore the various parts of self and the relational way that a strong attachment to God sets us up to do good research. By the end of the chapter, we hope you will feel freshly inspired to let your curiosity run wild and connect with God in the process.

CURIOSITY: A LONGING TO KNOW

Let us start with the beautiful Christian reality that we were created in the image of God: *imago Dei*. We are set apart from every other living thing on the earth in this way. What we see in the end of

Genesis 1 through the beginning of Genesis 2, as we read about being created in the image of God, will frame our approach in this book. First, God is a Creator. An innovator. He comes up with an idea (framed as a group conversation, reflecting God's complex relationship within himself) to make humans "in our image, after our likeness" (Gen 1:26). Second, he commands humans to "fill the earth and subdue it" (Gen 1:28), and he gives us a pretty extensive starter pack of supplies (Gen 1:29-30). If we are created beings who have an inborn inclination toward God's way of being, and he is an innovator, then it seems only logical that we would be natural innovators. Unlike God, however, we are not all-knowing and all-powerful. Thus, our innovation doesn't stem from a place exclusively within ourselves. While the scientific community may aim to arrive at the capacity to form life from nothing, so far we have failed to recreate this basic starting place of God. And even if we were to accomplish such a creative act, it would be merely a copycat effort at best. As created beings with a penchant for innovation, yet without God's unlimited knowledge and power, we have a different starting point for innovation: curiosity.

Imagine being handed a world filled with interesting things, some living and others nonliving, and being told to govern it. Perhaps this is not unlike setting a child in a sandbox with a pail and shovel, some trucks, a few figurines, a hose, and freedom to play. Any parent of a toddler who wishes to keep their house tidy would likely agree this seems like a messy prospect, but God is a daring parent who doesn't need everything to stay neat and clean. He wants us to play, build, and get our hands dirty along the way. Genesis 3:17-19 suggests that with the curse on the world came a resistance to our enjoyment of messy, exploratory play. Our minds matured with age and became jaded with a knowledge of evil, and mess became work. A world that was once a playground became a labor camp as we moved from free children to adult prisoners. From order to disorder.

What would happen if we were to pair redemption with the research process? What if we imagine engaging in God's design for us and reverse-engineer the process? While perhaps not fully possible within the clutches of a fallen world, in Christ we have an opportunity to live closer to our intended state. What if research helps return us to the very first state of play to which God invited us? What if fear or frustration or boredom didn't govern the research process? What might that look like?

Place yourself back in Genesis 1–2. Or perhaps envision yourself as that kid in the sandbox. You've been told to play, and freedom is all you have ever known. Imagine that you don't feel limited by the confines of the sandbox because you trust your parent, who told you to govern just that area. Your secure attachment to God allows you to be both fully curious and fully creative. What types of worlds might you build? Like a toddler, your free play is intermittently paused to reconnect with your parent. This is a reminder of your security to run off and play again.

In this framework, the freedom of exploration and innovation driven by curiosity is rooted in your sense of security in God. As such, a critical practice for Christians engaged in the research process is developing our relationship with God and pausing to reconnect with him. Genesis 3 and the rest of the Bible remind us that, if we explore and innovate without him, we are likely to wander from the sandbox. We may feel lost or fearful, or forget the excitement of the original command to govern the world with an incredible box of tools. Like children, we need periodic attachment moments to our Creator Father. Just a touchpoint that allows him to say, "I'm still here," and for us to feel the comfort and freedom of that reality once again.

Drawing Close to God: A Meditation for Researchers

We encourage you to record yourself reading this meditation slowly. After doing so, you can close your eyes and listen to your own voice praying these words. Take time to regularly connect your researcher heart with the Creator God.

The Prayer of the Researcher

Almighty God, Maker of heaven and earth, I humbly sit at your feet. Thank you for your goodness and your creativity. I long to know more about you and your world. What would you have me search for in this season of my life? I ask you to urge me toward your concerns for the world. Give me the courage to look under every rock that interests me, even when it feels heavy or scary to explore. Bring me peace when I sit in unsettled places. Give me joy when I get consumed or distracted. It is a joy to delight in your presence and explore your wonders. Thank you for all you have made.

God's Words to the Researcher (adapted from Is 40:28; 43:1-2; 2 Pet 3:9 NIV)

Do you not know? Have you not heard? The LORD is the everlasting God, the Creator of the ends of the earth. He will not grow tired or weary, and his understanding no one can fathom.

But now, this is what the LORD says—he who created you, Jacob, he who formed you, Israel: "Do not fear, for I have redeemed you; I have summoned you by name; you are mine. When you pass through the waters, I will be with you; and when you pass through the rivers, they will not sweep over you. When you walk through the fire, you will not be burned; the flames will not set you ablaze.

"I am not slow in keeping my promise, as some understand slowness. Instead, I am patient with you."

We were not designed to explore, innovate, and govern the world in God's absence. He did not set the world in motion and simply hand over the keys. He walked in the garden where man and woman were tilling the soil as their act of play and freedom. He made himself known to them and does so to us today. He created us to search for him, to imitate him, and to maintain a curiosity that would lead us into even deeper exploration, a never-ending venture into him and his community. Later in this chapter we will explore ways in which research is relational, but here we invite you to consider that the heart of the redeemed researcher is driven by a God-given and God-sustained curiosity.

FLOURISHING: THRIVING AS GOD INTENDED

God invites us to enter a place of shalom with him—bringing peace, wellness, and life to the research process. Shalom can be defined as "universal flourishing, wholeness, and delight."[1] If curiosity is the seed for research, and God is the soil in whom we are planted, what would it take for us to thrive in this garden of shalom as researchers? How might we flourish and blossom in this process of researcher development, from novice to seasoned explorer? The Harvard University Human Flourishing Program's "Flourish Measure" picks up on biblical anthropology (what is true about people) to share five domains that may be helpful for us to consider as we explore these questions: happiness and life satisfaction, mental and physical health, meaning and purpose, character and virtue, and close social relationships.[2] We will take each of these domains in turn, looking at how we might operate in each to flourish in the research process, then return to the analogy of a garden to draw our thoughts together.

Happiness and life satisfaction. Perhaps starting with happiness and life satisfaction doesn't feel fair if you are in a research course and have some daunting assignments ahead. You might imagine

---

[1]Cornelius Plantinga Jr., *Not the Way It's Supposed to Be: A Breviary of Sin* (Eerdmans, 1995), 10.
[2]D. Węziak-Białowolska, E. McNeely, and T. J. VanderWeele, "Human Flourishing in Cross Cultural Settings: Evidence from the US, China, Sri Lanka, Cambodia and Mexico," *Frontiers in Psychology* 10 (2019): 1-13, https://doi.org/10.3389/fpsyg.2019.01269.

happiness as being free of worry and full of only feelings of enjoyment, and perhaps *life satisfaction* as less struggle and more easy wins. We would argue that both happiness and life satisfaction are byproducts of growth and challenge. Accomplishing things and living the life we were designed for leads to feelings of happiness and satisfaction. However, this process does not have to feel unenjoyable. If you have a white-knuckling approach to your course, this is hardly a picture of flourishing.

We invite you here to ask, Does it have to feel hard? Is that the only approach? What if God wants you to flourish and thrive in every area of your life, including in your research methods class, in taking on a dissertation, or in submitting an article to yet another publisher who might reject your work? Let's return to the idea of work versus play. Approaching research as hard work is likely to feel—well, hard. We get lost in the mundane or confusing task and lose sight of the end goal of knowing something we didn't know before. In contrast, when we approach research as play, there is a mental switch that frees us up to simply enjoy ourselves. If you have ever hiked to the top of a mountain to gaze on a beautiful vista, you might be able to imagine what we are driving at here. It is both fun and difficult to hike to the top of a mountain. And those who do not attempt the climb do not experience the happiness and satisfaction that comes with looking out from the apex.

When thinking about research as play, there are developmental aspects to consider—just as there are when thinking about real-life play. Have you ever tried playing Monopoly with a five-year-old? Unless you just want a free-association experience and paper bills scattered around the room, you're better off trying Candy Land. Play is only play if you are at the developmental stage to understand and enjoy what you are doing. Similarly, when you try to tackle the results section of a research article in the early weeks of an undergraduate or master's-level research methods course, it will not feel like play. Very little happiness or life satisfaction comes from that experience. Ask yourself, What is my developmental phase as a researcher? Respond to this. It might be appropriate to just read an article's abstract and the discussion section to start. Choose an article with a title that sounds intriguing, or if you are not able to select the article yourself, try to connect with the reason it might have been assigned to you. Why this article? Why this topic?

To dive in further, grab a highlighter and mark any words you do not understand in the abstract or discussion sections. Ask your instructor to explain these words. Most likely, you'll be able to grab onto most of the discussion section, where you will read about the implications of the study. What do the findings of this article contribute to the world? What future research needs to be done? What ideas come to your mind that stimulate curiosity and excitement? Consider keeping a research journal in which you can write down these ideas. If you were going to do one of the future studies suggested by the article, what might it look like? (It's OK to imagine your name in lights as the genius researcher whose big breakthrough led to a revolutionary new mental health treatment, even though that's a bit like dreaming of being an astronaut one day . . .).

Notice that in this process you are engaging your mind and stimulating your curiosity once again. When our brains shut down and our eyes glaze over, research can be very boring to read. But a play mindset requires us to dive in, with pen, notebook, and highlighter in hand. These are our gardening tools as we dig and nurture the seed of curiosity in our God-soil. As you progress into later stages of researcher development, you can do this even when reading through paragraphs of statistics. Most of our students are surprised to find that they are able to engage the tougher sections of an article by the end of the research course. The first time that light bulb goes off and you recognize a good value for Cronbach's alpha or a correlation coefficient, happiness sparks, and maybe even a little life satisfaction occurs.

Mental and physical health. The second domain of flourishing is mental and physical health. Perhaps this is analogous to the sunshine and rain needed for our research garden. Much of this self-care domain will happen outside the research classroom as you sip a cup of tea, hike in the woods, or spend time cultivating your relationship with God. These practices enhance our work as researchers because they stimulate our brains and get our creativity flowing. This morning I (Kristen) knew I was heading into a day of working on this book, and my time was going to be shorter than I wanted. Even with that sense of urgency, I decided to take a brief visit to a nearby lake to go kayaking (my favorite form of self-care). Paddling along gave me an opportunity to think about flourishing, which gave me energy and inspiration to sit and write. Had I come to the computer one hour earlier and skipped kayaking, finding each word and idea would have been an incoherent struggle.

We'll be talking about researching with your whole self in the next section of this chapter, but for now it's important to note that we flourish best as researchers when we treat our inner researcher—our curious self—as an integral part of ourselves rather than as a hat we take off when we leave our class assignments or research projects. When you are taking that walk on a sun-filled day, you are not just checking off a self-care box. You are taking your researcher-heart into a new experience during which you can *notice*. Perhaps take time to notice which flowers are in bloom or what the wind feels like moving across your face. Consider asking yourself why the road turns in a specific direction and how it met a specific need. A simple cup of tea might lead us to wonder where those particular tea leaves were grown, how the plants are cultivated, and how tea has changed cultures over thousands of years. Who drank the first cup of tea, with whom, and what did this mean to them?

Other aspects of our mental and physical health must be nurtured to aid the process of research. It might sound obvious, but getting enough sleep, for example, enables our minds to stay awake and engaged when digging through a challenging article. Scheduling and time management are essential for getting our research tasks done without feeling frantic or rushed. We need to pace ourselves as researchers, taking one bite at a time and learning to chew slowly. If you look at the entire syllabus of your research course or think about all the work ahead of you for a dissertation, it's about as pleasant as shoving an entire steak into your mouth at once. You just can't chew it, no matter how juicy and tender it could have been one bite at a time. Bring yourself back to today: What is the one bite I can chew on and digest right now?

Any given project or study may take a lot longer than expected, or you may hit bumps along the way. At times, research can certainly feel like two steps forward and one step back. What coping strategies do you already use that might contribute to flourishing when the learning and research process doesn't feel easy? What stories will you tell about yourself as a researcher or the quality of your project? Internal messages such as *This is so tedious* or *No one will ever even read this anyway* discourage you, squash your inner researcher, and take you right back to research as work. If we are playing in the garden and feeding our souls with sunshine and water, we need to encourage ourselves with thoughts such as *This hard challenge is stretching me in some good directions* or *How might God be shaping and blessing me through this struggle?* Of course, a touchpoint back to your God-attachment is essential here as well. Sitting with him and sharing the moments of joy and struggle allows him to care for you throughout the research process.

Meaning and purpose. Meaning and purpose, the third domain of flourishing, represent the fertilizer worked into the soil to allow our research garden to grow beyond what only water and sunshine can produce. The difference between fertilized and unfertilized soil is the balance of nutrients that can be absorbed by the plant's roots. When we lack meaning and purpose on our research journey, it is easy to wither and wilt. A famous book by Simon Sinek called *Find Your Why* gets at the idea that meaning drives purpose. Sinek's book echoes the biblical truth that we flounder without a solid sense of what we are about. We can set goals and take steps to achieve them, but if we lose sight of why we headed that direction in the first place, we are likely to give up.

Perhaps this moment is a good time in which to pause and ask why you are reading this book. Chances are you have enrolled in a research course, or perhaps you are further along in the researcher developmental process and wanted to reconnect with your sense of purpose. What is your purpose for engaging in research? Before you mentally respond with *Because I have to*, let's ask in a different way: What meaning can drive research in your life? What fruit will you be able to bear that is not currently available in your life? What *aha* moments might you experience that could lead you to a deeper love of God or dependence on him? What other purpose could the research process serve in your life, both now and in the long term?

So far our exploration of meaning-making and research has focused on you as an individual. What can *I* gain from the research process? We must also think collectively about the greater purposes of our work as researchers and hold this as a guide throughout the research process. Returning to Genesis 1, when God commanded humanity to "be fruitful and multiply," he also said, "Fill the earth and subdue it" (Gen 1:28). Many dictionaries offer definitions of *subdue* that include "bring under control." God spoke a direct purpose and authority over all humanity from the very beginning as part of our identity as his image-bearers. If bringing order to the world is an integral part of who we are, then how are we to do that in an ongoing way without continual assessment of our world? Research is the process by which we understand what is in the world. These insights lead to strategies for ordering and subduing the earth.

Thus, when you engage in research you are connecting with a larger, collective purpose that is God-given. You are responding to the call to operate from a position of authority. (A side note: it is interesting that when a researcher becomes an expert, they are often referred to as an *authority* on their subject.) Bringing us back to your individual part in that bigger picture, when you answer God's call to research you can ask yourself, Where do I want to bring order to the world? Another way to explore your piece of the puzzle may be, What disorder in the world bothers me too much to let go of? The answers to these questions can be the start of your research agenda.

Character and virtue. Let's move into our fourth domain, character and virtue. What does it mean to develop as a researcher who nurtures a heart of character and virtue? Certainly, we want to uphold ethical principles of research, and these are not to be taken lightly. Research ethics protect us from corruption, both of the data and of ourselves. We'll explore these themes in more depth later. But the larger questions you must ask yourself are these: Who will I show myself to be as a researcher? As a counselor? Will the research questions I seek to explore and the way in which I conduct my research be driven by a character and virtue that reflects Christ?

Here we might imagine the Holy Spirit as the gardener in our research garden. He is a protector, a guide, a colaborer. As in

John 15, he prunes away the dead branches and serves as the source of life by which branches can grow. As we abide in the Spirit and he produces fruit in our lives, these changes will be seen in the contours of our research endeavors. Galatians 5 describes this garden fruit, highlighting the character and virtue of the Spirit. What crops are part of the Spirit's garden of shalom? Love, joy, peace, patience, kindness, goodness, faithfulness, gentleness, and self-control. This list provides a bouquet of the character and virtues that lead to flourishing, so let's pause to consider each.

Where does love blossom in your researcher heart as you move in authority over the earth? What types of research questions might you ask with love at the core of your curiosity? If you undertook the research process, or even the research course itself, with joy, what would that look like? Perhaps the squeal of delight of a child who has discovered a new type of creature in his backyard? *Look at this new thing! Can I keep it??* Imagine the fullness of joy at the next classroom show-and-tell. Might a conference poster session match this bubbling-over experience?

Consider peace. Shalom itself. In *Embodying Integration*, Megan Anna Neff and Mark McMinn write, "Our primary work as counselors . . . is to relax into the peaceful posture of rest known only to those who are deeply loved."[3] As counselor-researchers, peace is inherent to our posture toward the world. When we are comfortable in our own skin, rooted in a deep and secure attachment to God, we can enter the sacred space of helping others in a new way. We are not just keepers of peace but sharers. In much the same way, the peace-filled research process is one in which we are not seeking to posture or make a name for ourselves. We are deliberately and calmly moving through the work of exploration. We can

---

[3]Megan Anna Neff and Mark McMinn, *Embodying Integration: A Fresh Look at Christianity in the Therapy Room* (InterVarsity Press, 2020), 209.

follow one step and then another to see where the data lead us. Even when research deadlines loom or assignments are due, we have the opportunity through our rest in the Spirit to remain in a place of peace. This peace is not a feeling, although it may assist us in feeling calm. Rather, it is a posture gradually learned by those whose trust is actively in God. We return to him for our security. We are attached. As a result, it is in God's delight that we dwell as we engage in our research-play.

Research and patience go hand in hand. I (Kristen) remember when I first learned that a research study could take a year to conduct. I can now attest that from conception of an idea to publication in a journal, it is significantly longer than that. Each article you read was years in the making and took incredible patience in the heart of the researcher. (Not to mention this labor of love is typically unpaid.) What a testament to God's goodness and our formation by the Spirit when our research process is marked by peaceful, unhurried appreciation rather than the ideals of productivity. Rushing the research process leads to sloppy data and errors of all sorts. Ask the Spirit to grow your patience so it may help your research garden flourish.

What about the virtues of kindness and goodness? Do these accurately describe your way of being in life in general? As a researcher? What would it mean for kindness to envelop our engagement with members of our research teams or our participants? Might we find God himself expressed through us in these interactions? Are kindness and goodness byproducts of the results of our studies? When God saw his creation, he looked and said, "It is good." Does our research have such a depth of goodness that we can arrive at the end of a study and feel that same pride in our creation? Can we see that goodness as a reflection of God's image in us?

Next, imagine a life of faithfulness to the work of research, curiosity, and innovation set before you. Perhaps you sit at your retirement party and hear what others say about your life and the contributions you have made. Faithfulness as a lived virtue in the heart of the researcher empowers the commitment to see an exploration through to the end. It is a life of community rather than isolation, including mentoring and pouring into others. Faithfulness is a direct spiritual response to the calling God has placed on your life to explore and discover, to make meaning from what was unknown. Through the Spirit, the redeemed researcher has an opportunity to flourish in a life of faithful service to God and others.

Character and virtue were fully demonstrated by Jesus Christ in all these areas, but "gentle" is how he chooses to describe himself in Matthew 11:29. This description of his nature is included in his invitation into rest. To shalom. When the research brings weariness, the Spirit can minister to us in gentleness. We can align ourselves with him by agreeing with his gentleness for us. We do this by being gentle and compassionate as we still any inner voice of criticism or fear. In this way, we also practice self-control. In the mental health world, we might even conceptualize this as emotion regulation. As we exercise this virtue, we practice restraint and purposeful action in our research process. We step away for a time when we run into brick walls instead of barreling through. We pause. We listen. We hold tension. While the Spirit is at work forming our character and virtue for and through research, we flourish and become more expressive of our image of Christ.

Close social relationships. Now that we have taken time to smell the floral aroma of character and virtue, we arrive at the fifth domain of flourishing: close social relationships. Research is certainly not a solo sport. This reality was a challenge for me (Kristen) as I began my doctoral program. Over the course of my life, I had learned that my projects were generally better accomplished when I did the work myself. I can recall in elementary school being placed into project groups with the kids who were not motivated or hardworking. The teachers saw me as a student who could bring these others along. While this might have provided opportunities for leadership development, it did not instill in me a love for getting projects done with others. It was harder to carry the weight of the whole group than just to do a project by myself. Fortunately, meeting peers such as Paul taught me that my research and work is now made better with the help and perspectives of others. This book is just one example of the ways in which my own ideas are too limited without input and companionship. Research teams can create something that is organically alive and moving—a living organism that cannot exist except in the interactions of a flourishing group.

Aside from the work of any given project, researchers need close social relationships with their fellow researchers for inspiration and growth. In our garden metaphor, this idea is akin to companion planting. When tomatoes and basil, for example, are planted in proximity to each other in the garden, both flourish more than if they had been planted apart. Your colleagues who are planted around you—perhaps classmates, professors, or fellow members of professional organizations—can fuel your curiosity and creativity in the research process if you attend to these relationships. Notice the word *close* here—we are not simply talking about acquaintances with whom you have brief, surface-level interactions. These relationships develop over time, moving from classmate relationships, at which point we and others such as Henry Cloud and John Townsend began, and developing into those of colleagues, collaborators, and lifelong friends.

To flourish as a researcher, you must invest in these peers. When they ask you to read their paper or article, take the time to do so and offer genuine feedback. Get together monthly for check-ins on life and areas of curiosity. Repost the survey links of other researchers to help them along in the process of data collection. Share vulnerably about the challenges or doubts you have as a burgeoning researcher. Admit to your classmates (and your professor) when you don't understand part of an article. When working on a research team, share a reflexive journal in which you can write about your feelings and experiences in the research process. Take a look at the sidebar "Reflecting on the Research Process" for an example of a reflexive journal that we shared during a qualitative research project in our doctoral studies.

Reflecting on the Research Process

During our doctoral studies in 2019, we worked on a qualitative research project exploring how supervisors address values conflicts with counselors-in-training. Our team kept a reflexive journal, and here we share some of our entries with you, including one from our esteemed colleague Brian Fidler, PhD, LPC.

February 9—Kristen
What is a values conflict? For me, in the past it has felt issue-driven. My training in undergrad in integration (and really most of my comparison/contrast with biblical counseling) has felt very issue specific. I've changed a lot of my thinking over time on some issues. But what are the real value conflicts? Some of the issues . . . seem like issues until you are sitting across from a human being—it's not a debate but a person and a story. I've never had a values conflict in that moment. . . . Sitting in a session, what are the things that actually conflict with my Christian faith? I'll have to think more on that.

February 12—Paul
There is a tension for me in the overwhelming scope this project could have. I recognize a powerful bias or interpretive factor could be pushing for saturation and a theory when we do not have enough data because of the

fear that we will not find something substantive. I will need to reflect on this throughout the process and be held accountable through peer checking.

February 26—Kristen (after one participant interview was conducted prior to Human Subjects Review Committee approval)

We have a values conflict on our hands—seems fitting. Different members had different convictions about handling the HSRC process. I can see both sides—does it really matter? No. We'll get approved, and there is no actual difference between the before and the after. On the other side, in ethics, process matters. Considering yourself as the exception to the process is always dangerous. You don't know what you might not see. Also, what precedent are we setting as researchers? Imagine as a clinician if you started seeing clients before you had your intake paperwork established. Would you see someone without a consent to treatment in place? For how many sessions? That feels more risky than this situation, but what do I know about research and the risks we take on? (Not to mention that none of us are principal on this. . . . If I found out a student or supervisee took shortcuts on something with my name on it, I would be absolutely livid.)

We have the enthusiasm and the urge to drive forward with this research. We feel the time pressures. The process itself is flawed in the amount of time available versus the reality of scheduling interviews. How can we exercise patience in the midst of deadline pressures? How can we become better as researchers and as humans as a result of this values conflict?

What are some models that would help us resolve values conflicts as Christian researchers (individually and as a team)? Maybe we should be more directly open with [our professor] in person to tell him about what happened. Let him supervise us. See what he does. Be teachable in this moment.* The other thing is to notice the things within ourselves that make us squirm. Do I squirm about going outside the strict rules? Do I squirm about wasting time? What are my values, and what are they bumping into in this process? What is my reaction to my own inner squirm? Do I get mad, do I feel anxious, do I try to make everyone get along? I am big into team harmony, so my own squirm is people not getting along. I can go either way on the HSRC issue (although now that we have strict instructions that seems like a fairly giant lie to proceed with). But I think we have to be open, honest, and together as a team.

*A side note: this is the course of action we took, and the participant interview was thrown out.

February 27—Brian

I love group dynamics. It's a thrill to me to rub shoulders with people who are more gifted, smarter, more dynamic than me. It brings to light some of my deepest insecurities regarding inadequacy and insufficiency, and forces me to address them in light of our process. I love the chance to grow.

My weakness, though, is to defer when perhaps I shouldn't. At times, I can easily think someone else's idea may be better than mine, or the reasons for their process should be explored rather than overrun by my own. . . . I am learning to be more comfortable in that discomfort and to even make space for it. We're going to be asking supervisors to wade around in that moment of tension and to engage it with us. Perhaps it's only fair that as researchers we are willing to wade into those waters ourselves, engage our own space. I'm grateful for our team that we can do that. And I appreciate that I am learning to trust—trust my teammates, trust the process, trust my intuition and expertise.

We would be remiss not to discuss the close social relationships that extend beyond your formal research colleagues. Certainly people with more close friendships flourish more than those who operate in isolation and loneliness. Since we are considering research as play rather than work, we might think of anyone with whom you have a close relationship as a fellow explorer. Within the confines of a research classroom or project, you operate on a research team and pursue answers to research questions via data collection and analysis. But your parents, siblings, spouse, children, family, and friends are just as much a part of your lifelong pursuit of what is true. As we have suggested, the heart of the researcher does not turn on and off when conducting research versus living your personal life. Rather, your participation in the grand process of subduing the earth occurs every day in ordinary spaces with people who share your life. What quests have you shared with the people in your life? What order have you brought to God's creation with each other, and what areas of disorder might you hope to conquer next? To flourish with the heart of a researcher, you cannot go it alone.

RESEARCHING WITH YOUR WHOLE SELF

Now that we have built the foundation of how to flourish and live out this innate curiosity that God has given each of us, let's imagine what it might look like to integrate being a researcher into your identity. Could every part of you be fully activated and engaged so that you view yourself as an explorer on a mission? That unabashed kid in the sandbox? In Mark 12:30 Jesus tells us to love God with all our heart, soul, mind, and strength, with every part of who we are. Later in John 14:15, Jesus says, "If you love me, you will keep my commandments." Regarding research, by bringing every part of ourselves to the process of ordering and subduing the earth, we are enacting a robust love for God and keeping his command to humanity.

There are many ways to talk about parts of self. Heart, soul, mind, strength, as we've just mentioned. We might also consider Sigmund Freud's id, ego, superego or Richard Schwartz's exiles, firefighters, managers, and core self.[4] Marsha Linehan also gave us the concept of the "wise mind," in which our emotional and rational selves come together to help us make wise decisions.[5] Here we will follow a biblical understanding of personhood but use some words from our psychological heritage to help express ourselves. We will

---

[4]Sigmund Freud, "The Ego and the Id," in *The Standard Edition of the Complete Psychological Works of Sigmund Freud*, trans. J. Strachey et al., vol. 19 (Hogarth, 1923); Richard C. Schwartz and Martha Sweezy, *Internal Family Systems Therapy*, 2nd ed. (Guilford, 2020).
[5]Marsha M. Linehan, *Cognitive-Behavioral Treatment of Borderline Personality Disorder* (Guilford, 1993).

conceptualize our spiritual self (which we will refer to as the soul), our inner child, and our professional mind as they all work together to make up our researcher selves.

We begin with the soul, the seat of our identity, because whether we acknowledge this truth or not, we have been created as spiritual beings. Our identity is as *souled* persons. Sometimes we falsely dichotomize the spiritual and the physical, sawing ourselves in two as if we could shape-shift or turn off a switch. In the nature of our being, we are spiritually connected to an eternal and supernatural reality defined outside ourselves by our Creator God. Our whole being engages in the purposes of humanity, given to us by God, as we have already discussed, and the soul is what houses our researcher identity in an eternal kingdom. We live out a purpose that has ramifications far beyond what may be published in a journal. Our soul—our spiritual reality and identity—is fed by the Spirit. The Spirit anchors us, illuminating and growing the meaning/purpose and character/virtue domains of our flourishing.

As we acknowledge the centrality of our relationship with God, we invite you to attend to your relationship with him. You can follow the prayerful meditation shown in the sidebar "Drawing Close to God." Mindfully and purposefully offer yourself to your source of love, curiosity, and knowledge. Pray and ask him directly about your piece in his command to order the world. Invite him to reveal to you what he might have for you in this season of life as a researcher. Keep a journal by your side and consider writing your prayer to God along with anything that occurs to you in response.

As you sit in self- and God-awareness, are there any parts of you that feel held back from God? Any parts of you that are critical to a researcher identity and practice that are guarded, doubtful, or anxious? Much like Schwartz's exiles or Carl Jung's inner child, these parts of ourselves are directly connected to the process of research. Again, we invite you to revisit your childhood memories—what were your natural inclinations toward curiosity? What events chipped away at this curious play and made research turn into work? What happened that formed scared parts of you?

We recognize that every child is different. Some are more like daring inventors, and their curiosity leads them to try things. The Wright brothers, for example, were activating their inner-child selves when they first ran off the side of a sand dune in a homemade plane. Curiosity, trying and failing, innovating and building the world are what some of our inner children do. Others are more natural observers. Jane Goodall comes to mind, as her work in understanding the chimpanzee required a quietness of spirit that some researchers bring to the world. What type of child were you, and where does that show up for you now in your current developmental stage? Could that child be set free even in the midst of uncertainty or researcher impostor syndrome?

Finally, we consider our professional mind. Whether a student or graduate, if you are reading this book you have some connection to a desire to embark on a professional career as a counselor, helper, or researcher of some kind. This part of self might connect with Schwartz's managers, who keep all the ducks in a row and the outward appearance in check. However, engaging your professional mind in the work of research does not have to feel like an outworking of overresponsibility or posturing to appear impressive. Rather, your professional mind is the part of you that has developed all the way up to the adult self you are, ready to contribute to the world. It is akin to Linehan's wise mind in the sense that it balances both rational and emotional parts of you. In the helping professions, you regularly lean into emotions such as compassion and empathy. Research can tap into your rational, logical side and bring a greater balance to your professional expression and sense of self. For me (Kristen), my doctoral studies did just that—developing in me a love of research that engaged my logical mind in a way that had been understimulated in my counseling career. Certainly, good counselors use both logic and emotion daily, but the mathematical and logical figuring out of the data can bring a new energy to the engaged professional mind.

RESEARCH AS RELATIONAL

Up to this point, we have invited you to lean into God, the purpose he has given you, and your curiosity. From here we are ready to invite you to consider bringing your whole self to the work of ordering the world through research-play. But we do not do this for ourselves, nor do we engage in this process for the process itself. All our efforts to develop our hearts as researchers are for the delight of giving ourselves to God in worship and into the service of others. Through research we honor the Father, imitate the Son, partner with the Spirit, and love our neighbors as ourselves. With this in mind we hope you see that research is a relational interaction of receiving from and giving back to God for the purpose of blessing others in his world.

Have you ever seen a child draw a picture for their parents? Chances are it isn't very good on an objective level. But parents are rarely objective, and when a child hands a new piece of artwork to their loving parents, they are generally thrilled and find a way to display it. As people ooh and ahh over that drawing, the beaming parents are honored. This experience is not just a feeling of pride but an actual honor bestowed on them. The child has given them a gift that brings honor to them as they share, "Look what our child has done!"

In a similar way, we honor God our Father when we explore the world and bring him our findings. "Look what I made, Dad!" When we hand God our data born out of curiosity and poured over with all the parts of ourselves, he sees his own image in us. He sees the world he has made and the ways we have taken him up on his offer to tend the earth. Because he is God and not a human parent, he doesn't simply display our artwork for the world to see. Instead, he partners with us, allowing us to use our discoveries in conjunction with the Spirit to transform the world. With us, he changes lives through our innovative mental health interventions developed over years of research efforts. With us, he turns insight into new decision-making strategies and brings justice where oppression is uncovered. He returns honor by honoring.

As we participate in our Christian lives, we continually seek to imitate Jesus, the Son. With our whole researcher selves, we imitate Christ as we give ourselves to the mission of bringing order to the world. As he demonstrated, we can observe others and predict things from their behavior. As he did, we can act with timing and precision on a mission to conduct a true experiment. In John 5:19, Jesus says that the Son "can do . . . only what he sees the Father doing," and we follow in an analogous way. What is the redemptive work that we see the Son doing? How might our research be a catalyst for healing? Even as we participate in shalom, with rest and play as our approach to research, how might we, like Jesus, attend to the needs in front of us and respond with compassion? Could that type of attentiveness and mission drive our research engagement?

In John 21, Jesus challenges Peter even as he forgives him for his triple betrayal. He asks, "Do you love me?" and upon hearing Peter's reassurance he commands, "Feed my sheep" (Jn 21:15-17). After three years of following Jesus, from the initial call in John 1, Jesus again beckons to Peter, "Follow me!" (Jn 21:19). Notice the Son inviting you as you read these words: *Do you love me? Feed my sheep with all you explore in your research. Share your discoveries and knowledge with the church and the world. Follow me into places you do not yet understand.*

Find me in the spaces of inquiry, curiosity, and wonder. We pray that your researcher heart might respond to the Son with a resounding yes and amen. Or in the words of Isaiah, "Here I am! Send me" (Is 6:8).

Lest we strive to take on this calling in our own strength and ability, we remind you (and ourselves) that research is relational, and we partner with the Spirit as we work. Jesus tells his disciples in John 14:26 that he is sending his Spirit, the Advocate, who will teach us all things. Whether we are on a Christian journey or not, it is the Spirit who leads humanity into all truth and brings order into the world through our research. As Christians, we acknowledge and lean into this partnership, humbly aware that God's thoughts are higher than our thoughts and his ways higher than our ways (Is 55:8-9). In the words of Paul in 1 Corinthians 2:16, "'Who has understood the mind of the Lord so as to instruct him?' But we have the mind of Christ." We certainly cannot reveal anything in our research that God himself does not already know. In fact, through the Spirit poured out on us by Christ, we come to know higher thoughts than we can achieve on our own.

How do we acknowledge the work of the Spirit even as we begin to form a research question? Might it be that some major discoveries display the rumblings of the Spirit in the mind and heart of the unwitting scientist? Could it be that the burden on your heart—the area where you simply *must* bring order to the world—came directly from the Spirit of God? Perhaps that finding that showed up in your study, delivered through the labor of your surrendered whole self, was birthed by the hands of the Spirit. He has invited us into partnership, albeit an unequal one, in which he offers mutual respect and love where it is undeserved. He *allows* us to be researchers and to share *his* truth with the world as if we ourselves had the brilliance to discern it. And all the while he delights in it. He delights in you and all the things you want to know.

Through our acts of honoring the Father, imitating the Son, and partnering with the Spirit in our research, we also love our neighbors as ourselves. Research makes a genuine contribution to the world, enlightening neighbors we may never meet. When we consume research, we are blessed by the gifts of others who have gone before and left insights in their articles we read, a plate of cookies on our doorstep when we move into the research neighborhood. I (Kristen) remember the feeling of honor when I was cited for the first time in another author's research study. It was exciting to realize that people I did not know found my work, cited it, and built on ideas within my study. Of course, they had many citations of many researchers. We as researchers become a part of the research community (sometimes collectively called "the literature"). Just as we have received from researchers before us, we now are able to give. My research continues to ripple out in ways known and unknown to me.

Fortunately, the research well is deep, and there is plenty of room for more neighbors. There is no end to the things we will want to know. There will always be more studies to be done. In fact, sometimes research leaves us with far more questions than it answers. Once we uncover the first piece of the puzzle, we find five more hiding. God has sent us on a global scavenger hunt, and when we obtain the answer to one clue, it helps us collectively to share it with each other. So allow us to be your formal invitation into the relationship of the researcher community through the invitation of Mr. Rogers, "Won't you be my neighbor?"

CONCLUSION

We conclude this chapter by returning to curiosity and posing this question: What do you want to know? When the disciples began to follow Jesus, we are told in John 1:38 that he turned and asked them, "What are you seeking?" In a different way, we ask you the same. So, what are you seeking? How will you respond to the invitation we have presented in this chapter to give your whole self to the research process? Are you seeking answers to research questions? Or a greater knowledge of the depths of God himself? Or perhaps a combination? Maybe, before you can ask questions, you are in need of healing in an area of your heart that has become deadened to natural curiosity. If you resonate with this, we encourage you to ask and pursue Jesus for this healing and restoration.

We encourage you to take a look at the exercise in the sidebar "What Are You Seeking?" Whether you intend to be a good consumer of research as a clinician or a producer of research at a doctoral level, this exercise can help you identify your research agenda in light of all we have discussed in this chapter. We hope that working your way through this chapter has ignited a spark of imagination or inspiration. You have permission to daydream and wonder, to ask dumb questions (no such thing!), and to innovate. We look forward to citing your work someday.

What Are You Seeking?

In a notebook or journal, take time to explore these writing prompts to connect with your researcher heart and begin to identify the direction of your research interests. These prompts can also prepare you to engage in the classroom discussion questions provided at the end of this chapter.

1. What are three things I have been curious about or areas of disorder in the world that have bothered me across multiple stages of my life?
2. What are the ways I naturally relate to God? How can I use these ways of relating as I engage in reading and producing research?
3. Of the five domains of human flourishing (happiness and life satisfaction, mental and physical health, meaning and purpose,

character and virtue, and close social relationships), which ones stand out most to me as things I need in my life? What steps can I take to flourish as a researcher?
4. When considering the spiritual core, the inner child, and the professional mind, how do I see these pieces of myself working together? Is there any competition or conflict between them?
5. What types of articles excite me when I read the titles and abstracts? List five titles from a library database search that sound interesting.
6. If I imagine contributing to the world and loving God and my neighbor through research, what would I want my contribution to be?
7. Do I see research as a quest to discover truth that exists or as a process of creating meaning and new truths?

DISCUSSION QUESTIONS

1. What childhood memories connect you with the concept of innate curiosity? What are some events or experiences in your life that contributed to a squelching of curiosity?
2. Which parts of yourself do you most easily bring into this research class? Which parts are most hesitant?
3. In which areas of your life are you currently flourishing? What did it take to arrive at that place? What skills or traits do you bring to this course that could help you flourish as you learn?
4. How does research fulfill the command to love God and love your neighbor as yourself? How might that affect the way you approach this course?
5. Consider the word *innovation*. If you were to create a new and innovative mental health intervention, what steps would be a part of that process? How would research play a role? What parts of self would be activated in that process?

LEARNING ACTIVITIES

1. Watch "The Power of Wonder," a TEDx Wall Street talk by Jeff Hoffman.[6] Each student can individually brainstorm a list of five things unrelated to psychology or counseling that they are curious about and five things related to psychology or counseling they are curious about. Compare lists as a class and begin to group students around shared topics of interest.

2. Collect random objects from home or around the office and distribute one to each student. Have them study the object for two minutes and write down everything they notice. Once the two minutes are over, instruct them to do it again for another two minutes. Repeat for a third two-minute interval. Discuss as a class what that process was like and how their third observation period differed from their first one.[7]

---

[6]"The Power of Wonder: Jeff Hoffman at TEDxWallStreet," TedX Talks, YouTube, April 12, 2012, 11:30, www.youtube.com/watch?v=dcV4RXC-V94.

[7]This exercise connects to a well-known story called "Agassiz and the Fish," described in an article from the Gospel Coalition, among other sources. Justin Taylor, "Agassiz and the Fish," Gospel Coalition, November 16, 2008, www.thegospelcoalition.org/blogs/justin-taylor/agassiz-and-the-fish/.

TWO

Moving *from* Curiosity *to* Truth

I (PAUL) HAVE NO IDEA how old I was, but I remember it. With a slight twinkle in her eye, our playful, curly-haired teacher held out a small rock and a balled-up piece of paper in front of her, one in each hand. "When I drop these, which will hit the ground first?" she said. *Silly question*, I thought. *The rock . . . clearly.* Then our teacher invited us to raise our hands in a vote for *rock*, *paper*, or *together*. *Together?* I wondered. This option wasn't expected. In my confused state I didn't raise my hand for any of them. I am often a doubter, and my teacher had that twinkle in her eye, so my thought went something like this: *I wonder what trick she is pulling on us right now. What is this really about?* I didn't yet have a category in my mind for rock and paper hitting the ground together (which they did, by the way, just in case physics is lost in your memory somewhere, as it often is in mine). As I wrote those prior sentences I realized I should try this on my six-year-old daughter. So I did. Her response: "*What!* That's crazy!" She stood there with her mouth and eyes wide open.

Life as a human starts full of the unknown, the unexpected, and the intriguing. As we grow, we learn how the world works and what to expect in the context of the unknown. I think of this as a process of *doubt* (I don't know this), *evidence* (I have seen how this works), and *assimilation* (I can now navigate this). The wonderful thing about childhood is that our curiosity can lead us into all kinds of situations in which we doubt and then explore all the more. Hopefully this is within a safe and nurturing context that allows us to find evidence and assimilate what we find. What I am describing is the normal process of human development in God's world. We question, we find answers, and then we can attend to more. As we explored in chapter one, research is something you have done your whole life, starting as a curious child making memories. In this chapter we explore how research fits how you were made in God's world, and we invite you to sit back and reflect, rather than immediately jumping to "So how do I do research?" Our hope is that you will expand your view of how Christianity shapes research.

HOW THE BRAIN KNOWS

Our bodies are complex processing and learning machines. To be successful in life we need to process and make sense of all the stimuli that come into our awareness, so we know how to act and solve life's situations. However, before we can *make sense* of things, we simply *learn about* things. Learning is essentially neurobiological changes occurring in the brain as new stimuli cause neurons to wire together.[1] All the new connections we make get encoded in the brain by our hippocampus as events with details about time and place in such a way that we can retrieve all the information later. As we increase in complexity over time, our brains start to weave together generalizable patterns from episodes of memories to create *schema*, which are detailed maps of how we expect things to work in the world. Our quick and clever brain then compares events in our world to our schemas to make sense of what is happening as we try to predict what is likely to happen next. These

---

[1] Richard Keeling and Richard Hersh, *We're Losing Our Minds* (Palgrave Macmillan, 2012), 69.

making sense of things abilities allow us to adapt and prepare for what to do next.[2]

However, we don't live alone, and our brain-body functions occur in social contexts. Jean Piaget and Lev Vygotsky are commonly discussed in human growth and development courses and help us understand our contextual lives. Piaget discussed how children form schemas over time that help them conclude what is normal. He noticed that interacting with new information could lead to one of two things. First, the new information might fit with the child's expectation for the world, leading to assimilation, in which the information slots into their schema comfortably. Or new information might go beyond what the child knows, causing a rocky experience of accommodation, in which their schema has to be altered. As we get older, less information is new to us, so our schemas solidify and become a more completed mental models that are more resistant to change even if we do interact with new things.[3] This helps us understand why children are often open and willing to learn, while many adults appear less so.

If we hope to continue learning through research, humility enables us to remain open to not knowing—to realizing our model of the world is incomplete. This can be an uncertain position for many who prefer the safety and predictability of already knowing—*even if they don't really know.* This all means that curiosity can be threatening if it isn't accompanied by assurance in something greater than ourselves. We started to discuss in chapter one how as Christians we are anchored in God, and our assurance and stability are found in him, even if we are confused in his world. As God sustains

---

[2] Marlieke van Kesteren and Martijn Meeter, "How to Optimize Knowledge Construction in the Brain," *NPJ Science of Learning* 5 (2020): 1-2.
[3] Jack Balswick, Pamela King, and Kevin Reimer, *The Reciprocating Self: Human Development in Theological Perspective* (InterVarsity Press, 2016), 92; van Kesteren and Meeter, "How to Optimize Knowledge Construction," 2.

our identity and worth, we can curiously play with vigor. When we experience this surety, we can enjoy the experience of having our minds blown when the rock and the paper hit the floor at the same time. We don't have to know the answer first, we don't have to dismiss others who hold different views, and we need not be afraid to find more truth. Instead, finding new information and expanding our knowledge facilitates loving service in God's world as we cultivate the ground and illuminate God's beautiful creation.

Now let's add in the work of Vygotsky, who suggests that our social moment, with all its values, language, and meaning, significantly shapes development. Each culture suggests to its children how to understand themselves through the community's collection of unique messages about how people and the world can and cannot be. Therefore, rather than learning about the world and expressing themselves in a neutral context, Vygotsky says that children's self-understanding is an internalized reality shown in outward expressions.[4] In short, the child is (and you were) given a worldview through a shared experience.[5] This means that throughout your development you came to know the world and engage with it through a cultural heritage that appeared normal and perhaps monolithic.

As we trace developmental theory and neuroscience, we hope to expose that what you know of the world is complex and valuable, and you can trust what you know, *and* what you know is contextually bound and socially relevant. For example, there is a reason most people dress up to go to a wedding or sit down during class. How you think about the world, the doubts that arise, the questions you curiously ask, and the way you criticize or assimilate evidence is underpinned by what you have learned in your places,

---

[4]Holbrook Mahn, "Vygotsky's Methodological Contribution to Sociocultural Theory," *Remedial and Special Education* 20, no. 6 (1999): 341, 343.
[5]Balswick et al., *Reciprocating Self*, 94-95.

times, and cultures. You will, like many, probably struggle to ask questions beyond your normal. You may also need a lot of convincing to trust something new, and so may anyone who comes across your future research.

An Illustration of Knowing in Context

Let's tie this discussion together with an example from a woman named Margo. Read closely and see whether you notice how she is shaped in community and how this affects her journey toward becoming a researcher.

> Margo is twenty-four years old and grew up in Chicago attending a nondenominational church and quality (but not fancy) schools. She would tell you that she remembers snuggling up with her mom most evenings and feeling welcomed in her home. She never knew her dad, but she did know her large extended family and Latino roots. Growing up she was loud and fun and enjoyed her sisters. Margo's mom would add that during the early years she would sing calming songs of affirmation over her sweet girl and that struggles with discipline would almost always end with hugs and reminders of acceptance. Margo was always close to her mom and aunts, sharing her life with them.
>
> Margo loved school because her friends would always gossip together but had each other's backs. She struggled with math but didn't care too much because she was affirmed by teachers and her mom about her well-rounded academic thriving and wonderfully creative personality. Margo learned her questions were welcome, and her home was safe even when she saw that others were living differently around her. Her mom was often stretched and worked hard to provide for and take care of the kids, which was common for the women she knew. As Margo grew older, a good friend turned into a solid boyfriend, but they separated due to different career and school journeys. She grieved but bounced back.
>
> Margo is beginning a research class in her master's program. When asked what she was curious about, Margo reflected and recognized that she felt systemic cultural bias against her culture and

the prevalence of overworked and burned-out families. She wanted to know how the women in her social circles had thrived and cared for those who hadn't. Her first research idea was to understand the role of creativity in enhancing the resilience of Latina women. She couldn't shake the idea that there might be a critical link.

What can we learn from this account of Margo's story? She asked a research question prevalent to her experience. She defined it in her terms and with culturally normative goals (resilience) in mind. She had learned she could ask hard questions and that people would talk to her. She knew she could pursue what she cared about. She valued her intrinsic worth and that of others. She had learned to see localized cultural dynamics. She pursued what she considered effective (creativity). We could say more, but these are just a few examples that display Margo's schemas, sociocultural learning, and willingness to expand her knowledge *within* her prior expectations. What else do you notice?

A research assistant helped Margo to recognize how her prior learning had shaped how she thought about research. Together they considered the following questions: How do systemic racism, creativity, and resilience relate? What assumptions is Margo making about Latina culture based on her experiences? Would she be too close to this research question to be objective, and did that matter? How might someone from a different cultural context understand the idea of helping Latinas? Are there other methods for this research that might be as effective or yield different results?

We can affirm Margo and her questions and recognize that she has insider knowledge about what Latinas in her community would experience and how they could benefit from creativity. At the same time, this example shows how easy it is to be limited by what we already know and reduce the scope for what we could know. We could encourage Margo to notice any doubts about what helps Latinas thrive in Chicago and become curious. She could seek evidence in prior literature and then pursue a research agenda. She might learn of new evidence that underpins strategies to support this community. If Margo is humble and allows for mismatches between her expectations and any new evidence, learning could lead to culturally appropriate support and change.

SOCIAL KNOWLEDGE AND MEANING

How have you come to see and engage with the world as you do? To answer this question, let us tie together what we discussed about our brains (neuroscience and Piaget) and learning in social contexts (Vygotsky), adding a framework for our particular view of the world. Understanding this will help you understand how you already approach research.

Charles Taylor, an influential philosopher, agrees with Vygotsky that, as people with learning, synthesizing, and predicting brains, we are in dialogue with the world. We actively participate in exchanges of information, love, creativity, relationship, and more with those who matter to us. Those who matter to us teach us their language of life; we do not define ourselves from our own understanding.[6] That is how we build shared communities and culture that are expressed in images, stories, legends, and all manner of common experiences and values. As we engage in a community (with those we love), we learn and accept what Taylor calls a *social imaginary*, which describes the ways the community "imagine[s] their social existence, how they fit together with others, how things go on between them." The social imaginary is "shared by large groups of people . . . [and] makes possible common practices and a widely shared sense of legitimacy."[7]

For example, in the West we have learned that seeking authenticity is normal, and we express it through our choices. From here on, think of your *imaginary* as a *story* that tells you how to be normal and explain life within your specific community. Imagine a community that all learns to walk sideways, and in this community, everything is built for sideways. The doors are narrower, cars are different, hiking is eventful. Sideways is normal, and it is comfortable.

---

[6]Charles Taylor, *The Ethics of Authenticity* (Harvard University Press, 1991), 33-34.
[7]Charles Taylor, *Modern Social Imaginaries* (Duke University Press, 2004), 23.

We value the things that support our sideways lives—they aren't questioned. In this community it is really odd when we spot someone walking forward. They don't seem to fit. They experience and interpret our narrow doors differently. They value different things.

While this metaphor is limited and a little fanciful, we hope it helps you see just how much our understanding of life sets our expectations. We will use the terms *imaginary* or *story* interchangeably throughout the book to refer to this idea of what we automatically think of as *normal* and *how things work*. Our imaginary isn't ultimate truth, but it is the reality we learned. It isn't perfectly aligned to God's story, but over time, we hope our story moves toward his own.

We share large parts of our story (imaginary) with those around us, and what is thought of as valuable by our group is produced by a backdrop of events and institutions that help it to make sense.[8] Authenticity is part of our modern Western story because it rests on the backdrop of Enlightenment thinking, and more recently on pop culture. In a way, we live in a dialogue with pop culture, and it fuels our community's story, telling us that things such as seeking authenticity are good. We hear it in songs, see it in social movements, fashion, and more. Other shared experiences such as the Bible, the stock market, or the Constitution also tell us what to value. It is hard to always see, let alone escape, the dominant stories in any culture because they seem normal. For example, take Martha in the Bible. In her day, she lived among influences that taught her a story in which she valued service and doing. Those things fit snugly within the story about life she shared with many women at the time. Mary, sitting at Jesus' feet, seemed so strange—she didn't act according to the story.

---

[8]Taylor, *Ethics of Authenticity*, 37-39.

DOUBT, EVIDENCE, AND ASSIMILATION IN THE CHRISTIAN LIFE

The Christian life is no different. We participate in a story that rests on what we deem to be significant. The Bible shapes a Christian understanding of life that is dramatically different from that of the wider culture. Even though diversity is seen among Christians, our general shared story is more similar than it is different. For example, our shared story, found in the Bible, leads Christians to value forgiveness very highly. This is critical for us to reflect on as researchers because we interpret what we don't know and would like to know from within the influence of our understanding of what is normal. For example, many of us are curious how to make the most of this life and how to live well. That likely didn't strike you as an odd statement to read. Why? Because it fits with the biblical and the Western imaginary. Making the most of life fits both. However, issues such as abortion and sexuality fit differently in the biblical and Western imaginaries. Any big differences in guiding stories will likely lead researchers to ask different questions, assume different values, and start in different places. It is unlikely that you would find a modern, Western liberal conducting research from the starting assumption that abortion is morally wrong. Why? Because that doesn't fit their story of the world.

John's Gospel makes clear that Christian's have a story through which to see and understand everything else in the world: "These are written so that you may believe that Jesus is the Christ" (Jn 20:31). The redemptive story of the Bible can be summarized like this: (1) God created a good world for his glory, our delight, and enjoying relationship with him; (2) the fall brought separation from God, and the subsequent curse left us dislocated and exposed; (3) Christ came and made payment for the curse, our disobedience, and united us once again to our loving Father; and (4) Christ will return and finish his kingdom work, and believers will suffer no more and enjoy his goodness forever. When we experience the Bible as an authoritative backdrop for life, it casts a powerful view of life. But remember, we never internalize a pure Christian story, as it is contaminated by other competing stories such as modern individualism, within which we also live.

As Christians, we can wisely ask ourselves, What is the story I really believe about how the world works, and how does it shape what I am curious about? What secular or Christian beliefs does my imaginary hold? After all, we hold a blend of biblical and nonbiblical beliefs because of our lives. So, let's be honest with ourselves here. What can we do if the Bible's story seems to speak *against* what we are actually curious about because we have more deeply internalized a secular imaginary?

Scripture and C. S. Lewis both help us here. There are many places where Scripture explores how our hearts and agendas are allied to the sinful nature, which promotes the *self as the ultimate authority*, filled with our own interests and pleasures (Ps 51:5; Rom 5:12; Gal 5:19-21; etc.). Do you ever struggle to see past yourself and your desires? We do. The current Western Christian culture provides a truly mixed imaginary, formed by many influences. For example, individualism has parented us all. Jesus offers us relief and an invitation back to his story: "Our old self was crucified with him in order that the body of sin might be brought to nothing, so that we would no longer be enslaved to sin" (Rom 6:6). "Those who live according to the flesh set their minds on the things of the flesh, but those who live according to the Spirit set their minds on the things of the Spirit" (Rom 8:5). Paul reminds us that Christ's redemptive work binds us to himself so that we can value his story. This story becomes our own when we work it out over time (Phil 2:12), reminding ourselves of the Christian story by living in it through fellowship, worship, encouragement, correction, and all forms of sibling love (Rom 15:14; Col 3:2; 2 Timothy; Heb 10:25).

This isn't our trite encouragement to "be a better Christian"; we simply know that our experiences and choices shape us as people and researchers. In *The Weight of Glory*, C. S. Lewis reminds us that our deep human desires are good and point toward our design. Lewis also says that nothing fully satisfies us now because our desire is ultimately for the eternal, infinite God and his delight in us. Amid the fall, our desires are rather confused and muddled, and small pleasures can distract us, making the Christian life look dull.[9] Lewis would say it makes sense that we have a fascination with (and often research) approval, personality, comfort, health, sex, and many more such things, forgetting they are just a part of God's good gifts. But he'd also point out that we have only scratched the surface and can barely fathom the fullness of what personality, comfort, health, or sex were designed to be.

Lewis invites us to strain forward beyond our desires and see where they come from and what they are intended for in God's world. When God's story and language take root in our heart, we see these pleasures differently; our curiosity shifts, our actions change. Christian community can help us see through our new eyes. We need personal and academic friends as well as churches and actions that focus on God's kingdom. This is how we gradually become steeped in the language and values of the Christian imaginary. It will cause us to be enthralled by God, ask our questions in line with his story, and find answers we understand within that story. We hope you join us in the excitement of a vision of research that is steeped in God's world.

---

[9]C. S. Lewis, *The Weight of Glory* (HarperCollins, 2001), 26, 33.

THE ISSUE OF APPROACHING RESEARCH

Atheistic and religious approaches to psychological research vary. The central concern is this: Each group knows that what you assume to be the fundamental realities of life frame the questions you ask about life, which in turn dictates what answers you can find and what solutions you might enact. For example, if you ask a young American atheist in this present cultural moment, "Is shame ever good?" it is probable they would say emphatically, "No!" However, if you asked the same question to someone from a collectivist culture, perhaps in rural China, they may say, "Of course! It helps people know what to do." The young American assumes the value of personal autonomy and freedom, making self-inhibiting emotions harmful, whereas an older Chinese native may assume the value of conformity and community, and therefore self-inhibiting emotions are helpful to organize people's behavior. The Chinese native may never have asked, "Is shame ever good?" because the question doesn't fit well within their imaginary in the first place. These two people hold different assumptions about what is helpful and healthy, leading to different responses to the same question. This is an example of how community is a guiding authority, shaping people's stories and the assumptions and actions they take.

Hopefully, you can feel some of the tensions that arise as we consider knowledge and research in our social contexts. Now we describe the approaches of different imaginaries in a little more detail to really get you thinking. Before reading on, take a look at figure 2.1, which provides a visual way to organize the concepts we are going to introduce you to in this chapter. You will see that imaginaries are the biggest context for understanding life and each one has ideas about what is true and how to find out more truth. Research attempts to find more truth, but we go about this process with different methods and assumptions based on the bigger context. We invite you to refer to the diagram as you continue to help organize your thinking.

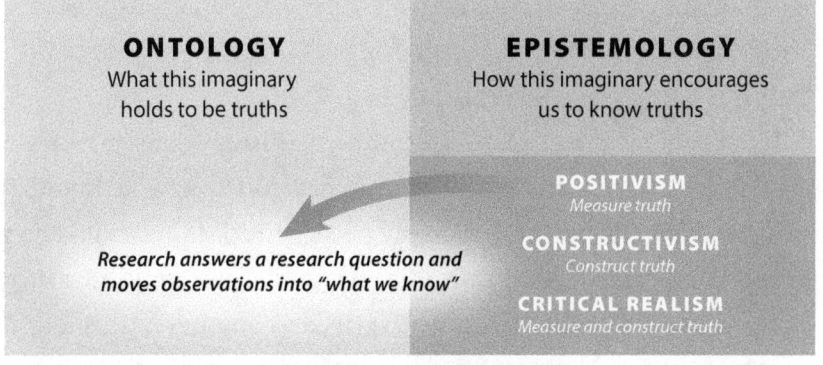

Figure 2.1. Imaginary or story that explains life (e.g., secular naturalism, theistic naturalism)

As stated above, our *imaginaries* or *stories* were learned in our social contexts, and getting curious about them helps us describe, recognize, and see the limitations of how we think the world works. As we do this, we will start to see what assumptions we hold and how this shapes our thinking, theorizing, perceptions, and actions.[10]

Here are two different imaginaries that alter someone's approach to research. Secular naturalism is a widely held story, and those who live by it say that the world is a product of naturally arising occurrences and that the laws of nature will explain life as it relates to all people at all times. Another imaginary, called relativism, disagrees and asserts that personal experience changes life itself, and there is no knowledge that applies to all people; instead, we all participate to construct knowledge. These two stories about the world are quite opposed in their search for truth and end up using different research methods that fit with their assumptions about life and truth. Here lies a problem. If you do not agree with, or

---

[10]Roger Erdvig, "A Model for Biblical Worldview Development in Evangelical Christian Emerging Adults," *Journal of Research on Christian Education* (September 2020): 285-86.

value, the underlying story (and its assumptions) that guide a research study, it is incredibly hard to find the research trustworthy or use the findings because the whole process will feel illogical or misguided. This has presented the research community with a critical question: Can you accept things as true if you disagree with the underlying view of life from which they came?

This problem didn't just occur; it has a history. Starting in the eighteenth century, the world quickly developed new technology and radically altered the way many people lived. Industrialization in the West came with a prevailing view that we could measure, order, and predict life—faith wasn't needed anymore. This led to people using empirical studies in an attempt to understand things and create solutions, such as medicine. As this happened, people started to grow wary and reject the supposedly untrustworthy wisdom of mysticism and oratorical traditions such as the Bible. The idea was this: If you could measure and observe a set of facts (or things) and record how they interacted, then you could be sure that you understood how something worked—done and done. This is just like the idea of dropping a piece of paper and a rock and measuring when they hit the floor, because it can give insight into the workings of gravity. This knowledge of gravity could then be applied to other contexts such as flight engineering. This is a great example of the secular naturalistic imaginary. In short, industrialization and modernization made the felt need for faith, prayer, and God less immediate because we felt as if we could finally answer our own questions and fulfill our own needs. The only problems that remained were considered to be a result of gaps in our knowledge.

Even though modernization seemed to answer how life works, people of faith and those who valued personal experience disagreed. The issue is this: Can't our personal experience and our interpretations actually alter what we call true? Some say yes. Two ideas will help this all make sense: *ontology* and *epistemology*. In everyday language, ontology is a claim about the reality of things and processes, such as how gravity holds things down, or how the hormone oxytocin leads to pleasurable feelings. And epistemology describes the process of how we know what we know.[11] For example, how do we know that gravity works as it does, or how do we know that oxytocin is pleasurable?

Now let us return to the conundrum that some people disagree that you can just measure things and find out truth. Opposition to secular naturalism (the you-can-just-measure-the-laws-of-nature position) can be *ontological*. For example, a Christian would say there is an actual God who operates in the world and is a part of how things really are, even though you can't measure him. A second opposition to secular naturalism could be *epistemological*. A Christian might say they know God not because they can see, touch, and measure him but because they *experience* him internally and through prayer.

What we are noting is that you can measure things that affect your life, and you can't measure everything that makes life work—such as God. There is a way to work with the "it's only accurate if you measure it scientifically" position while allowing for God. Theistic naturalism allows for more than just measuring to explain how things *are* and *work*. This is good news for Christians (and others) who want to research experiences of God and matters of our experience. C. John Collins, a keen biblical scholar and scientist, explains that theistic naturalism gives us more options for knowing truth by suggesting that nature and natural laws not only exist in a measurable way but also serve and express God's purposes, which

---

[11]Danica Hays and Anneliese Singh, *Qualitative Inquiry in Clinical and Educational Settings* (Guilford, 2012), 34-35.

are often beyond the measurable.[12] Collins is saying that although things can be measured by themselves, they were often made by God to interact for bigger reasons and purposes, and it is these bigger reasons and purposes that explain how we experience life. The theistic naturalist story has space for faith and theology to explain life in this world. The theistic naturalist is OK with controlled scientific experiments but also recognizes that these types of experiments may miss a fuller understanding of the complexity of life. This is a story of life that allows for gaps in our understanding while still holding a bigger truth, which frees us to ask different questions and interpret findings differently from a secular naturalist who wouldn't allow for faith or theology (or the actions of God).

Collins also addresses the imaginary of relativism (the belief that no specific knowledge can apply to, or account for, all people's experiences).[13] In relativism, knowledge is relative because people individually partake in finding information and interpreting its meaning. While we agree that people and their interpretations are involved, we think people are still sharing a look at real and actual things that can be known. So far, we hope you see that allowing for God in our explanation of life allows us to research our curiosities with confidence. We can know that we are discovering something of God's world, and it will fit within the wider pattern of what God is doing across his creation.

We invite you to consider with us what assumption you have in your own story of how the world works. Are we really thinking like secular naturalists (we can only measure things)? Like relativists (it's all up for interpretation)? Or like theistic naturalists (nature is measurable and serves a God who authored meaning)? This is really asking: *What imaginary are you actually using as you*

---

[12]C. John Collins, *Science and Faith: Friends or Foes?* (Crossway, 2003), 481-82.
[13]Collins, *Science and Faith*, 481-83.

approach research as a Christian? Perhaps this sounds odd, but you can mentally assent to the idea of the Christian story as explaining life while actually living out a different story (e.g., secular). This can happen knowingly or blindly.

Let's look at a concrete example that shows how different guiding stories change what is possible for research to measure. A Christian researcher may have a theistic imaginary and want to understand how a relationship with God affects people's well-being. This theistic position allows the researcher to have a research question in which God directly matters. If this researcher sets about researching this question with only secular-naturalistic methods (as is common in much quantitative research that uses data points and statistical analysis), this would require the researcher to break down the idea of a relationship with God into observable data points, such as feelings of closeness to God or time spent in prayer—which aren't actually God. The original theistic question allowed for information about truth (God) that the secular methodology can't account for.

Table 2.1. Example summary

Imaginary/Story	How Life Works	Methods That Fit
Secular naturalism	There is reality only if you can measure it	Observation of definable data points
Theistic naturalism	There is order beyond what is measured	Observation of definable data points Hearing personal experience grounded in an imaginary

Table 2.1 summarizes the imaginaries and methods in this example, in which observable things that happen in relationship with God are understood as one part of what makes a relationship with God. Just measuring these observable things will misrepresent the spiritual-experiential nature of relationship with God. I wouldn't personally feel that observable things like "felt closeness" or "time spent in prayer" fully capture the quality of my relationship with

God and how it affects my life. Sometimes I can feel very distant from God but remain convinced of his goodness and grace. Therefore, researchers need to think carefully from conception to completion and check whether the methods fit the story. In the above example we would encourage the researcher to choose a methodology that is able to explore personal experiences of the spiritual-experiential aspect of relationship with God. Doing this could find new truth about the experience of relating to God that couldn't be found before. One thing I (Paul) have found is that when my imaginary that has generated my research interest is at odds with the imaginary behind my research methods, I feel a bubbling confusion and concern that the work isn't really grasping what I intended. I have learned to pause at these moments and consider the guiding stories in play.

It is a little on the wild side to fully accept that our story of how the world works guides interpretations of research data, meaning secular-naturalistic and theistic researchers who are both interpreting one set of data may come to different conclusions. Here is an example of how this has occurred in my (Paul's) clinical life. I am a Christian who has read a good deal of research on attachment, and it is not uncommon for the secular naturalist authors to conclude that their findings provide evidence of pair-bonding behaviors and evolution. I have often struggled to accept the starting assumption of evolution in these interpretations because it seems to me that mutuality and security in relationships are assumed to have developed rather than being a part of our created design. Therefore, I agree with the secular naturalist that attachment exists, and we can learn a lot by measuring this phenomenon, but my imaginary allows for a different understanding of its origin and full purpose.

Of course, as a Christian I must recognize my theistic-relational imaginary comes with its own assumptions, and I see attachment research as partial evidence of my imaginary. The key thing is that I want to consciously allow my theistic imaginary to carefully guide my interpretation rather than doing so blindly. We hope you can start to notice that some of the ways your imaginary is influencing how you read the research you interact with. Notice what you learn about yourself, how you explain the findings, and how this orients you to future questions.

As we just introduced, you, the reader, might have a different imaginary from an original researcher and therefore doubt the research's value. This means we need to *justify our approach to our research*. For example, if you do not believe God exists, then research that suggests a relationship with God leads to human flourishing may aggravate your imaginary. You may be tempted to reject this study or see it as misguided and covering over other psychological phenomena. You might question how the researcher even measured the idea of a relationship with God. What is a relationship with God in the first place? How do you capture such an elusive concept? And even if you can measure this, does it apply to everyone, or just the Christians who were studied?

If the imaginary (with its assumptions) behind a research study is not clearly articulated, rationally discussed, and its limitations recognized—no matter how effectively the research was conducted—it is hard for readers to treat it with respect or trust any claims of truth. Especially when we research and communicate across imaginaries, the need to build trust by demonstrating our theoretical approach and a matching methodology is high.

A DIRECTION FOR CHRISTIAN RESEARCH

These issues that lie behind research can be complex. I (Paul) have personally experienced confusion and frustration about how to approach Christian integration in counseling research—the area I am most curious to explore. Colleagues have helped and supported me through honest dialogue and pointed me to scholars who have tackled these issues before us. I want to share with you some helpful encouragement I have received to provide the beginning of a road map for your research journey. I hope it encourages you that there are paths to navigate the concerns above. Remember, right now we are inviting you to expand your thinking with these realities and not expecting you to fully flesh out your new way to research.

Wonderful Christian scholars and researchers have shared solutions to the methodological conundrums brought about by research that arises from different imaginaries. We want to share two perspectives as food for thought. One typifies much social research, and another offers attempts at a more holistic theological perspective. First, a *levels of explanation* approach to integrating psychology and Christianity holds a theistic imaginary for life and salvation but also leans heavily on secular naturalism to make discoveries about the world. Proponents of levels of explanation suggest that we live with multilayered explanations of reality, and we can engage in research and discussion at the appropriate level (and imaginary) for the desired discussion.[14] David Myers gives the example of *love*, in which different professions can describe and research love from their imaginary with its assumptions.[15] A physiologist describes and studies the bodily arousal of love, the social psychologist studies desirability and emotive changes in love, and the theologian considers love as a goal and ethic for relationships with one another and God. Each layer is seen to build on top of the others to create a more robust understanding of God's world. Both synthesis and disagreement occur between these levels, and

---

[14]David Myers, "A Levels-of-Explanation View," in *Psychology and Christianity: Five Views*, ed. Eric Johnson (InterVarsity Press, 2010), 49-50.
[15]Myers, "Levels-of-Explanation View," 51.

it can be hard to fit them together into a coherent picture. Positively, though, each level can use research methods suited to its specific level without fear of misrepresenting the bigger picture, because the bigger picture is only ever thought to be what the combined parts show us. Here guiding imaginaries are given little consideration and therefore secular research can be easily used.

We note that the levels-of-explanation approach is one of five views of integration often cited in integration literature. The other four views can all influence a research agenda, and we encourage any interested readers to investigate the other views and think about their implications. What do you think about the levels-of-explanation idea?

Paul Watson offers an alternative approach for Christian (and secular) researchers by inviting the often-warring factions arising from different imaginaries to one table of collaborative scholarly discussion.[16] Watson recognized that synthesizing data that arise from different interpretive frameworks is problematic at best because you are disagreeing about how you can know things and what things are even *for* in the first place. This leads to some seemingly chaotic and competing data, and you can't simply synthesize them, as was the case with love above. And, as discussed before, many secular researchers have not valued theistic (including Christian) levels of interpretation and preferred to reject them because such levels don't fit with how they understand the world. Watson would prefer we stop privileging one level of explanation over others, but this leads back to the conundrum of which imaginary is correct and acceptable.

Watson's helpful desire is that all researchers *acknowledge* their imaginaries and how they influence their exploration of any

---

[16]Paul Watson, *Psychology and Religion Within an Ideological Surround* (Brill, 2019), 4.

phenomena.[17] Practically, Watson urges two things. First, that each researcher be open about their imaginary, which means they clearly express how they come to *know* things and how they interpret what things are *for*, no matter what the dominant cultural view. This requires that researchers *know their imaginary* and allow it to guide their questions, methods, and interpretations throughout the research process. Second, researchers ought to be willing to hold generous dialogues about the truth they have found from *within their imaginary*. Watson suggests this approach will promote mature dialogue and a process through which we can come together to construct a greater understanding of human flourishing. We believe Watson is onto something important and exciting because it allows a Christian research approach to be taken seriously. What is your immediate reaction to these generous dialogues?

Let's explore an example: Joshua Knabb and Kenneth Wang wanted to understand a *Christian experience* of relating to God to help *all researchers* understand how this affects Christians specifically. They provide a wonderful example of *knowing* and *stating* their imaginary faithfully by clarifying at the start of their work that they are researching a relationship with God from a "within perspective."[18] Knabb and Wang let their Christian imaginary frame the idea of God and relating to him. They explain it this way: The Bible is a source of knowing (epistemology) for Christians who have a relationship with God, and therefore it is reasonable to conduct research that uses biblical terms and ideas because it captures Christians' lived experiences.[19] The authors use the normal rigor of scholarship yet stick to a robust Christian

---

[17]Watson, *Psychology and Religion*, 74-76.
[18]Joshua Knabb and Kenneth Wang, "The Communion with God Scale: Shifting from an Etic to Emic Perspective to Assess Fellowshipping with the Triune God," *Psychology of Religion and Spirituality* 13, no. 1 (2021): 68.
[19]Knabb and Wang, "Communion with God Scale," 68-69.

imaginary that flows through their literature, from their questions, to their methods, to their discussion. Knabb and Wang are clear that their findings apply to Christians and avoid the error of overgeneralizing their findings, while offering them up for dialogue. This example encourages us as Christians to own our imaginary, pursue our curiosity, and share our findings. We hope it inspires you too.

Collins, whom we heard from earlier, wants to give you confidence that Christians have much to offer in these types of discussions, stating: "I believe that the Christian [imaginary] makes the best account of science: it shows us why science works (the same God who made the world made us to rule it); it shows why we like science (God made us curious); and it shows why science reveals natural gaps (because God has carried out supernatural actions as well as maintaining nature)."[20] Given these strengths of a Christian imaginary in research, we appreciate Watson's desire to help us bring our contributions to the work of discovering truth. It is exciting to be able to contribute to what is known about our world in a distinctly Christian manner.

We want to be straight with you. The social sciences normatively expect a secular-naturalistic imaginary that makes it difficult to bring a Christian imaginary into contemporary scholarship and research. Academic journals and editorial colleagues have traditionally been resistant to Christian imaginary research precisely because it is challenging to prevailing assumptions. However, behind researchers such as Knabb and Wang a path to discussion (akin to Watson's vision) is emerging. While these thoughts are just the beginning, you can develop as a researcher over time and engage topics with Christian savvy throughout your approach.

---

[20]Collins, *Science and Faith*, 483.

And we need not worry that we won't be able to line up alongside our secular colleagues. Eric Johnson reminds us that faithful Christian research will "result in a psychology significantly different from late modern psychology *only where* Christianity has something distinctive to contribute."[21] It is critical to understand this point. Christians are not to dogmatically claim they alone have access to truth and the full understanding of human realities—that is to forget Watson's point about generous conversations. Instead, we can stand in humility and assert that a Christian imaginary does indeed allow access to different questions, methods, and interpretation that bring meaningful contributions to understanding life. And so too will research from an explicitly Muslim, humanist, or any other imaginary. We hope that as we peek behind the curtain you can appreciate both the complexity and beauty of carefully considered research.

Getting Practical

If you find the theoretical discussion about imaginaries hard to follow, or just find yourself asking, "What does this mean for me now?" rest assured we have been there ourselves. Here are some practical action steps to help you develop on your research journey. We draw on Johnson's work to help us.

1. Remember this definition: An *imaginary* describes how you expect the world to work, what you have learned is important, and it is generally widely shared within cultures or subcultures.
2. Get to know your *imaginary* by asking the following questions: How do you think people react and what they value? What matters in life and for mental well-being? Get to know your assumptions. Johnson suggests the Christian intellectual community (which includes you) engage in a form of identity politics and actively embrace their

---

[21]Eric Johnson, "The Three Faces of Integration," *Journal of Psychology and Christianity* 30, no. 4 (2011): 351, emphasis added.

minority identity, solidify their voice in writing and action, and enhance their distinctive research influence in the larger culture.[a] How can you solidify your identity as a Christian researcher?

3. Research applications: What questions do you have about human life that come from within a Christian imaginary? Read what has previously been understood about your area of curiosity from inside and outside your imaginary. Revise your questions based on assimilating your reading. Ask for support to develop and refine research methods that support your questions.

4. Interpret research findings by generously understanding the social imaginary of the authors. You can often discern this from the literature review and discussion sections. Consider what limitations are present in the research based on their starting assumptions.

5. Engage in winsome dialogue. Not everyone will appreciate research that represents minority perspectives or methodology. Winsomely defend and promote your work, which is a lot easier when you have followed the points above. Return to seeking synthesis to add evidence to the patterns of truth we have.

[a] Eric Johnson, "The Three Faces of Integration," *Journal of Psychology and Christianity* 30, no. 4 (2011): 347-48.

TWO APPROACHES TO THE ILLUMINATION OF TRUTH

We have seen that our internalized understanding of how life works changes our default approach to thinking about, understanding, and interpreting everything. Within any imaginary, we still have to consider how we can find stuff out through research. Thus we now focus on epistemology—the *how* we can know part. Trustworthy researchers share with us their *how I came to know this* (their method) so that we can understand how they found their evidence. A good research method does at least three things: (1) effectively answers the research question being asked, (2) honors the theoretical arguments the researchers made to arrive at the research question, and (3) provides trustworthy findings through the accurate collection, analysis, and interpretation of data. For example, if you told me that you discovered that physical and psychological pain is the key to long life, I'd sure like to understand how you found this evidence, as it defies my current beliefs.

Let's consider two different approaches you might have taken to this pain research that represent the two main ways of knowing: Perhaps you discovered the role of pain by rigorously studying objective data such as increases in hormones, negative life situations, and numerical reports of pain, and then analyzed these data with statistical processes. Or perhaps you discovered the role of pain by interviewing thriving elderly people and asking them to point to the most meaningful and sustaining factors in their lives. Very different. The first is a positivist approach, while the second is constructivist.

Regardless of a researcher's guiding story, positivism and constructivism are the two major approaches to finding knowledge. Positivism holds that it is possible for researchers to accurately and objectively state universal truth claims as a result of observing and experiencing phenomena as it arises.[22] Researchers like this approach within social-scientific research, as it attempts to provide coherent and concise knowledge about life that can serve the public interest. Central to this process of discovery is (1) stating a hypothesis (what we think we might find), (2) systematically measuring the appropriate variables (things that can be objectively measured), and (3) analyzing the data to verify whether the hypothesis is correct. If we do this process with integrity, we can find data that uphold or reject a hypothesis and can be generalized to broader situations represented by the research.

---

[22]Hays and Singh, *Qualitative Inquiry*, 39.

Researchers who use a positivist philosophy in their methodology have allowed prior literature (what we already know) to shape their hypotheses, kept strict boundaries with research participants, avoid researcher values and biases, and use well-known statistical methods to control for extra variables that could confuse the data.[23] What we just described is often referred to as the idea of pure science that can objectively discover truth. However, critics of positivism are plentiful, arguing that research findings often fail to represent all people, resulting in marginalization and minimization of various groups. This can happen when research doesn't measure a representative sample, when the researchers' imaginary influences the hypothesis, and many other ways.

In contrast to positivism, the constructivist paradigm accepts and works with unique human experiences, not assuming one person's experience will explain others. Constructivists accept that various experiences emerge from interacting with different people, no matter how similar some aspects of their lives might be. As a simple example, take two children from the same neighborhood of the same race, gender, and socioeconomic standing. One child could learn that always saying thank you is necessary for parental approval, while the other child learns they need only to smile. You can see this could alter what they *know* to be polite. These children are different—there is no one understanding of politeness. Constructivism is an approach that assumes that universal truth cannot exist due to each person's subjective experience. To account for the fact that people do interpret and experience things differently, a constructivist paradigm for research requires that researchers recognize their values and biases, then detail how these might affect research questions, methods, and any interpretations they make.[24]

---

[23]Hays and Singh, *Qualitative Inquiry*, 39.
[24]Hays and Singh, *Qualitative Inquiry*, 40-41.

This process requires researchers to carefully detail whom findings represent, because the research participants also have a unique set of experiences, values, and biases.

As you would assume, making space for each person's experience significantly limits what generalizations are made and leaves claims of certainty behind. Importantly, we think that Christians need not panic over constructivist claims that we each interpret and create meaning. As we explored earlier, God created each of us with brains that develop neural pathways and the ability to build schemas that tell us how the world works. We all need these schemas to make sense of our everyday lives. Each one of us has a different childhood and understands nuances differently, and we also recognize that our personal reality cannot possibly capture all of God's world.

If only there were a middle ground. One where we could know universal facts and still allow for personal experience. Thankfully, there is: critical realism, which navigates between positivism and constructivism. Critical realism holds that subjectivity is a human experience, while also recognizing that this doesn't preclude our developing knowledge of how things are for all people in general. Christian philosopher Michael Polanyi suggests that scientific discoveries emerge in the context of different imaginaries with all their unspoken implications, and yet confirmation of these discoveries can occur through persuasive patterns of truth.[25] (Can you hear the echoes of Watson's approach from earlier in the chapter—more dialogue!) In short, we might do things or experience things differently, but if you watch enough people, over enough instances, you will see repeat patterns that point to a general human reality. Patterns of truth are critical and actually are the focus of both

---

[25]Ted Newell, "Can a Christian Be a Constructivist?," *IAPCHE Contact* 212 (September 2009): 3-4.

positivist and constructivist research. R. Burke Johnson and Anthony J. Onwuegbuzie say it a little differently but argue for a similar idea, saying that as people create and experience individual realities, we should call them "multiple perspectives, opinions, or beliefs."[26]

This approach allows us to hold space for a shared reality that unites these perspectives, opinions, and beliefs. These thinkers and researchers understand that we all live in the same world together and that objective truths are present, even if we experience them differently. Christian students, researchers, and clinicians can rest assured that there is space to hold one's experience of life as genuine, while humbly recognizing that our experience, along with other patterns of truth, point toward an actual reality made by God the Creator. It is worth knowing that *mixed-methods research* has gained popularity because it combines both positivist and constructivist methods to seek patterns of truth that can be thoughtfully applied to people's lives.[27] This is encouraging because mixed methods create space for curious exploration around diversity yet bound that exploration within rigorous measures of what we are discovering.

A CLOSER LOOK AT POSITIVIST AND CONSTRUCTIVIST METHODOLOGY

We hope our discussion of imaginaries (guiding stories) and ways of knowing (epistemology) has prepared you to appreciate the key roles of both qualitative and quantitative methods in any research toolbox. Our hope below is to draw on our reflections so far and

---

[26]R. Burke Johnson and Anthony J. Onwuegbuzie, "Mixed Methods Research: A Research Paradigm Whose Time Has Come," *Educational Researcher* 33, no. 7 (2004): 16, https://doi.org/10.3102/0013189X033007014.

[27]Johnson and Onwuegbuzie, "Mixed Methods Research," 23-24.

help you see how both qualitative and quantitative approaches can be implemented and trustworthy.

Typically, those seeking truth using a positivist philosophy adopt quantitative research methods. This approach is where you will find tightly defined variables that can be measured, controlled studies, numerical data, statistical analysis, and discussion of probabilities, statistical significance, and reliability. If these terms are new or confusing, then rest assured that your research class and textbook will help you make sense of them. For now, we'll simplify and say that we sometimes playfully describe quantitative research as the application of logic and math to expose patterns of truth. The main foci of quantitative researchers are

1. to be measurable
2. to be generalizable
3. to be replicable
4. to show causation—the golden standard

To meet these standards, each of the following steps are usually included in quantitative research:

1. Identify the research problem.
2. Formulate testable research hypotheses in the light of past literature.
3. Select a research design that answers the research question by testing the hypotheses.
4. Define and operationalize each variable that will be measured.
5. Sample the target population in a randomized and representative fashion and provide participants with informed consent.
6. Conduct the research according to the predefined method.
7. Organize and analyze the collected data.
8. Formulate conclusions and disseminate the findings.

Here is a research example that shows a positivist philosophy and its associated quantitative method: To discover how to help Christians develop felt intimacy in their relationship with God, researchers create hypotheses about effective interventions from past literature, current practices, and theory. The researchers make measurable (operationalize) their definition of intimacy in relationship with God and specify objective measures and how they will be kept from bias. Next, researchers sample a Christian population and randomly assign participants into different groups that each receive a different intervention hypothesized to increase intimacy with God. One group receives no intervention to serve as the control group for comparison.

The researchers use the objective measure of intimacy both before (pre) and after (post) the intervention and gather numerical data. The researchers look for change (variance) in participant scores using statistical analysis and discern whether the differences are statistically significant, which means they are unlikely to happen by chance alone. A significantly greater degree of variance in scores for one intervention group over the others suggests which intervention leads to the greatest reported change in levels of intimacy with God. Other Christians represented by the sample may find the results beneficial in supporting their personal experience of God. Of course, the research may also find no differences in the groups, and the researchers may return to the literature to consider what variables may have accounted for a lack of change. This may lead to iterations of research that slowly provide what Polanyi calls a persuasive pattern of truth in regard to helping Christians with intimacy with God.

Critical to quantitative research are issues of validity and reliability that help establish trust and relate to our chapter's central question, "How do we know what we know?" The simplest way to understand validity and reliability is with an analogy. You place an order in my bakery for three of your favorite apple pies with a flaky crust and large apple slices. Later, I provide you with three pies that all fit the description, and you conclude *I am doing what I said I would*, demonstrating validity as a bakery. If I provide you with three pies of varying flakiness and odd-sized apple slices, I am less accurate, and you would trust me less next time. I am showing you less validity, as I didn't do what I said I would. Validity is a measure of accurately doing something. However, you may be more interested in just receiving pies than in how good they are. You order three pies every week, but you are not concerned with what type of pie, and our bakery delivers on time, every time. You can count on us. Reliability is a measure of *replication* but not accuracy. Reliability is concerned with whether the quantitative method would work on repeat or whether the finding was a one-off. For an informative classroom activity, refer to Nader Nassif and Yassif Khalil, who use the pie analogy to explore validity and reliability concepts.[28]

In short, quantitative research produces trustworthy information to contribute to the persuasive pattern of truth when it is accurate (valid) and replicable (reliable). In practice, the research must represent those whom it says it represents (sampling), must be conducted with strict adherence to the method (avoids confounding variables), and must measure what it says it measures (operationalization of variables and appropriate measures). Further, inferences must be true to the data gathered (statistical methods and discussion). Baking is much the same. If you follow the same accurate recipe with precision and don't add anything or take

---

[28]Nader Nassif and Yvette Khalil, "Making a Pie as a Metaphor for Teaching Scale Validity and Reliability," *American Journal of Evaluation* 27, no. 3 (2006): 393-98, https://doi.org/10.1177/1098214006288786.

anything away, then you can be trusted to provide a consistent product that doesn't mislead you or give you any nasty surprises.

In contrast, those seeking truth using a constructivist philosophy often utilize qualitative research methods. This approach is where you will find exploratory questions, named biases, interviews, observations, calls to action, and the use of code books and interpretation. These steps can lead to accounts of life, collated stories, detailed explanations, and findings that expose patterns very different from the original research agenda. We sometimes describe qualitative research as collaborative acts of observing others and inviting readers into these experiences and their meaning. Qualitative research covers a broad set of goals and methodology, often making it feel elusive or confusing. For example, here are just some of the goals of different methodologies: to uncover lived experiences, to understand how a construct is understood within a specific context, to report a singular case example, to decode patterns of interaction, to provide voice to a marginalized group, to describe cultural phenomena, and to stimulate action among participants through empowerment. Diverse indeed. But there is a through line—discovery.

We simplify the major components of research within most qualitative traditions as

1. Identify the research problem, often in conjunction with the population in question.
2. Formulate purpose statements, which may include research hypotheses.
3. Select a research tradition that achieves the purpose statement.
4. Detail a projected method to engage the target population and gather data.

5. Articulate and account for researcher participation, with particular attention given to values and biases.
6. Conduct the research, often allowing ongoing reflection and methodological flexibility.
7. Organize and analyze the collected data, often in iterative stages.
8. Articulate the experience of participants, formulate conclusions, and disseminate the findings.

Here is the same issue of assisting Christians to develop felt intimacy in their relationship with God, but seen from a constructivist philosophy with its commonly associated qualitative method. First, a constructivist research team understands the construct of intimacy with God to be contextually bound and different for Christians across culture, race, age group, religious tradition, and more. The team defines a specific cultural group and seeks to understand that population's understanding or experience of both relationship with God and intimacy. They may discover that within the focus culture, relationship with God and intimacy do not belong in the same sentence. The team explores the religious traditions around relationship with God and seeks to understand the population's current experiences, including whether they desire any change in their experience. If the population desired change, researchers may collaborate with them to discern the type of change desired and culturally acceptable change strategies.

You can imagine how this process could take a long time and include multiple iterations of research methods. In time, the team collates their findings from focus groups, interviews, and observations, using the cultural group's own words to highlight their needs and experience to a wider audience. Here we see a different type of evidence, one of lived experience, contributing to Polanyi's patterns of truth.

Qualitative research can't be assessed for trustworthiness in the same way as quantitative research. Positivist ideas of validity and reliability just don't fit. Instead, a range of terms have been used to capture qualitative research that is considered authentic, believable, and free from outside or inside disturbance. These include *truth*, *value*, *credibility*, and *goodness*. We follow Danica Hays and Annaliese Singh, agreeing that the term *trustworthiness* is helpful because "in essence, the validity of your study is the truthfulness of your findings and conclusions based on maximum opportunity to hear participant voices in a particular context." Therefore, assessing the trustworthiness of a qualitative study asks whether the study speaks truthfully about what it claims to discuss. To achieve trustworthiness researchers can self-assess their process through the lenses of credibility, transferability, dependability, and confirmability.[29] When qualitative research satisfies these standards, trustworthy evidence can be added to the persuasive pattern of truth.

SYNTHESIZING RESEARCH AND ADJUSTING OUR SOCIAL IMAGINARIES

This chapter has prepared you to consider synthesizing research findings into your understanding of the world. Let's look at what happens when we do this synthesis even if we are not aware that it is happening. Each of the data gathered started with someone's doubt about how the world works in detail and a curiosity to answer the question. Depending on the researcher's imaginary, the issue may be understood differently, and this can be explained by the researcher. Next, the researcher employs a philosophical

---

[29]Hays, and Singh, *Qualitative Inquiry*, 192.

approach to the idea of discovering truth that aligns within their imaginary and uses complementary methods to find evidence of patterns. Finally, various readers (students, counselors, psychologists, parents, clients, politicians, and more) take pieces of this new evidence into their mind, where it bumps into what they knew before. If the reader is discerning of good evidence and humble enough to accept its lessons, they may expand their schemas and operate accordingly.

Changing our minds is often hard. The bigger the gap between what we previously thought and what we are invited to realize, the greater the struggle is. And sometimes, the greater the rewards are. When you first truly accepted the radical news of the gospel, it was a great reward. When you first learned something unwanted (Grandma has cancer, global warming is proceeding faster than we knew), it may have taken time to accept, and you likely wanted verification from another source (e.g., What do Grandma's doctors say? Show me the scientific weather data).

Synthesizing new and divergent data can be tiring and time consuming, but the key traits of self-awareness, humility, and discernment help in the process. These traits go beyond your technical knowledge and allow you to effectively read and assimilate research. Self-awareness allows you to understand your starting assumptions that stem from your imaginary. Humility allows you to accept that you may not know, that you may have distorted views, and that you can learn from others. Discernment allows you to look carefully and critically at research to evaluate validity, reliability, and trustworthiness. We encourage you to practice these traits so that they develop. For example, when you note methodological concerns, do not throw out the research but seek to understand the researchers' choices and what you can learn. Remember, it was another image-bearer who found the limits of our understanding, got curious, attempted to provide evidence, and has invited you to converse with them about their interpretation.

CONCLUSION

While theoretical information doesn't always present as immediately applicable, we hope you have seen that your story of how the world works shapes the way you interact with research. Research doesn't always start from the same assumptions, and this makes a big difference in how it is conducted and discussed. We want you to feel confident to think critically about where this research came from, and having a grasp of positivist and constructivist ideas can certainly help. Most importantly, we want to encourage you that building persuasive patterns of truth can be a real pleasure when we are honest about our starting points, our biases, and our approach. We don't need to prove it all, to everyone, all at once. Step by step. New patterns are a delight and provide our brains with unexpected challenges in God's incredible world. This chapter has laid the foundation for the next, where we consider why we care about what we do and how to expand our research curiosity to love our neighbor.

DISCUSSION QUESTIONS

1. If God's Word provides truth and reality, are you comfortable with the idea that you are still engaged in a process of discovering and interpreting truth? Why or why not?
2. Do you find yourself more immediately drawn to positivist or constructivist approaches to finding evidence about God's world? Why do you think this is?
3. What were the dominant social narratives of your culture growing up? How do you see that your *imaginary* (how you

imagine the world working) has been shaped by your culture's understanding of life?
4. What is your normal disposition and response toward being given new information? Are you skeptical, open, excited, reticent, hostile? Why do you think this might be?
5. If you had to summarize chapter two to another student, researcher, or counselor, what would you say?

LEARNING ACTIVITIES

1. In small groups, discuss what information (or evidence) you would need about one another to feel as though you could care for each person well. Notice and name any differences between the information you stated you would need within the group. What does noting these differences expose about how you may personally approach research and the discovery of truth?
2. In pairs, take it in turns to ask the other person ten questions that can be answered with objective facts, such as: How old are you? How many siblings do you have? When you have finished, consider how much more you know that person. Discuss together whether this information (or evidence) has helped you know the truth about one another. Do you need anything else?

THREE

Honoring Diversity *in the* Kingdom

I (PAUL) WANT TO SHARE two real-life vignettes. First, my good friend recently sent me a text message with a link to a fantastic pair of headphones. Not earbuds but the real expensive ones that only diehard audiophiles know about. He said, "I'm thinking about these. . . . They have great control via the app, lossless streaming, and incredible acoustic range." He has been into 1920s–1930s big band music and loves all the tones and nuances. Just discussing the music, he visibly lights up. Throughout our text exchange I could tell he was excited but nervous. He wanted the joy of the music while avoiding the disappointment of what could turn out to be a regrettable purchase.

Second, my eleven-year-old son and I were taking trash to the dumpster in the alley behind our house when a well-groomed, purring cat sidled up to us. The cat kept following us and meowed more earnestly. My son said, "Dad, I think it's lost," which we debated a little until he said in a gentle voice, "Get your phone out and take a picture. We could put it up around our street and help it get home." Our family had recently had conversations at dinner about the fear of losing our dog Clo, and through more discussion I realized my son was feeling deeply for the well-being of the cat's whole family. He wanted good for them. He wanted this family to be reunited.

These vignettes reveal the power of what each person cares about. Our *cares* shape our concerns, motivations, and actions. My friend cares about rich musical experiences and resourcefulness. My son cares about the well-being and emotional experience of others. These are fairly typical things to care about, and I suspect you can relate. In general, we refer to the things we care for as things we *value*. Much has been written about values, but in simple terms, a value we hold is the culmination of our ascribing goodness, worth, and desirability to specific objects or experiences. When we have ascribed goodness, worth, and desirability to things, it affects our opinions, actions, and goals related to these objects and experiences.[1] This is so normal that Gordon Allport suggests that the priorities that flow from what you value act as a dominating force in your life.[2] Our actions reveal our values, and our values reveal the stories we have internalized about what is good, what is pleasurable, what will bring happiness or success, and everything else.

Research questions are no different. They expose researchers' values that have become active pursuits. The researcher cares to find the right question and its answer because it feels meaningful. For example, I might ask, "What is the most effective method for helping economically distressed people reduce negative rumination and subsequent mental health concerns?" My hope in that study is to help relieve suffering in low socioeconomic status communities. I care about it! Given that we all care about different things, we can affirm the diversity of questions that arise in us alongside a field that states we need to do more to affirm and attend to human diversity

---

[1] Peter M. Allen and Liz Varge, "Complexity: The Co-Evolution of Epistemology, Axiology and Ontology," *Nonlinear Dynamics, Psychology, and Life Sciences* 11, no. 1 (2007): 19-50, www.ncbi.nlm.nih.gov/pubmed/17173728; Benson Irabor and Andrew Onwudinjo, "Ethical Responses to a Changing World of Axiological Questions," *Theology, Philosophy and Education in the 21st Century* (February 2023): 181-94, https://doi.org/10.13140/RG.2.2.15587.63524.
[2] Gordon W. Allport, "Values and Our Youth," *Teachers College Record* 63, no. 3 (1961): 1-8, https://doi.org/10.1177/016146816106300301.

through research.³ Sadly, though, values come in many shapes and sizes, with openness or hostility and both positive and negative impact. This chapter is critical to help us wrestle with what we are valuing, how it affects others, and how we can be shaped as Christian researchers who act ethically with our curiosity.

Here are examples of prior research that show a diversity of cares and manage them positively—we hope it gets you thinking. Our first example is research that cared to understand racial and ethnic distress. One study sought to find the barriers for African Americans seeking care for depression, finding that shame and denial played key roles and needed to be addressed.⁴ Another considered how proximity to peers who died by suicide created a clustering effect among Korean adolescents and suggested monitoring friendship groups after such an event as a preventative strategy.⁵ Other studies asked questions that show a care for the benefits that are inherent to cultures. A fascinating example considered how cultures provide different forms of resilience in the face of traumatic events, acknowledging unique variations.⁶ A second study considered how factors of well-being (gratitude, self-esteem, and optimism) that had been studied in the West may arise among Japanese individuals.⁷ A third question researchers asked explored

---

³Jared Hawkins, Roy Bean, Timothy Smith, and Jonathan Sandberg, "Representation of Race and Ethnicity in Counseling and Counseling Psychology Journals," *The Counseling Psychologist* 50, no. 1 (2022): 123, https://doi.org/10.1177/00110000211041766.

⁴Mario Cruz, Harold Pincus, Jeffrey Harman, Charles Reynolds III, and Edward Post, "Barriers to Care-Seeking for Depressed African Americans," *International Journal of Psychiatry in Medicine* 38, no. 1 (2008): 71. https://pubmed.ncbi.nlm.nih.gov/18624019.

⁵Won-Seok Choi, Beop-Rae Roh, Duk-In Jon, Vin Ryu, Yunhye Oh, and Hyun Ju Hong, "An Exploratory Study on Spatiotemporal Clustering of Suicide in Korean Adolescents," *Child and Adolescent Psychiatry and Mental Health* 18 (2024): 54, https://doi.org/10.1186/s13034-024-00745-9.

⁶Jessica Tyler, Nancy Darrow, Aisha Outlaw, and Jennifer Guffin, "Lived Experiences of Utilizing Cultural Resiliency to Navigate Traumatic Loss," *Journal of Counseling & Development* 101, no. 2 (2023): 180, https://doi.org/10.1002/jcad.12462.

⁷Norberto Nawa and Noriko Yamagishi, "Distinct Associations Between Gratitude, Self-Esteem, and Optimism with Subjective and Psychological Well-Being Among Japanese Individuals," *BMC Psychology* 12 (2024): 130, https://doi.org/10.1186/s40359-024-01606-y.

the appropriate use of counseling interventions in diverse contexts. For example, researchers adapted and trialed emotion-focused therapy with underserved refugees suffering from posttraumatic stress, leading to culturally attuned recommendations.[8] Finally, other studies have engaged the intersection of psychological and spiritual factors. A recent study examined how church messaging affects LGBTQ+ Christians' expectations about how they may be accepted amid church communities, which led the researchers to offer recommendations around providing support to LGBTQ+ Christians.[9] These examples are just some of the ways that valuing diversity expresses itself in our research questions.

Despite the diversity of ideas in the research above, we recognize that there is a darker side to the ways in which research has contributed to bias and oppression over the course of many decades.[10] Some have directly expressed concern for both the accuracy of social-scientific research and the potential for negative impact it could have on clients if values are left unchecked. Paul Pedersen and Anthony Marsella suggested in 1982 there was an ethical crisis in crosscultural counseling, with harm resulting from misapplication of assumptions, assessments, and interventions.[11] There had been a troubling pattern of researchers imposing their values onto others. Both individual and systemic changes are needed to move counseling research into a truly diverse and multicultural space,

---

[8]Davorka Marovic-Johnson and Emily Brown, "Counseling Refugees with Posttraumatic Stress Disorder Using Emotion-Focused Individual Therapy," *Journal of Mental Health Counseling* 46, no. 2 (2024): 96, https://doi.org/10.17744/mehc.46.2.01.

[9]Juan Carlos Hugues and Steven Rouse, "Everyone Belongs Here: How Affirming and Non-Affirming Church Messages and Imagery Cause Different Feelings of Acceptance in LGBTQ+ Christians," *Journal of Psychology and Theology* 51, no. 4 (2023): 523-36, https://doi.org/10.1177/00916471231185811.

[10]Joseph Ponterotto, "Racial/Ethnic Minority Research in the Journal of Counseling Psychology: A Content Analysis and Methodological Critique," *Journal of Counseling Psychology* 35, no. 4 (1988): 410.

[11]Paul Pedersen and Anthony Marsella, "The Ethical Crisis for Cross-Cultural Counseling and Therapy," *Professional Psychology* 13, no. 4 (1982): 492.

which is why we have seen increasing emphasis on diversity competencies. We can learn how to become a part of the solution as we engage self-awareness, reflection, learning, and a process of formation. Core texts within a research or cultural diversity class handle the issues of historical, socioeconomic, ethnic, cultural, and political bias and oppression that have emerged from a predominantly affluent, White, and Western approach to and ownership of psychological research. We both have clients and friends who have been deeply affected by some constellation of these issues as they manifested as micro- (and macro-) aggressions in cultural dynamics, ill-fitting interventions, or colorblindness.

Social Justice and the Whiteness of the Psychology Field

Think back to your first theories class. It is likely that you learned some major names such as Sigmund Freud, Carl Jung, Alfred Adler, Abraham Maslow, Carl Rogers, Burrhus Skinner, Albert Ellis, Aaron Beck, William Glasser—do you notice a trend in these figures? Sometimes we put all their pictures on one slide to show our classes visually that all these men (ahem, *men*) are White and Western. The modern field of psychology was birthed in Germany by Wilhelm Wundt. Throughout Europe and later the United States, the study of psychology took hold. The leaders of the field were White men, with rare exceptions such as Anna Freud, Mary Ainsworth, Karen Horney, and Virginia Satir. These women's contributions never soared to the heights of their male colleagues, evidenced by the fact that they might receive a footnote mention in a counseling theories course. It wasn't until 1989 that Kimberlee Crenshaw wrote her seminal work on intersectionality, and only since the 1990s have the fields of psychology and counseling begun to truly pay attention to issues of diversity. It took until 2014 for the American Counseling Association to add social justice and multiculturalism to its code of ethics as mandates for the profession.

We have a unique challenge and opportunity as researchers developing in the twenty-first century to diversify our field. Actions such as minority scholarships by the National Board of Certified Counselors play a crucial role in increasing the number of people of color entering counseling and psychology work, and we can do more. In research, we can live out our faith by engaging in social justice as we recognize and seek to change the historical Whiteness of research teams and study participants. Even more than this, we need to acknowledge that much of what we have established as true in counseling and psychology is not as generalizable as we have believed. Our base of knowledge is inherently biased and skewed, driven by the questions Western, White researchers have asked and measured in Western, White, and often male and college-educated populations. As researchers and as clinicians, we must maintain a deep awareness that our understanding of human behavior is slanted. If you are in the majority culture, your bias is likely even greater because the things you have learned in psychology from White theorists generally match your own cultural observations.

We do not name bias or injustice to heap shame on the profession. Instead, we encourage you to observe your own potential "White guilt" reactions if you are in the majority culture. Our goals in naming these truths are (1) to validate the oppression, bias, and microaggressions that have occurred in psychological research and counseling rooms, and (2) to raise up a diverse generation of future researchers and clinicians who will carry us forward in the work of Christ-honoring multiculturalism. Will you join us in that work?

A key path to becoming part of positive change is to understand how our values shape our questions and curiosities and what we do in response. This chapter is designed to help you do just that. Let's start by considering the question, How do we end up with the *values* we have? Or, said colloquially, *Why do you care about that?* (or *not care about something else!*). We have said we value objects and experiences, but where do our ascriptions, loaded with bias and prejudice, come from?

The answer lies in what shapes our imaginaries, as we discussed in chapter two. The grand story of Christianity is one of *good living* that should drive our lives and actions toward one another. We can call this way of *good living* a Christian ethic. Now, you might think ethics usually show up as a handbook (ACA or APA, anyone?), a set of principles, a formalized set of practices, or even a shared group commitment (such as licensing board ethics) that instructs us how to live well within a specific area—what has this to do with values? But ethics come from somewhere—the shared stories about the *good life* that suggest what to value. Stories of the good life emerge as people wrestle with sources of knowledge and experience, and for Christians this emerges from God's revelation of the good life in the Bible.[12] Christian ethics can be thought of as instructing us how to live toward the design of flourishing for which we are made. It is wonderful that both Christian ethics and counseling and psychology ethics reject alienating or dehumanizing practices. The Christian ethic provides specific and substantial help toward finding a way to dignify all people through diverse and responsive research. We shall see why, but first we help you consider the values you have.

WHY DO I *CARE* ABOUT *THAT*?

To answer the question "Why do I *care* about *that*?" we said we must consider how a rich set of interwoven factors has taught us to ascribe goodness, worth, and desirability to specific objects and experiences. This experience is far more powerful than our intellectual commitment to an external set of ethics such as the ACA or APA ethics codes. In this section we lay out the factors that teach values (social imaginaries, sin, culture and community, and family of origin) and attempt to show you how they mingle

---

[12]Keith Stanglin, *Ethics Beyond Rules: How Christ's Call to Love Informs Our Moral Choices* (Zondervan, 2021), 22-23.

together in our experiences, challenging our ethical living and research practices.

Imaginaries and the interruption of sin. As we saw in chapter two, our imaginary is our story of how the world works. This story accounts for our whole explanation of life. You might be getting a sense of just how important your imaginary is in shaping what you care about. James Sire pushes the point, saying our understanding isn't abstract but is "situated in the self—the central operating chamber of every human being. It is from this heart that all one's thoughts and actions proceed."[13] If your central story—your understanding of the world—tells you that honoring diverse perspectives is important, you will proceed to demonstrate openness to others. Think of it like this: If your imaginary is the grand story, then values can be seen as the all-important characters that bring the story to life—parts of the whole that are ascribed goodness, worth, and desirability.

Interestingly, the story itself asserts which parts of the story deserve to be valued. Sometimes with clarity, sometimes not. For the Harry Potter fans out there, you might recognize that the story of Hogwarts and the wizarding world organized how you feel toward Dumbledore, Harry, Snape, and the other characters. You learn how to relate to each of them over time because of the story itself. But for the music enthusiasts, the complex arc of genres and their artists intentionally allows space for people to be divided around what is good music. This allows people to divide *within* the music story around artists such as the Beatles or Taylor Swift. Hogwarts's story makes it easy to like Dumbledore. Music's story leaves much more room around the Beatles or Taylor Swift.

---

[13]James Sire, *Naming the Elephant: Worldview as a Concept* (InterVarsity Press, 2004), 143.

As Christians, we believe God's world comes with a wonderful and powerful story, which leads to ways of good living and *theoretically* teaches us what to value. We have discussed the biblical story with its four movements (creation, fall, redemption, and consummation). This story explains our world and values like this: In the beginning God creates (Gen 1–2) creaturely people with limitations, needs, and a desire for loving connection (Gen 2:18; Ps 73:28). Critically, "creation is not a static state of perfection before humanity messed it up, but an ongoing project awaiting fuller realization, extension, and fruitfulness."[14] When humanity is tempted and falls into sin, we are alienated from God. As a result, we know all too well how sin distorts our relationship with each other, creation, and God himself (Gen 3). In total confusion about life, humanity pursued many ways to find peace and fulfillment without God. Humanity is tricked, lost in sin and division, with each believing they are superior to the other (Gen 11:4; Eph 2:8-10). Our ability to internalize the good Christian story is disrupted by sin (doubt, shame, distrust, and fear) that generates values deep in our hearts that move against a Christian ethic of love. Paul the apostle shows us how the Corinthians were *led astray* just as Satan led Eve astray (2 Cor 11:3). What once appeared as good and sustaining looks quite different through jaded and wary eyes—values change.

Miroslav Volf captures Satan's cunning so well: "Evil is capable not only of creating an illusion of well-being, but of *shaping reality* in such a way that the lie about 'well-being' appears as plain verity."[15] The trickery of sin is that it seems self-evident to us that esteeming (valuing) our needs and pursuing happiness through indulgence

---

[14]Tim Harris, "Shalom, Gospel and the Mission of God," in *Flourishing in Faith: Theology Encountering Positive Psychology*, ed. Gilles Ambler, Matthew Anstey, Theo McCall, and Matthew White (Wipf & Stock, 2021), 65-80.

[15]Miroslav Volf, *Exclusion and Embrace: A Theological Exploration of Identity, Otherness, and Reconciliation* (Abingdon, 1996), 89.

and self-fulfillment is wise. We have been led astray, right into the trap of desiring (valuing) what will not sustain us but make us feel comfortable. Our disorientation to God's story leaves behind a story vacuum, and worldly imaginaries enter in, further shaping our values in such a way that it appears we are pursuing what is truly good when we may be astray.

What a problem for diversity and ethical research when we live by an ethic that is less about *others* and more about *self*. When our values seem good, we celebrate their promotion, we fund research that aligns with them, we author interventions to uphold them, and we instill training programs. Can you see the direct links to the problems that have plagued our research agendas? It's hard to see others rightly, it's easy to fear, it's easy to assume our way is right, and it's easy to advocate as we deem fit.

Now we are ready to see how the gospel reshapes our values to fuel us toward ethical living. It begins in the restoration that comes in Christ. As Volf says, at the heart of the Christian faith is that we need not be perceived as innocent to be loved but ought to be embraced even as wrongdoers.[16] This is a powerful value statement about honoring people. And this is precisely what happens in Christ: "Father God is buying back his lost children by sending his eldest son, his heir, to 'give His life as a ransom for many' (Mt 20:28)."[17] True joy, well-being, and the rest we crave are realized when we both rest in God's reuniting salvation *and* absorb the beautiful way of life God teaches us to value—a life of creational intention, productivity, and intimate family life.[18] This (our) story's pinnacle is coming in consummation, when we will be at peace

---

[16]Volf, *Exclusion and Embrace*, 89.
[17]Sandra Richter, *The Epic of Eden: A Christian Entry into the Old Testament* (InterVarsity Press, 2008), 45.
[18]Harris, "Shalom, Gospel and the Mission," 79.

with God and restored to full creativity and intimacy with all others (Rev 7; 21–22). As we wait for this amid life's pain and confusion, our story is "God as the ground of human wellbeing: 'Be holy, because I the Lord your God am holy' (Lev 19:2 NRSV). 'We love, because God first loved us' (1 John 4:19 NRSV). Or in modern parlance, "We flourish, because God flourishes."[19]

Even without a Christian imaginary guiding us, we can still discover something of human well-being because people are still God's creatures, and if we study them well, we see something of the truth. However, when our interpretive story is muddled, we can use good insights for misguided ends. A simple example: *If it makes you feel good, do it.* We all know through one experience or another that overindulgence, or just following your feelings, doesn't work. It starts with desire and ends in a type of death. The biblical solution to changing our values is to soak in the reality of God's abundant love. When we do this we absorb a Christian imaginary, in which good living is about others, and it makes sense deep in our bones. We can actively soak in the story by living in Christian community that enacts the story. We can enact lives in which Jesus is the Redeemer, in which we believe the kingdom is coming, and we let these truths shape our values. When the story changes, our values change, our motivations change, and our research changes.

Culture and community. We come to the next factor that shapes our values. People within different cultures and communities enact all manner of values based on their shared stories (imaginaries) and their separate stories (life experiences). Even when values overlap between cultures, their prioritization is different. Local communities generally share some agreement around a grand story giving rise to what we call cultures. Garrett McAuliffe states that culture includes

---

[19]M. Anstey, "And God Saw It Was Good," in Ambler et al., *Flourishing in Faith*, 63-64.

"attitudes, habits, norms, beliefs, customs, rituals, styles, and artifacts," and these elements coalesce into internalized and expressed stories that "express a group's adaptation to its environment."[20] Over time, the stories expressed in and through a social environment shape and reshape cultural values. Fascinatingly, advances in neuroscience show that the origins of culture-making start in infants, who have a "well-integrated self at birth, an effective self. But [they must] work out what to do with this motivated life. . . . One of the first things to learn is the meaning of the world: to learn the meaning of other older person's actions."[21] By watching others and participating in sociocultural life, we have come to an awareness of how to interpret, think, and respond. Culture is so powerful that it shapes our understanding of others' thoughts and emotions; how we look at others' faces; our economic life; our religious beliefs, unity, and experience; what we want from artificial intelligence; and much more.[22]

Many volumes explore how cultures are formed and sustained. For our purposes we highlight two core processes that relate to living in a fallen world. First, *ethnocentrism*, which is the strong sense of importance people place on their own ethnic groups. Boris Bizumic, Conal Monaghan, and Daniel Priest explain that humans tend to

---

[20]Garrett McAuliffe, "Culture and Diversity Defined," in *Culturally Alert Counseling: A Comprehensive Introduction*, 2nd ed., ed. Garrett McAuliffe et al. (Sage, 2013), 8.

[21]C. Trevarthan, "Neuroscience and Intrinsic Psychodynamics: Current Knowledge and Potential for Therapy," in *Revolutionary Connections: Neuroscience and Psychotherapy*, ed. Jenny Corrigall and Heward Wilkinson (Karnac Books, 2003), 67.

[22]Francois Quesque et al., "Does Culture Shape Our Understanding of Others' Thoughts and Emotions? An Investigation Across 12 Countries," *Neuropsychology* 36, no. 7 (2022): 664, https://doi.org/10.1037/neu0000817; Caroline Blais, Rachael Jack, Christoph Scheepers, Daniel Fiset, and Roberto Caldara, "Culture Shapes How We Look at Faces," *PLoS One* 3, no. 8 (2008): e3022, https://doi.org/10.1371/journal.pone.0003022; Viviana Zelizer, *Economic Lives: How Culture Shapes the Economy* (Princeton University Press, 2011), x; Samuel Stroope, "How Culture Shapes Community: Bible Belief, Theological Unity, and a Sense of Belonging in Religious Congregations," *The Sociological Quarterly* 52, no. 4 (2011): 568, https://doi.org/10.1111/j.1533-8525.2011.01220.x; Xiao Ge, Chuchen Xu, Daigo Misaki, Hazel Markus, and Jeanne Tsai, "How Culture Shapes What People Want from AI," *CHI '24: Proceedings of the CHI Conference on Human Factors in Computing Systems*, 95 (2024): 11, https://doi.org/10.1145/3613904.3642660.

live as if everything revolves around us and our kin. Even when a culture's diversity is high, people still tend to have few friends that are dissimilar to them; we are drawn to self-ism.[23] For instance, it wasn't historically normative to pay attention to cultural and racial bias amid research because we didn't value, let alone recognize, the importance of diversity. Take one example: The Asian American community was historically labeled the "model minority," suggesting they function well, are somehow immune from cultural conflicts, and adjust easily. This perception left members of this cultural group with increased performative pressure and a lack of support.

A second core process is *mainstreaming*, which identifies how being saturated in a continual flow of similar information shapes what we perceive as normal.[24] Similar messages from personal relationships, media, institutions, advertising, and more interact in "a continual, dynamic, ongoing process of interaction among messages and contexts."[25] What happens next is that we inevitably think, feel, perceive, and make choices from *within* the view of our culturally cultivated story.[26] In short, our relationships and culture have mainstreamed repeating messages in our story that shape our values. In the end, things from *within* the story seem *self-evident*. Anything from *without* seems strange and improbable. Consider the idea of Botox. It was odd (or at least niche) a while ago, but now it is common. Why? Because its supposed benefits and necessity for our culturally defined ideals of beauty are being mainstreamed to us through social media, advertising, and relationships.

---

[23]Boris Bizumic, Conal Monaghan, and Daniel Priest, "The Return of Ethnocentrism," *Advances in Political Psychology* 42, no. 1 (2021): 29-30.
[24]*Cambridge Dictionary*, s.v. "Mainstreaming," accessed May 13, 2024, https://dictionary.cambridge.org/us/dictionary/english/mainstreaming.
[25]George Gerbner, "Cultivation Analysis: An Overview," *Mass Communication & Society* 1 (1998): 180, http://dx.doi.org/10.1080/15205436.1998.9677855.
[26]Glen Scrivener, *The Air We Breathe: How We All Came to Believe in Freedom, Kindness, Progress, and Equality* (Good Book Company, 2022).

Cultures and their communities become expressions of their own *self-evident* values. Let's be honest, who doesn't like to fit in and feel like part of a group (even if it's fitting into a group that likes to *not* fit in)? We all want the experience that our attitudes, habits, norms, beliefs, customs, rituals, styles, and artifacts are good and support our flourishing. This makes people hold tight to the culture that sustains their coherent story about the world and limits their curiosity about the lived experience of others. Engaging a new culture with different values can be challenging and revealing, as many young clinicians and researchers discover.

Even amid people who long to express themselves and their creativity in positive cultural and communal ways, the reality of the fall is seen as self-preservation and fragmentation. We are no different and suffer from what Romans 12:3 describes: No one should "think of himself more highly than he ought to think, but to think with sober judgment." It is hard to soberly reflect on our cultural values. As mental health providers, we must engage in cultural self-examination to discover our values and learn to see multiculturally. What a struggle when our "heart is deceitful above all things, and desperately sick" (Jer 17:9).

Whatever story your culture mainstreamed (through media, celebrities, economics, etc.) shaped what you value, and we display these values in our research curiosity. So, we invite you to ask yourself, What has my culture mainstreamed to me? What is lacking in cultural messages that my Christian story supplies? Where are these messages in conflict? What can I see or not see about the needs and experiences of others? Am I reactive to the needs of others, and why? What values do I hold about personal growth and well-being that limit my research curiosity? And do I need to change what I am exposed to so that the mainstreamed messages I absorb change?

Beyond Bracketing

Bracketing is the standard practice for addressing values conflicts in research and counseling, and the concept is central to many ethical decision-making models.[a] Bracketing is a tool to help the novice researcher gain awareness and control of biases by stepping back and seeing differences between values we were taught to hold versus ones we do hold. The idea is that you set aside your values and just use the secular researcher values you were taught. While it is important for any researcher to seek as much objectivity as possible, Christians with deeply held religious beliefs may find that the bracketing approach creates cognitive dissonance and feelings of forsaking one's values. Therefore, the idea of setting aside values in order to research and practice ethically may not resolve the experience of values conflict for Christians.

We propose an alternative model to the resolution of values conflicts using concepts from James Fowler's stages of faith and Lawrence Kohlberg's stages of moral development to go beyond bracketing.[b] You may choose to do a deeper dive into these theorists and their work; we apply their basic ideas here. We believe that the use of bracketing reflects Kohlberg's stage four of moral development, characterized by "doing one's duty in society, upholding the social order, and maintaining the welfare of society or the group."[c] We also view bracketing as occurring in the Fowler's stages three and four of faith development, defined by an awareness of one's own values.

The advanced counselor who is attending to values conflicts that emerge amid their work can begin to see beyond binary categories and hold multiple views in tension. In the higher stages of faith development, we are able to lean into the reality that faith is much bigger than ourselves, and we recognize the implications of both personal and systemic sin and redemption. Fowler describes a "quality of the transcendent" in this highest stage.[d] What if we as researchers, instead of merely setting aside our values, were able to hold their complexity while also allowing for further complexity and diversity of values in God's world? Rather than getting stuck on the black-and-white thinking that sometimes surrounds values conflicts, we might love our neighbor, a deeper, central aspect of our faith, as each person holds different but honored values. This approach is not an amputation of values, but it is a healing of the fractured self as we attend to people amid complexity.

Rather than merely bracketing your values, evaluate where you are within the stages of faith and stages of moral development. Do not merely recognize your bias and set it aside for the sake of research, but instead do the internal work necessary to expand your thinking. This work includes racial-identity development, spiritual growth, and sometimes trauma work. Once you are able to recognize your biases, ask yourself where they come from. Explore the art of looking at the world from the perspective of another. Practice nonjudgmentally holding in tension views you hold with the conflicting views of another. Here you will hold your own values, honor the values of others, and allow diverse values an appropriate place within research. We believe that this inner work, essential for counselor-researcher development, will move you beyond bracketing into a framework of justice and broader Christian ethics for the research process, as we've been discussing in this chapter.

[a]Michael M. Kocet and Barbara J. Herlihy, "Addressing Value-Based Conflicts Within the Counseling Relationship: A Decision-Making Model," *Journal of Counseling & Development* 92, no. 2 (2014): 180-86, https://doi.org/10.1002/j.1556-6676.2014.00146.x; Colleen M. L. Grunhaus, Victor E. Tuazon, Edith Gonzalez, and Nathaniel J. Wagner, "A Counselor Education Case Study: The Counselor Values-Based Conflict Model in Action," *Counseling and Values* 63, no. 2 (2018): 164-79, https://doi.org/10.1002/cvj.12086.
[b]James W. Fowler, *Stages of Faith: The Psychology of Human Development* (HarperCollins, 1995); Lawrence Kohlberg, *The Philosophy of Moral Development: Moral Stages and the Idea of Justice* (Harper & Row, 1981), 409-12.
[c]Kohlberg, *Philosophy of Moral Development*, 410.
[d]Fowler, *Stages of Faith*. 209.

Family of origin. The final category we explore that affects our values and ethics through experience and learning is the close-knit interactions of family. I say "close-knit" not to indicate a felt love or closeness (although this is often the case) but to indicate the consistent and inescapable impact of our first caregiver experiences as they socialized and taught us.[27] In the early stages of

[27]Colette Sabatier and Lyda Lannegrand-Willems, "Transmission of Family Values and Attachment: A French Three-Generation Study," *Applied Psychology* 54, no. 3 (2005): 379, https://doi.org/10.1111/j.1464-0597.2005.00216.x.

life, we are in this context most of the time and start utterly dependent on these people for nurture and sustenance, creating a huge need to understand what is going on so we can fit in. Importantly, a caregiver's approach to their children is shaped by their reasons for having children, and this shapes their goals and actions. Did your parents think children were desirable for group survival, satisfaction, personal growth, or something else? Each of these motivations could lead your parents to emphasize things such as independence, affection, obedience, and skill formation differently. As our caregivers enacted behaviors they valued, we as children observed them and imitated them.[28] Do you remember your caregivers explicitly emphasizing value-driven behaviors such as sharing? I sure do. Of course, as children grow, exposure to diverse people and experiences challenges children's values, causing them to try out and adopt different values from their caregivers.[29]

Experiences of attachment are important in how children learn values. If they feel free to ask questions or challenge valued behaviors, this is completely different from living in fear. Attachment relationships develop early with those who comfort and support us, and these relationships form our cognitive-affective schemas. Optimally, these schemas are filled with a sense of internal security and confidence in self and others.[30] Of course, insecure attachment can form when we are not sure about the availability or responsiveness of others, but whatever our experience of attachment, our schema shaped our behaviors and interactional patterns when we

---

[28] Diana Boer and Klaus Boehnke, "What Are Values? Where Do They Come From? A Developmental Perspective," in *Handbook of Value: Perspectives from Economics, Neuroscience, Philosophy, Psychology and Sociology*, ed. Tobias Brosch and David Sander (Oxford University Press, 2015), 131, https://doi.org/10.1093/acprof:oso/9780198716600.003.0007.
[29] Boer and Boehnke, "What Are Values?," 131-35.
[30] Sabatier and Lannegrand-Willems, "Transmission of Family Values," 380.

were in distress.[31] Secure attachment helpfully gives rise to an increased sense of self and positive obligation toward others, while insecure attachment gives rise to identity challenges and ineffective or antisocial behaviors.[32] If you felt safe going to your caregiver, it changed the learning dynamic of the relationship, and you could foster trust, connection, and the ability to learn through bold questions. If you were insecure, you were probably more rigid.

I (Paul) was somewhere in the middle as a child. Sometimes I rejected what was being told to me, but sometimes I just accepted it to stay in my mum's good books. Can you think of a rebellious child who defines their own path? Or a submissive child who simply learns the caregiver's desires? Studies have shown our learned behaviors link directly back to our values; for example, studies have found that living with secure attachment leads people to place more importance on values that allow flexible and adaptive communal responses.[33] This means that when we trust our needs can be heard and responded to, we are less anxious to take care of ourselves and become generous in caring for others. Our family life affects how we see people and what concerns we might be curious about.

Sin, of course, has a large part to play in our family learning. Children struggle with prosocial values such as sharing or delaying gratification, not just because they are developing but also because they are learning to manage the desire to feel better right now. We are exquisitely primed in our early years to be incredibly selfish. The value-related experience of "if I share now, I'll feel good about

---

[31]Mario Mikulincer et al., "Attachment Theory and Concern for Others' Welfare: Evidence That Activation of the Sense of Secure Base Promotes Endorsement of Self-Transcendence Values," *Basic and Applied Social Psychology* 25, no. 4 (2010): 299-300, https://doi.org/10.1207/S1532 4834BASP2504_4.

[32]Sabatier and Lannegrand-Willems, "Transmission of Family Values," 381.

[33]Mikulincer et al., "Attachment Theory and Concern," 310.

myself later" seems a long way off. Children are a great example of the divided heart we hear about in Romans 7. Plus, our caregivers struggled with their own sin, pursuing things they hoped would satisfy them, such as rest, wealth, money, appearance, or approval. This too taught us what to value. However, the good caregiver imperfectly battles to give themselves to their children and we experience this complex web of values.

Consider with us how parent choices can shape children: A parent might love the restorative feeling of peace and quiet after a hard day. Nothing wrong with that. However, when their three-year-old is joyfully making a racket most days, the parent's restoration is disrupted, and the parent habitually quiets the child with screen time, especially when the child is emotionally dysregulated. This child might feel entertained but not curiously engaged and learns to push away difficult feelings. The child might come to value alone time and peace and quiet like the parent. Fast-forward, and as a grown researcher this person shows a deep bias toward promoting peace and quiet, contemplative practices as optimal regulation. These practices have their place, but are they a full reflection of healthy variables such as coregulation, intimacy, comfort, and sacrificial living? And does this budding researcher have awareness for cultural differences around the idea of peace or appropriate intervention? While not catastrophic, this example demonstrates how family life amid the fall, with all its rough edges, shapes our values and research curiosity.

The human experience. We considered why we care about specific things and how they come to dictate our view of good living. We laid out how the important factors of imaginaries, sin, culture and community, and family of origin all shape our values and change how we live in response. Finally, we briefly explored how each of these factors in the context of the fall leads to researcher bias, which is the soil for acts of privilege and oppression. Now we draw these factors together and follow Paul's personal life to see how these factors weave together and affect cares, curiosity, awareness, and engagement with God's diverse world. Notice how the factors in Paul's life informed his curiosity as a researcher, and imagine what problems this could create. Watch for how Paul describes good living, the impact of culture and community, the influence of family dynamics, and of course, the fall:

> I grew up in southern rural England in the late eighties, and by the time I began my PhD in counselor education and supervision, I had learned that our loving God had a master plan for his world. This is a plan in which the joy of the Trinity is shared between God's people in creative and productive communal life that invites healing and growth. However, that was a stark shift from childhood, when I didn't feel there was a coherent story for life. Church never seemed to connect to the week, even though I repeatedly sang, "He has the whole world in his hands." It didn't feel like that growing up—it was too messy! Christianity was taught as a way of life where you put others first—yet everyone seemed more concerned about themselves? At home, I knew my parents loved me, but life seemed like a complicated game of give and take, navigating other people's reactions and needs before your own. My life experience left me with real questions. Did I fit in? I'm sure I am loved, but does anyone actually care about me?
>
> At school I learned that being cool mattered, a little extra weight is shameful, girls are confusing, and if you work hard enough, you'll get somewhere. I learned that people help when they want but most of the time leave you alone, expecting you to figure it out. This applied to sports too, as I played basketball daily until my back pain overtook me. I simply couldn't push through it, but I never asked about changing it and put up with it. School and college continued, and I couldn't decide what to study. I felt like I didn't know myself, but the full story is I didn't have self-confidence and feared failing at what I loved. I sought advice about degrees, but it was given without the advice givers understanding me, so I tried and left a business studies degree. Twists and turns occurred as I tried again, felt encouraged in my faith, and ended up with an advertising degree. But instead of an advertising job, I pursued an internship with a church because I had grown in my love of Jesus

and thought I might be interested in becoming a pastor. I spent my internship in a middle-class, White, suburban, commuter town near London. It was a lonely time with everyone traveling so much and having little energy for social engagement.

Finally, at age twenty-four I was struggling with so much back pain I had a big surgery with a long recovery, during which I experienced true dependence again (I couldn't wash or dress myself), and for the first time since being little, I felt the freedom to have needs I couldn't meet and the wonder of being truly cared for. During recovery I began to appreciate slow mornings with my infant daughter, sipping tea after a cold morning at the park, and not being productive. Not long after this I sought out a counseling degree, perceiving that I longed to work with people in pain who all deserved access to care.

How people live shows you how they really believe *life works*, and this comes through in Paul's words. He struggled to believe God had a good master plan when he was younger because of confusing experiences. He also didn't emphasize a relationship with God, comfort, or positive experiences in community. Paul does state a vision of flourishing creativity and productivity, yet tells a story full of self-doubt and thwarted efforts. Finally, there is no mention or experience of people who are different from him or of learning from others. His story is particularly White and middle class, with normative middle-class concerns and social training. Can you imagine the difference if he had lived in Kolkata, India, was adopted into another country, or grew up on the poverty line? This isn't to denigrate anyone's experience but to highlight how context shapes us.

So, how do you react to the information that Paul's dissertation topic explored how having a relationship with God develops character virtues and how these virtues lead to well-being in our lives? Is it surprising that Paul was deeply curious about virtue formation, asking questions such as, "How can we live well with one another?" Doesn't it fit his story that he wanted to know more about how a relationship with God might shape us? He was fascinated to explore how we really feel satisfaction and secure in life, and whether that relates to God. Can you see these curiosities and questions flowing out of Paul's life experiences?

Our imaginaries, cultures, and lives leave us with blind spots that relate to bias within our research, but these biases may be a good thing. Paul's research would not have happened if he didn't have a unique intersection of experiences: English-familial-cultural-relational-Christian. We wouldn't have the same data from over two thousand Christians showing how God affects their character virtues. You might not be doing a dissertation but a senior or master's thesis (or something else), and your experience may give you curiosities that would help extend research into much-needed places. Where might your unique cares and questions lead us collectively? We don't want you to see your perspective as bad—not at all. Yet we all need to embrace how biased and specific we are. There is tension here. We have the potential to expand, include, and exclude. It is wise to consider what effect our research questions might have and whom they faithfully represent. We hope you are becoming more aware of the potential for your curiosity to be limited and specific in God's world. We are all affected by these issues, and our intention is to raise them and proactively engage them without shame. After all, biased curiosity and limited vision are normal in our human lives.

Seeking Out Diverse Samples

When we take a convenience sampling approach to research, we are likely to have nondiverse samples of participants who are similar to ourselves. To do the hard work of diversifying research, we have to willingly inconvenience ourselves. Having learned the hard way during my dissertation research, I (Paul) have implemented a careful approach to expand my personal curiosity and plan for robust participant selection.

First, when studying how spiritual formation and mentoring affected counselors' efforts to integrate their faith into counseling, I wanted to make sure the racial diversity of my sample mirrored the counseling population. I decided to research racial diversity among counselors, and a 2019 Bureau of Labor Statistics study found 88 percent of counselors were white. While diversity in the field is still lower than in the general population, I brainstormed how to build from my own mostly White connections and find participants from across America. As a result, I limited personal contacts and recruited from a Christian university with strong diversity, a Midwestern ACA mailing list, and a national listserv of counselors. This strategy did not guarantee robust diversity but provided a greater likelihood. My final sample was 85 percent White, a little more diverse than the national average.

Second, when studying the issue of suicide (one of my clinical interest areas), I have purposefully sought out perspectives on this issue that differ from my own, in terms of both causal factors and therapeutic responses. This has been challenging. For example, the first time I came across the Collaborative Assessment and Management of Suicidality (CAMS) approach to suicide prevention, I was a little shocked that this approach simply acknowledges suicide is a *good choice*, inasmuch as it is effective at ending someone's experience of psychological pain.[a] Proponents of the CAMS approach advocate for life and alternative coping strategies, yet they aren't scared to value the desire of people to end their pain even if it meant extreme measures. This was at odds with anything I had heard in the church previously. Instead, I had heard versions of the idea that suicide was unforgivable and a self-focused attitude that ignored the provisions of God. Ultimately, I had to reconcile my imaginary that God is our provider and comfort with the data that showed how effective the CAMS approach was at helping people stay alive. I am glad to say that I now see how the CAMS approach fits well within a Christian approach to counseling, not least because it forces me to humbly depend on God.

[a] David Jobes, *Managing Suicidal Risk: A Collaborative Approach*, 3rd ed. (Guildford, 2023), 4.

EXPANDING CARES AND CURIOSITY

Having seen how our values, or what we care about, develop in a relatively narrow manner, we now consider how to expand and enrich our *cares*, whether we come from a majority or a minority. It all starts with learning from God's heart for diverse people, which forms the Christian ethic for diverse engagement. We personally find this inviting, motivational, and formative for our researcher eyes, and we hope you will too. In this section, we explore how internalizing God's story shapes us and provides for curious engagement with others in research. Finally, we share practical tools to help you become researchers who are multiculturally competent for the well-being of others.

God's heart of diversity. So, what is God's heart for the diverse? It starts with the Israelites in the Old Testament and with the precious idea that Jesus would come as Messiah and King for all the nations (Is 9:6-7), and his governing would increase forever and provide peace in God's great kingdom. Later on, it blew the minds of God's followers in Jesus' day that the Messiah intended to mediate God's covenant to *all* humanity—"For God so loved the world, that he gave his only Son, that whoever believes in him shall not perish but have eternal life" (Jn 3:16).[34] God didn't want separation. The Israelites often operated with a story of exclusivity in their minds, like what we often see today across culture wars. Yet God knew all along that his story is about reconciling all those who believed in him, loved him, repented of sin, and followed him. We invite you to open up your heart and mind to the story of Genesis to see what God designed for us *all*.

In the Garden of Eden, God gave a beautiful home of diversity and creativity and invited the man and woman together to

---

[34]Richter, *Epic of Eden*, 217.

participate with him in creation by imaging him. You can image him in a deep desire for intimacy and creative delight. God invites you to enjoy a life in the Trinity, of giving and receiving—he invites you to enjoy being separate and together with others.[35] The beautiful life we are called to is communal intimacy, in which seeing one another and laboring for them is a delight.[36] When Eve eats the fruit and passes it to Adam, secure intimacy is broken, trust is undermined, and shame enters the story. This is critical to us as researchers because this is the beginning of division and separation, from God and each other. We weren't made to maintain separation. But with the curse people are selfish, or culturally insensitive, and it feels hard to care for them. The curse, with its distrust, self-preservation, and separation, becomes the foundation of *our* story. It is different from *God's* intended story. God was the first to see each of us, to have questions that were for our good, that are intended to heal us: "Where are you?" (Gen 3:9). Your questions that seek the good of diverse people follow your Heavenly Father.

If we rejoin God's story in the New Testament, we see Jesus declare all foods clean again, removing separations. The passages that deal with these food issues show that separation and division from others is a key issue that Jesus' kingdom will overcome—all can now eat together without restriction (Mk 7:19; Rom 14:20; 1 Cor 8:9). All people are invited to intimacy, imaging God in community, and the creation of beauty. The apostles were tasked with bringing this new life to the ends of the earth (Acts 1:8) as a precursor to the day when every culture and nation will bring their treasure into the kingdom of God (Rev 21:24-26). It is a beautiful story to know

---

[35] Volf, *Exclusion and Embrace*, 128.
[36] Ross Hastings, *Theological Ethics: The Moral Life of the Gospel in Contemporary Context* (Zondervan Academic, 2021), 79-84.

that we will all stand shoulder to shoulder, feeling no envy, jealousy, fear, or shame, but only delight, joy, interest, care, and favor. This is what excites us as researchers. We were made to see and delight in one another, to create good for one another, to research what *they*, not just *I*, need.

As this story becomes our story—our imaginary—it alters how we interpret the world. For example, we start to deeply believe that our Indian, Lebanese, or Sudanese sister has been made to image our God and create beauty in a way we may not. We get curious. If we lean in together and peer past the surface divisions, what can the other teach me? What might I find out about flourishing in God's world? We are shaped by God's story and accept that differences, cultures, and identities create challenges and confusion but ultimately express God's glory. We hope this gives you confidence that truly Christian research *is* diversity-honoring research. You can love as Christ has by asking curious research questions about the diversity of people's lives that is often discussed using the language of the biopsychosocial-spiritual.

Curiously engaging the biopsychosocial-spiritual. As we have named, God has called us into a creative partnership with himself and others to bring beauty. Counseling and psychology research is one way to do this, and it occurs in the sandbox we discussed in chapter one. Just as kids dig in, explore, play, and build in the sandbox, we too can join in God's sandbox through diverse research. We have so much to explore here as our biological lives, psychological lives, social lives, and spiritual lives intersect within us and between us. What a sandbox our biopsychosocial-spiritual lives provide.

Diverse lives are the sandbox because we develop in dynamic relationship to sociocultural environments. Jack Balswick, Pamela King, and Kevin Reimer use the term *relational developmental systems* to capture this idea that each part of the system in which we live affects the others, with no simple linear effects.[37] Everything from your relationship with God, time in school, church, culture, grandparents, friends, food, geography, and age—to name just a few—affects you and your well-being. Developmental theorists, psychologists, and counselors have been exploring for a relatively short time, and you can join them. We hope you are excited with us that there is so much to explore. Cast your mind back to chapter one's invitation to curiosity. What is it that you value and have become interested in amid the relational developmental systems of people's lives? How might you view your curiosity within the cultural system in which you live?

To stimulate your curiosity for the beauty of diversity, let's break down the biopsychosocial-spiritual in God's world. First, *bio-* includes the human body with all its parts and functions and considers how it has been distorted by the curse of the fall. Our brains and bodies are fantastic. Are you interested in the impact of cultural trauma on the brain and how this affects self-perception? Are you curious how imbalances of neurochemicals such as dopamine might relate to mood disorders and whether this could be different in Asian compared to Latino biology due to population genetics? Do you wonder about racially different bodies' experiences of pain amid cultural messages?

Psycho- refers to psychological factors and how we express ourselves. For instance, we form schemas and personality patterns in response to significant relationships, stress in the environment, and experiences of trauma or conditioning. Our internal worlds—our minds—powerfully influence our lives. Are you fascinated by culturally esteemed personality traits and how they support

---

[37]Jack Balswick, Pamela King, and Kevin Reimer, *The Reciprocating Self: Human Development in Theological Perspective*, 2nd ed. (InterVarsity Press, 2016).

flourishing? Have you wondered how diverse experiences of attachment affect resilience?

Social factors describe the impact of culture and social dynamics on our psychology. Consider how each culture relates, supports, discourages, organizes, and expresses itself in different ways that shape us. Have you wondered how you might date or experience marriage differently if you lived in Europe or Africa? Are you sensitive to how family history has altered your perception of career and opportunity?

Finally, *spiritual* engages experiences of transcendence, interconnection, and stories of meaning. Do you wonder why religions captivate people and motivate them? Are you curious about the connections between flourishing, worship, and service?

The intersections of these variables are plentiful. Researchers can follow their curiosity to locate variables across the biopsychosocial-spiritual and ask what we know about how they relate. For example, take the bio- variable of neurochemical imbalance and the spiritual variable of a relationship with God, and investigate their interaction. Or take the social variable of cultural approaches to grief, the psycho- variable of resilience, and the spiritual variable of hope, and explore how hope and resilience relate and affect well-being in the face of grief. Then do this across different cultural groups. The playground is simply huge, and God is invested in the redemptive possibilities of it all.

PRACTICAL TOOLS

The options for our curiosity are expansive, and *we* are the limiting factor. We want to help prepare you to ask even more curious and insightful questions that both delight you and attend to diverse communities. Here we offer you tools to assist in personal formation and engagement in research practices. These tools have helped us as researchers pay careful attention to how we label variables, how we design research studies, and how we interpret and share data so that we do not import bias, miss the needs of others, or come to limiting conclusions.

Formation of the self. We have explored God's heart for his diverse creation and how this establishes the Christian ethics of diversity. As we seek to join God's story and to value diversity and the needs of others, we understand this as an act of spiritual formation. Formation is an active, embodied pursuit, and John Clark and Marcus Johnson explain how this requires "the renewal of our minds and transformation of our whole person into the image of our incarnate God and Savior."[38] Colossians 3:2 urges us to "set [our] minds on things that are above, not on things that are on earth." We aren't forgetting the earth and what we notice; instead, we are mindfully allowing God's story and its values to meld with our earthly cares. Renewing our minds is an embodied act because our actions relate closely to our thinking and the imaginaries that shape the stories we hold dear. As we practice mindfully noticing what we attend to, this will illuminate our values. Then, because we don't change much just because we want to, we can place ourselves amid the influence of *God's story* through community, thought partners, church, Scripture, and more so that God's story will infuse our old one. Our old cares can start to seem distant or foolish, and space for the other is created.

C. S. Lewis in *The Weight of Glory* helps us notice just how different our engagement for others would be if we dwelled fully in the biblical story:

> It is a serious thing to live in a society of possible gods and goddesses, to remember that the dullest and most uninteresting person you can talk to may

---

[38]John Clark and Marcus Johnson, *A Call to Christian Formation: How Theology Makes Sense of Our World* (Baker Academic, 2021), 22.

one day be a creature which, if you saw it now, you would be strongly tempted to worship, or else a horror and a corruption such as you now meet, if at all, only in a nightmare. All day long we are, in some degree, helping each other to one or other of these destinations.[39]

If we recognized one another as such precious creatures, would that change how we cared for them? Prioritized research to serve them? Let us hold our cares to the light of God's story.

We have found that dwelling on the biblical story with God as our loving King and provider fosters humility and rest. Humility is a freeing virtue that is defined by an accurate appraisal of self as finite and in need of help, a lack of concern for self-importance, a strong sense of one's worth for relationships, and transcendence of the self that provides for an orientation toward others.[40] This is the sweet gift of God to us in his story. He tells us just who we are and how much we are loved. Yet, accepting our limitations and expanding our engagement with others is still complex given the fall, as a result of which we are predisposed to in-group preference and self-preservation. This posture makes sense in a world without God, in which limited resources and pain tempt each group to separation and suspicion as they seek their own survival (ethnocentrism again). God's bigger story can change us through provision and coming redemption, a state in which satisfaction isn't the highest goal. When we know we are beloved children of the King, we can turn our attention to the good of the other.

Developing humility is possible in contexts that steep us in God's love. Our acceptance of our limited selves, and our curiosity for the world, is formed when we experience sustaining community (God's hands and feet), *and* this is anchored by the story

---

[39]C. S. Lewis, *The Weight of Glory: And Other Addresses* (HarperCollins, 1980), 45-46.
[40]Caroline Lavelock et al., "Still Waters Run Deep: Humility as a Master Virtue," *Journal of Psychology and Theology* 45, no. 4 (2017): 287, https://doi.org/10.1177/009164711704500404.

we recite and remember (God's story). Humble stability enables us to bracket (hold) our own experience because we are not in distress. Then we can attune, listen, and empathize with the needs of others. We invite you to reflect on *where* and *how* you are engaging in a sustaining community that delights in truth together. Is this present in your life right now? If so, how can you lean in? If not, where could you find it?

Finally, forming ourselves is critical because we influence our colleagues and research participants.[41] If we hold self-focused or misguided assumptions about others, we run the risk of spreading our views through small and large interactions, interrupting the work of beauty. For example, we might omit the humble act of mentioning that we are uneasy around this group of people and inadvertently bias our colleagues through hesitation. Or, more overtly, we may provide research participants with negative relational experiences as we remain cold or distant. In short, the humility afforded by the gospel allows us to be aware of our automatic reactions to others. We encourage you to sit in the experience *and* teaching of God's story as you are formed. We encourage you to use tools such as self-reflective journaling and sharing your struggles in a supportive community as you mindfully allow others to shape your curiosity.

Approach to variables. We have discussed how the process of formation requires that we spend time with others, hear their stories, and let them inform us about their experience of pain and well-being. As we are open to the voice of others, we will start to see their needs as they do. It is critical that we are open to the participants' (those we are talking to or researching) names and

---

[41]Stephanie Reich and Jennifer Reich, "Cultural Competence in Interdisciplinary Collaborations: A Method for Respecting Diversity in Research Partnerships," *American Journal of Community Psychology* 38, nos. 1-2 (2006): 1-7, https://doi.org/10.1007/s10464-006-9064-1.

descriptions of their experiences so that we do not alter what they are communicating.[42] With practice, we can learn to filter out our own labels. When we do this, we will have variables to define and measure that represent and matter to these specific people. This act of humility presents a technical challenge because the scientific community often labels phenomena differently from participants' colloquial terms. For example, what most people mean by intimacy isn't what attachment researchers mean by intimacy. Or what middle-class White researchers mean by distress doesn't necessarily align with what a working-class immigrant means by distress. A participant's culture has mainstreamed so much data in their lives that they come to unique cultural understandings of different phenomena. We honor our participants and provide effective research by checking that the labels and language we use for variables describing the phenomenon the participants experience makes sense to them. While this slows the research process, it safeguards its utility. More importantly, it upholds a Christian ethic of diversity, agreeing that these specific people are full of dignity, and we create beauty by serving them well.

We hope you see that we are attempting to go beyond simply gaining knowledge of diverse groups, instead using self-awareness of our values, biases, and assumptions to allow skillful engagement with others.[43] Another way to skillfully engage is to offer our research questions to multiple participants, carefully asking them to articulate their experiences and talk among themselves to find their own consensus about our questions. If their consensus agrees with our questions, we can be more confident that the language we

---

[42]Bonnie Nastasi, "Cultural Competence for Global Research and Development: Implications for School and Educational Psychology," *International Journal of School & Educational Psychology* 5, no. 3 (2017): 208, https://doi.org/10.1080/21683603.2016.1276817.

[43]Derald Sue, "Multidimensional Facets of Cultural Competence," *The Counseling Psychologist* 29, no. 6 (2001): 798, https://doi.org/10.1177/0011000001296002.

use will represent them. If not, we can adjust. We do already have some well-established variables that represent specific populations that have been prioritized in the past. For example, White, male college students have historically been highly featured in assessment and research design (a problematic bias), and therefore in researching that group we may already have accurate definitions for variables. The key here is not to set up arbitrary rules to guide us but to instill wisdom and curiosity to discover the depths of the human heart. After all, the "heart is like deep water, but a man of understanding will draw it out" (Prov 20:5). When we truly understand people from their perspective, we can love them well through our research language.

Research method design. After becoming curious about the flourishing of specific people and learning how they experience specific variables, we are ready to move further into the research process. This starts with selecting an approach to our questions that facilitates mutual informing, which we might call a culturally responsive design.[44] Typically, qualitative research designs allow for innovative strategies in which we hear from and respond to our participants. Mixed methods (quantitative and qualitative) can build from cultural specificity and deepen understanding. To select an appropriate method, it is wise to reflect on the dynamics of culture and power that surround the research agenda and our participants. But is a carefully selected method enough? The Christian story reminds us of the potential for the corruption of our hearts and our tendency to use power to seek our own ends. If we are the privileged, how do we hear the oppressed (unheard, hostile, or fearful) participant?

---

[44] Caroline O'Hara, Catherine Chang, and Amanda Giordano, "Multicultural Competence in Counseling Research: The Cornerstone of Scholarship," *Journal of Counseling and Development* 99, no. 2 (2021): 202-3, https://doi.org/10.1002/jcad.12367.

We suggest going beyond the standard considerations of multicultural competence to our Christian ethic for research. We recommend you use self-awareness, reflexivity, and reflective questions designed to treat others as image-bearers: "How has this community been subject to the ideas and desires of others?" "How might this community experience and interpret being studied?" "How might I demonstrate a posture of open curiosity in a manner that they will understand it as such?" "Can I remain open to what this community will teach me?"

As we design research studies, it is a fun challenge to discern the godly wisdom in common cultural methods. We can uphold our Christian story of assisting in flourishing and beauty in part by adopting elements from multiculturally competent research practices that align with our imaginary. This includes careful selection of instruments (assessment tools and scales), the process of participant engagement, and interventions that affect the variables (dependent variables) we are measuring.[45] We briefly discuss practical considerations for these elements of method design in an attempt to support humble research.

Selection of instruments. We must remember to check the norming group used to develop any assessment tools or scales. Norming refers to the population used to construct the instrument, and it tells you whom the instrument most likely represents, including any group biases. It is unwise to use an instrument that does not include your population in its norming group, as this may distort your findings. This is not least because your population may understand the instrument differently, which approaches our second concern with instruments. Does this population comprehend your study, your instructions, and your personal

---

[45]Tracy Robinson-Wood, *The Convergence of Race, Ethnicity, and Gender: Multiple Identities in Counseling*, 4th ed. (Merrill Prentice Hall, 2012).

engagement? If not, you will need to develop new methods of explanation or measurement. Instruments must also work similarly and be accessible for a range of participant identities because diversity always exists within groups. We can check our instruments beforehand for their flexibility. Last, an instrument may not be appropriate within a specific culture, as it may cause offense or interpret variables according to the researcher's paradigm. This includes interviews in which a researcher's questions are not carefully worded and end up being guided by the mainstreamed language of a culture.

Researchers who are shaping themselves with humility to recognize the diversity of God's world will be sensitive to these issues that limit representative measurement. Solid preparation will mean learning about the culture you are engaging in, speaking with the population you wish to study, and having them review instruments and provide feedback. You may even choose to codevelop instruments and interview questions to avoid harm, confusion, or bias.

Participant engagement. We have already stated that participant engagement might be necessary in early research design. Here we focus on conducting the research. We are required to give informed consent so that participants know what they are agreeing to. This act starts to build trust and provides an opportunity to demonstrate cultural awareness. It is wise to indicate to participants how you have accounted for cultural differences and will receive their feedback and requests. The idea of informed consent itself may be strange in certain cultures, and we can help by explaining how this process stems from our own cultural ideas. Next, consider your use of technical language, style of speech, pacing, and tone. You may expect to communicate one thing but be seen as doing another. Learn about cultural norms and customs so that your participants are well disposed toward you. This is a simple act of hospitality that seeks their welfare. Last, consider how you will contact participants to invite their participation. Is this approach normative for their culture? If not, prepare to do this with sensitivity. Do they have access to the technology you expect? How might this cultural group respond? Will they be fast or slow, direct or indirect in their communication, enabled or burdened by participation?

We could summarize this section like this: remember participants' lived context and learn how to wrap your methods around its shape without compromising the standards of rigorous research.

Interventions. This includes elements of research aimed at changing a dependent variable, such as providing counseling or using psycho-education. When we use evidence-based techniques, we must again consider the norming groups and cultural context of the evidence base. It is possible that interventions that are positive in one cultural context are harmful in another. Check the literature for similar research areas to your own and discern what has been found as successful or limited. If necessary, consider altering your research to accommodate the need to learn more before providing interventions—this is still necessary research, as it seeks this group's well-being. This draws us into our second point, which is the need to check how interventions are understood across cultures. For example, education in America is often used as a springboard to think and discuss, while for other cultures it is regarded as direct instruction to be followed. If your intervention teaches only *general principles* to participants of a *direct-instruction culture*, you are likely to cause confusion and see little benefit. Remember, interventions might have an unexpected impact. If you introduce something new to a system, the system will adjust to it in some form, so pay attention.

Imagine a culture that permits limited discussion of emotions and commonly uses repression. An American might consider this as unhealthy and introduce tools to get in touch with feelings, hoping to expand the group's self-awareness. How might this affect a culture that has never engaged emotions relationally? Can you foresee challenges? And finally, after any intervention it may be necessary to debrief with the participants to discern the true impact. How and when to do this requires consideration in the light of the participants' culture and not our own. We may discover that providing follow-up care or support is necessary to avoid harm to our participants as we work toward the goal of facilitating flourishing in their lives.

Research data interpretation and dispersal. We come to our final aspect of research that we can prepare for. Have you ever miscommunicated because you misconstrued someone's meaning? Yes? I'm not surprised; it happens daily because we are subject to our brain's quick filtering processes, which seek to make meaning according to what we know. To avoid biased interpretations of any data, we need to carefully engage it in a manner that allows it to show us the answer, which can take time, patience, and multiple reviews. Member checking is an effective strategy of taking any interpretations of the data back to the participants and asking them whether it lines up with their experience. It is humbling when our interpretation doesn't fit well but saves us from harming the group with biased information. Further, as we share findings, we can share information about the culture they represent. Helping our readers understand the participants' context as we did protects them from misapplying any findings. We should assist our readers in the process of applying findings by humbly and carefully thinking through its implications. In some situations it can be helpful to have the participants of the research become community partners in sharing any implications, in part by assisting them in self-advocacy. Finally, we must always carefully consider and state possible limitations and biases in our work to assist generalization.[46]

It is worth heeding the caution of Caroline O'Hara, Catherine Chang, and Amanda Giordano, who urge us to consider all research as part of a system in the world in which researchers, participants, readers, culture, politics, and the psychological field all apply their influence, with the result that research is never neutral; rather, it facilitates the status quo or can assist in change.[47] Let us be curious pursuers of change that leads toward beauty.

CONCLUSION

We have seen that our everyday life shapes us, so it is no wonder we have specific values that are diverse and different from one another. It can certainly be challenging to reflect on all the ways we have been shaped, so we encourage you that it is OK to do this over time and with care and compassion. We know that it takes time and intention to position ourselves in such a way that we learn to delight in diversity and begin to open up to the cares of others. This is a transformative process that might seem scary at first, or threatening to your own sense of self, but we promise it is worth it.

As we grow in wisdom, we will know when to hang on to deeply rooted cares because they will bring flourishing in God's world and when they instead limit our interpretations and curiosity. With God as the foundation of our Christian ethic of diversity, we can rest assured that supporting all people is our kingdom call. Each of us will contribute to this great project differently. We hope you

---

[46]Derald Sue and David Sue, *Counseling the Culturally Different: Theory and Practice*, 3rd ed. (Wiley & Sons, 1999).
[47]O'Hara et al., "Multicultural Competence in Counseling Research," 201.

are inspired to allow your loving Heavenly Father to shape you and show you what he has in store for you.

DISCUSSION QUESTIONS

1. From the perspective of the mainstreaming effect of your culture, what is the goal of life?
2. How is your identity as a researcher shaped by God's story about you and the world thus far?
3. What mainstreaming contexts will you place yourself into to develop humility and space for the cares of others?
4. What are some ways you can posture yourself to attentively connect with and learn from others?
5. What intersection of biopsychosocial-spiritual variables are you curious about?
6. How could you find out whether your understanding of these variables is the same as the one held by the population you would like to research?
7. What struck you most about making the research design process align with the cares of God for his people? Why do you think this struck you?

LEARNING ACTIVITIES

1. In groups of three, start by sharing areas of research in which you are most interested. Name specific variables and research questions if you have them. Once you have each shared, invite the other group members to reflect back to you what values (or cares) they hear in your interests. Discuss what you are becoming aware of in this process.
2. In groups of three or four, find a research article that focuses on crosscultural study. Read the author's abstract, introduction, and research questions. Then discuss as a group how

you would approach and explain the study to these research participants. Once you have done this, read the method section of the paper and discuss the research's strengths and any changes you would make to the sampling or methodology to diversify the sample or protect the welfare of these participants.

FOUR

Measuring God's World

SOMETIMES THE MATH ISN'T MATH-ING. At whatever point that happened to you in your educational experience, it may have shaped the entire direction of your life. When I (Kristen) have asked my counseling students why they entered the profession, one of the themes in their answers is that they considered the medical field but hated math. So here we are, in the soft sciences, muddling our way through the math we thought we had left far behind. For some professors tackling the research course, your dissertation process may have been that giant math hurdle after which you swore you were going to clear your brain of the mess of statistics that had entered in. And yet, you drew the *research straw* when course loads were being assigned.

There are others of you who are perhaps secretly delighting in the activation of an unused part of your brain. You are arriving at the quantitative portion of your research class with excitement, but you may be hesitant to admit it to a fellow student who is telling you about their math aversion. Let us encourage you to be fully you in this experience. Rise to the occasion and push yourself to create your own challenges rather than coasting. How can you dive deeper? What teaching strategies would you use if you were covering this material as an instructor someday? What questions spin off your first and second and third layers of questions? As empathetic as you may be, a tentative climate in the research classroom does not have to dictate your approach to discovery and learning.

In this chapter we are going to explore quantitative aspects of the research process. To do that well we need to step away from math for a bit, regardless of which feelings we have about the subject. We need to look at the larger picture of God's established systems of order and connect with the beauty and meaning in these ideas. We start the survey of beauty by looking at the idea of normal distribution.

According to the central limit theorem, which developed over time from thinkers such as Abraham de Moivre in 1733 and Pierre-Simon Laplace in 1810, among others, you will find that a bell-shaped curve best represents normality of data—yes, most data actually fit the same curve shape overall.[1] Of course, there are some who argue about the randomness of data and point out evidence that the central limit theorem is not always true. With any theory, it is important to note that it is at best an approximation of reality.[2] Overall, it is widely accepted that the natural pattern of data, under typical conditions and with an adequate sample size, will be distributed in the shape of a bell. Amazingly, 68 percent of all the measurements in a data sample will be one standard deviation away from the mean in both directions, 95 percent will be two standard deviations away, and 99.7 percent will be three standard deviations away. It's poetic. (Despite our efforts to step away from math to see the wider picture, 68-95-99 is helpful to memorize.)

Rather than asking, "What does a normal distribution tell us about what we can do with our data?" let's ask, "What does a normal

---

[1] Hans Fischer, *A History of the Central Limit Theorem: From Classical to Modern Probability Theory* (Springer, 2011), 5.
[2] Aidan Lyon, "Why Are Normal Distributions Normal?," *The British Journal for the Philosophy of Science* 65, no. 3 (2014): 621-49.

distribution tell us about God and his established order in the universe?" We are not looking for a trite answer here. Rather, we encourage you to pause your reading and think for a moment. Beyond the typical answer that God is a God of order, frequently ripped from its context in 1 Corinthians 14:33 and applied to science, how might we envision the kingdom of God and the nature of God himself as we consider the bell curve? It might feel neat and tidy, but normal distribution means that we are not all the same. As we saw in chapter three, God's heart for diversity is represented as we look at a concept such as variance (how things differ). Is a normal distribution fundamentally fair? Is it God's design that some are born with an IQ of 70 and others 130, both two standard deviations away from the mean and yet divergent in privilege and capacity? Or are those questions a direct example of cultural bias, in which we as Americans have decided to use IQ as a means for evaluating a person's worth? If God is just, loving, and fair, then he must have a different view of this bell shape we keep seeing all around us. In heaven, will there still be a normal distribution of characteristics? It seems unlikely that we will all morph into a single, uniform, perfect creature even in a state of sinlessness and complete redemption.

From this line of thought, here is an observation for you to chew on: God makes art out of random patterns. He finds so much beauty in the differentness of his creation that from it he extracts a design. Each individual is a dot on the data chart, created by the hand of God and shaped by a combination of divine intervention and random probability in a broken world. When the individual data points—seemingly arbitrary or even unfair in some cases—come together, a picture emerges. From humans to birds to rocks, it is the same bell-shaped picture, with all the brilliance of an intricate pointillist painting. Perhaps we are displayed in the gallery of heaven that showcases the glory of the Creator.

A second observation: God sees a much bigger reality than we do. Normal distribution represents only a single-dimensional view of these God-driven patterns. Thousands of years of human history had passed before even that bell curve took its shape and spoke to us about God and data. Most Christians would agree that God is infinite, deep, vast, and complex. Even scientists such as Albert Einstein, Stephen Hawking, and others without a faith in God have undertaken quests to uncover and make meaning from multidimensional truths. What if a two-dimensional curve beside a thousand other curves creates a sculpture rather than a simple painting?

Research brings us here. Curiosity and inquiry and critical thinking brought us to a place of imagining a gallery filled with the creations of the divine Artist. This example sets the tone for the journey we are taking in this chapter to see the glory of God and his kingdom in quantitative research. So far we have seen God's love shine through in the breadth and variation of his creation, placing value on the full spectrum of a normal bell curve. For the remainder of the chapter, we will dive deeper into the Bible and examine the major types of quantitative analysis you will come across, including descriptive statistics, correlation, between-subjects comparisons, within-subjects design, and regression. We will use a researcher's perspective to enhance our interaction with the Bible, and we will read the Bible to inform us as researchers.

DESCRIPTIVE STATISTICS

It seems fitting to turn to the book of Numbers to consider descriptive statistics. As it turns out, God seems to like to count things. Moses, Aaron, and the tribal leaders listed in Numbers 1 were being obedient to God as they counted the men of each of the twelve tribes of Israel. These are the most basic of statistics—simply giving a count, a percentage, or a ratio. Yet anyone who has ever attempted data collection will surely tell you that arriving at those numbers is far from simple. We personally would not want to volunteer to take Moses' place and oversee a massive census, even with the tech we have now.

If you read the book of Numbers past the first couple of chapters, you'll see that the counting is not just for the fun of calculating sums. Rather, it is the beginning of making organization and meaning within a society governed by God. He appoints leaders, assigns tasks, and provides a legal system for his people. The provision of order offers a sense of safety as well as authority. God reveals the ways of his kingdom and sets clear expectations for his people. More than that, he includes them in carrying out laws and rituals. He provides them with festivals to remember his faithfulness, and he gathers them together as a community. This is the power of counting amid social life: Each person matters and contributes to a greater whole.

We see other examples of descriptive statistics in the Bible, from the Jewish calendar system to the feeding of the five thousand. In the latter instance (see Lk 9), Jesus tells his disciples to seat the people down in groups of about fifty. The text does not indicate Jesus' reason for this instruction, but it sure makes it easier to count to five thousand when you have one hundred groups of fifty. There is something valuable in the vastness of that number, so easy to multiply and record in later testimony.

Despite this quantitative way of documenting a miracle, God is not always a "bigger is better" kind of God. Sometimes lower numbers are preferable, as we see in Judges 7 with Gideon's army. Here God says, "The people with you are too many for me to give the Midianites into their hand, lest Israel boast over me, saying, 'My own hand has saved me'" (Judg 7:2). Of the thirty-two thousand in Gideon's army that day, twenty-two thousand (68.8 percent) were too scared to fight and immediately bailed at the first opportunity. God continues to decrease the number and tests them based on how they drink water. In this instance, kneeling down and directly drinking the water is unacceptable, while using one's hand to cup the water sets one apart. In this quantitative study, only 3 percent of men drink water using their hands.

What an odd experiment to set up, with no particular explanation why that was the measure of who should remain in the army. Since God was looking to reduce the army to a very small number, perhaps he chose something that he was well aware 97 percent of men in that time would do. Here God wants a small number to make it very clear to Gideon and all Israel that they rely on him for victory. He is the savior, more than able to demonstrate his power with or without them. The place of numbers in this example helps us feel disoriented and then in awe of God. The descriptives bring illumination.

A final example that builds on this theme occurs in 2 Samuel 24, in which David completes another census. This time, unlike with Moses and Aaron, counting the people is not something God asked him to do. Rather, it is the arrogant heart of King David that leads him to want to count the "valiant men" in Israel (800,000) and Judah (500,000). After singing songs such as "The LORD is my rock and my fortress and my deliverer" (2 Sam 22:2) and describing the worthlessness of men compared to God in 2 Samuel 23:5-6, there is a shift in the writing, and we read of the "mighty men" by King David's side. When we arrive at 2 Samuel 24, God is angry. Does the writing capture a progression of thought and a shift in heart on David's part? It is not entirely clear. However, we see that his counting of his troops does not go over well with God. David loses 5.4 percent (70,000) of his men to disease within a few days as a punishment.

What are you taking away from these examples? How do they make you reflect on the nature of God and the human condition?

We find the passages come alive with a different kind of meaning, challenge, wonder, and beauty because of the descriptives. They affect our heart.

A further question we can consider is, When does quantitative research honor God, and when might it anger him? We posit that descriptive statistics can be used for God's glory to enhance the understanding of the world and the people in it, and they can also be manipulated and used for ill-gotten gain. Even the ethical codes of secular psychology and counseling organizations caution against the misuse of data and conflicts of interest. In an article from Lifeway Research, Bob Smietana describes the ways in which pastors can use descriptive data inappropriately to drive home seemingly Christian values.[3] Smietana describes fear-mongering on topics such as divorce rates or the percentage of young people leaving the church. Christians, including pastors and church leaders, are just as prone to believing misinformation and misapplying descriptive statistics as any of us. Anxiety can be a powerful emotion, leading to what Smietana calls "the sky is falling phenomenon." Proverbs 20:23 comes to mind here, as unequal weights or false measurements are called an abomination to God. We have an ethical and spiritual mandate to use data accurately and carefully.

If we lean into a search for data that are true, honorable, commendable, and excellent (Phil 4:8), what might they tell us? What light can current research shed on both earthly and supernatural realities? Could that influence how we live and worship, in spirit and in truth (Jn 4:23-24)? Our first step in exploring these questions is to look for peer-reviewed, scholarly research. It may seem that information is constantly at our fingertips, but a search engine will not present quality research most of the time. However, we

---

[3]Bob Smietana, "False Facts: Why Pastors Love Bad Stats," Lifeway Research, January 7, 2014, https://research.lifeway.com/2014/01/07/false-facts-why-we-love-bad-stats/.

cannot blindly trust a peer-reviewed article either. Sometimes low-quality studies sneak through and get published anyway. We need to take an active role in evaluating the truth, not just as we conduct research but also as we consume it.

Let's take a look at a few examples of descriptive statistics from current research. Barna Group and Lifeway Research are both well-known Christian research groups that provide a lot of information about spiritual realities via descriptive statistics. (Note that in this section, we will report findings in a linear fashion to highlight studies that illustrate descriptive statistics. However, we do not encourage you to write literature reviews or research papers in this way. Be sure to take a look at the sidebar "Blending Your Sources" to note the difference between linear versus blended use of sources.)

First, in 2021 Barna Group reported that 38 percent of pastors had thought about leaving ministry in the prior year.[4] This finding isn't surprising considering that pastors had the impossible job of leading churches that couldn't physically gather, in some areas for the better part of a year, during pandemic shutdowns. Thankfully, by March 2024 pastors were feeling better, with 59 percent endorsing that they were "very satisfied with their vocation."[5] If we take these two examples of descriptive statistics at face value, we could assume that there is an upward trend (as indeed we suggested with our choice of wording—"feeling better"). We see the word *pastors* and we may assume that the sample is generally the same, even if not the exact same participants. But what if a whole lot of those pastors who were thinking about leaving ministry

---

[4]"38% of U.S. Pastors Have Thought About Quitting Full-Time Ministry in the Past Year," Barna Group, November 16, 2021, www.barna.com/research/pastors-well-being/.
[5]"New Data Shows Hopeful Increases in Pastors' Confidence & Satisfaction," Barna Group, March 6, 2024, www.barna.com/research/hopeful-increases-pastors/.

actually did leave between 2021 and 2024? What effect would that have on the outcome of the second study? In that case, those pastors surveyed in the second study would represent those who never wanted to leave in the first place. If you remove the dissatisfied pastors from the sample group, suddenly 59 percent feeling "very satisfied" is not actually a change.

Looking at these data in a different way, the first study reported that 38 percent of pastors were thinking of leaving, and the second study found that 59 percent were "very satisfied." For all you quick math-ers out there, 40 + 60 = 100. While a few percentage points might have changed between measurements, ultimately one way of reporting the data emphasizes the nearly 40 percent who are thinking of leaving, and the other highlights the almost 60 percent who are very satisfied. Hopefully you can clearly see that descriptive statistics are easily manipulated and require a careful eye to discern what is true past the headlines. Figure 4.1, provided by Barna Group in the March 2024 article cited earlier, offers a fuller picture, comparing apples to apples.

Figure 4.1. Barna survey of pastors

Source: "New Data Shows Hopeful Increases in Pastors' Confidence & Satisfaction," Barna Group, March 6, 2024, www.barna.com/research/hopeful-increases-pastors/. Used by permission.

Despite the useful comparison in this figure, we still do not know the number of pastors who actually did leave the ministry between each of these surveys. We also do not know exactly why these numbers varied or whether they changed to a statistically significant degree. Note that the sample sizes are adequate, ranging from 413 to 584. On visual inspection, you don't have to be terribly amazing at statistical analysis to imagine that there is not a significant difference between 38 percent, 42 percent, and 41 percent (the three middle data points). This difference is likely pretty close to a normal margin of error (representing the normal inaccuracy within research). We might find statistical significance between the January 2021 measurement and the March 2022 measurement (the highest and lowest data points), as well as between March 2022 and September 2023 (the final measurement). If there is not a statistically significant difference between the first and last measurements but those two are potentially significantly different from the central-most data point, then we could at least venture a guess that a trend emerged for a period of time. From January 2021 to March 2022, pastors' desire to leave ministry appears to have significantly increased. Then from March 2022 to September 2023, we see a potentially significant decrease back to baseline.

What does all this tell us, other than providing an interesting look at how to understand and interpret descriptive statistics? We suggest these data points help us refine our curious questions—questions that start with the data and emerge around it. For example: When considering a spiritual reality, what does it mean that even at the lower baseline and ending data points, about one-third of pastors were thinking of leaving ministry? What would be the spiritual impact if around 30 percent of churches were being led by individuals who did not want to be there anymore? Where is God in all this, as Christ seeks to lead his bride into a new and coming kingdom? What is the spiritual impact of pastor discouragement and burnout on their own spiritual lives as well as the spiritual well-being of the congregations they are still trying to lead? How are these pastors seeking God in the midst of contemplating leaving the ministry? Are they seeing themselves as failures in their callings, or are they sensing God leading them into a new season?

Additional research is needed to shed light on these questions, and it is a line of research that I (Kristen) have conducted and continue to explore. Anecdotally, we have personally known pastors who have left the ministry within the past few years, and we've heard stories of ministry trauma, burnout, and crises of identity and faith. We have seen former pastors shift into fields such as real estate or sales, and more ministry-adjacent careers such as teaching and coaching. Some are fully deconstructing their faith directly as a result of the pain and disillusionment that they experienced in ministry. Our hearts are heavy with these realities, deeply feeling the spiritual weight and gravity for these individuals and for the broader church. These spiritual realities drive us to prayer and back into research, to produce and consume research on topics such as pastoral burnout, spiritual abuse, and church trends that affect what discipleship looks like in a digital and modern age.

From a clinical perspective, all of this research is absolutely essential to treating individuals, couples, and families facing these types of issues. Recently, I (Kristen) received a call from a couple in ministry looking for couples counseling. Within the prior year, they had left the church they had served for decades. They described symptoms of burnout, which led to a sabbatical, during which they sought to determine whether to leave the church. Upon their return, the church board presented the pastor with a list of grievances and accusations and dismissed the couple from their position. They were left stunned and shaken. Sadly, this story is one we have heard multiple times with varying details and circumstances. Pastors and spouses experience burnout and ministry trauma, and they seek out counseling often after the situation has already hit a crisis point or they have left their church.

On the flip side, we have had many clients who experienced church hurt and spiritual abuse at the hands of pastors they trusted. All these clients need evidence-based care as they work through their trauma. If you are clinically practicing in this kind of space and marketing yourself as a Christian counselor, you are likely to have on your caseload both pastors hurt by their congregations and individuals hurt by their pastors. Understanding research works hand in hand with our softer clinical skills to help us avoid bias and treat each client with dignity, respect, and quality care.

Jesus preaches in Matthew 7:7 that if you seek the truth, you will find it. As you deepen in your development as a researcher, consider pursuit of the truth a central part of your identity. Is this not the heart of the spiritual journey? Through the study of research and learning how to conduct, evaluate, and apply it, you will be more able to discern what is true. Soon enough you will spot bad descriptive statistics in a headline or social media post, and you can be a voice in helping the church avoid misinformation. You can also bring to light what is true by producing and sharing excellent data. In addition, you can apply research to provide evidence-based care and healing to those who seek your help. All of these are facets of the worthy calling of the Christian researcher and clinician.

Blending Your Sources: How to Write a Good Literature Review

One of the most frequent bits of feedback I (Kristen) give to my graduate counseling students is this: Blend your sources. When you are writing a literature review, it can be convenient to read an article and then write about it. Pick up the next article, write about it. Sentence by sentence and paragraph by paragraph, you are whittling away at your references list and getting that paper written. However, the end result of this approach is linear reporting of sources. This is an advanced writing concept for researchers, moving past the basics such as, "Make sure you actually read your sources," "Don't plagiarize," and "Follow an outline." After you have those ideas mastered, you are ready to really write well using this idea of blending sources. Here's what this looks like in a paper:

> The recent literature provides insight into XYZ topic. Source 1 showed a difference between variable A and variable B. They used an ANOVA to show group differences on the variables in question. Source 2 also showed a significant difference, and their regression showed how variable A is predictive of variable B. Source 3 added to this knowledge, telling us more about variables A and B and measuring variable C as well.

In the above example, we are hearing about three different sources in a linear fashion, much like a list. It is a summary of each study one by one. Generally, this approach leads students toward simplistic writing and accidental inaccuracies. You'd be surprised how many papers we have seen in which the sentence from the above example, "Source 3 *added to* this knowledge . . ." ends up citing a study that occurred prior to the other two! What can sound like a nice transition sentence is factually untrue and likely more an effect of reading the articles in that order. We would also discourage you from starting a sentence with, "Studies have shown . . ." when citing only one source. If you say "studies," we want to see at least three references to back up your claim. Another red flag shows up if you cite only one source in a given paragraph or, worse, rely on a single source for multiple paragraphs or pages.

Blending your sources is the alternative to linear reporting of data, and we strongly recommend you practice this on each assignment. This approach is more challenging because it requires strong outlining prior to writing your paper and careful note taking as you read your articles. A good literature review should directly set up the variables you are analyzing in your research study. Thus, your literature review outline should look something like this:

I. Introduction *(do not use an APA heading—the word* Introduction *is omitted)*

II. Variable 1 *(use an APA heading)*

    A. Point 1 (multiple sources)
    B. Point 2 (multiple sources)
    C. Point 3 (multiple sources)

III. Variable 2 *(use an APA heading)*

    A. Point 1 (multiple sources)
    B. Point 2 (multiple sources)
    C. Point 3 (multiple sources)

IV. Variable 3 *(use an APA heading)*

    A. Point 1 (multiple sources)
    B. Point 2 (multiple sources)
    C. Point 3 (multiple sources)

V. Purpose Statement *(heading may be optional)*

VI. Research Questions and Hypotheses

As you describe what we know about variables 1, 2, and 3, you are using what you have gathered from the recent literature to point to the need for your study. Because you are writing in a fashion that should lead us to believe your study is essential to add to our body of knowledge, you want to avoid linear summary. Instead, blend your sources by citing multiple studies at the end of most sentences and certainly within paragraphs. You are making assertions and backing up your claims with multiple references. Here's what good blending of sources looks like:

> It is well-established within the literature that variables A and B are significantly related (Source 1; Source 2; Source 3). While there is speculation as to the exact nature of the relationship, some studies have attributed the correlation to XYZ (Source 4; Source 5). One author posited this theory as to the relationship (Source 3), while another offered a different point of view (Source 1).

In this example, we have five different sources, and we are using them to support our own points. We are discussing the existing literature without summarizing one study at a time. Blending your sources means you are focused on the data itself rather than reporting on individual studies. If you perfect this skill, you'll be well on your way to thinking and writing like a researcher.

CORRELATION

Let's take one step deeper to look at correlation, a statistical analysis used to evaluate relationships. It's right there in the name—*co-relation*. What does x have to do with y? You can have positive correlations, in which x and y move together in the same direction. Perhaps number of sit-ups per day and core strength. You've likely heard that "correlation does not equal causation," the axiom of every researcher. However, you could imagine that, generally speaking, if you do one hundred sit-ups per day, that would be likely to have a positive relationship on your core strength. There are a host of other variables involved that stop us from saying sit-ups cause one to automatically gain ripped abs. But a statistically significant relationship exists.

Correlations can also be negative. In this case, x and y move together but in opposite directions (i.e., when x increases, y decreases). You will also see this referred to as an inverse correlation. An example of this might be social anxiety and party attendance. The higher one's social anxiety, the fewer parties one attends. Again, there are a whole lot of other factors that could play a role in that correlation, particularly for any one individual. Generally speaking, however, those variables are likely to have an inverse relationship when evaluating a representative sample (which a normal distribution of scores on a social anxiety scale would indicate).

Positive and negative correlations describe linear relationships. You can draw a straight line on a graph to show the movement of x with y. Relationships can also be nonlinear but still exist as a measurable correlation. These relationships are often referred to as *curvilinear*. You'd expect to see this when looking at something such as hours of sleep and quality of life. Initially, you might assume this is a positive correlation: The more sleep you get, the better your quality of life. This idea would certainly be true if you are thinking from the perspective of how you would feel if you suffered from insomnia for more than a night or two. But what happens if you sleep too much? Imagine a person who is sleeping fourteen or sixteen hours per day. Would their quality of life keep going up? While we are not pointing to an actual study here, we could imagine that after a certain point of eight to ten hours of sleep, the statistical relationship turns into a negative correlation. Thus, you have a curvilinear relationship, in which the line on the graph goes up, hits a peak, and then descends. This draws an arc shape, like an upside-down *U*.

How can we examine correlation through the lens of Scripture? What examples do we see in the Bible, and how does that contribute to a greater understanding of God himself? The book of Proverbs is a good place to begin, filled with a plethora of "if this, then that" types of statements. In Proverbs 10:1 we see a positive correlation between the wisdom of a son and the happiness of his father, and in Proverbs 11:9 we see a positive correlation between righteousness and life. Proverbs 13:12 gives us an example of a negative correlation: The length of time until one's hope is realized is inversely correlated with emotional well-being.

However, we have to be careful that we don't slip back into "correlation equals causation," which is a temptation when reading the Bible. For example, Proverbs 10:4 says, "A slack hand causes poverty, but the hand of the diligent makes rich." While we agree that work ethic is one factor that can contribute to poverty, it is certainly not the whole picture. Surely we could all think of rich people who did not get that way via diligence (and Proverbs also recognizes that reality). What we are missing here are a variety of covariates, or other risk factors for poverty. If we are looking too deeply for causation, we miss what God is actually saying about the correlation in this particular verse. This causation line of thinking has been misused by Christians to blame others for their own problems. We need to read Scripture with a careful eye just as we would a research study.

Other examples of correlation in the Bible can be found in stories in which God's people made observations, formed hypotheses, tested these hypotheses, and arrived at a conclusion. For instance, in Exodus 17, when the Israelites are fighting the Amalekites, they observe a correlation between Moses' hands being raised and victory in the battle. We can see that they arrive at that conclusion through a series of observations by the use of the word *whenever*. We don't know how many times this raising and lowering of his hands occurred before they understood the correlation, but it was enough for Moses' arms to get pretty tired. In our modern age, we might dismiss such an event as a mere coincidence. What supernatural realities might we miss with such a supposedly enlightened approach? Allow us to suggest that a quest for the truth via scientific observation and study is enhanced, not diminished, by the incorporation of faith. Through faith, we have potential to see the relationships between the natural and the supernatural.

At times the Bible makes claims that have potential to be quantitatively tested. For example, in 2 Peter 1:5-7 we see a list of variables that are positively correlated with effectiveness in Christ. These variables are faith, virtue, knowledge, self-control, steadfastness, godliness, and brotherly affection. Peter actually describes the inverse correlation: As these variables increase, your ineffectiveness decreases. Whether we want to frame it around effectiveness or ineffectiveness, this seems like something measurable.

If we could quantify the constructs of faith, virtue, knowledge, and so on, we could measure the correlations involved and gain clarity on the construct of effectiveness. Peter seems to suggest it has something to do with knowledge of Christ and remembrance of all he has done, but research might illuminate this point even further.

What have researchers already done to examine these constructs? This question is essential anytime we begin to wonder about a topic we might want to research. As clever as you may wish to be, it is most likely that your thinking—or some version of it—has already been tested by other researchers. As a researcher, you always want to build on the foundation of others who have gone before you. One professor of ours told us in our dissertation preparation that when we found the study we wished we had been the ones to conduct, we had finally hit the gold mine. Rather than being disappointed that someone else had already asked our questions, we could see that study as a sturdy foundation from which to build with clarity.

One study we wish we had been the ones to author was conducted by Jeong Kim and colleagues in 2016.[6] These researchers developed and tested the Adapted Inventory of Virtues and Strengths (AIVS), a forty-six-item instrument measuring emotional transcendence, practical wisdom, integrity, courage, and commitment to action. Their article is a wonderful example of factor analysis, but frequently in scale development authors use correlation as a secondary way of demonstrating construct validity. Additional measures of life satisfaction, resilience, and psychological well-being were correlated with the AIVS factors. All five

---

[6]Jeong Kim, Christine Reid, Brian McMahon, Rene Gonzalez, Dong Lee, and Phillip Keck, "Measuring the Virtues and Character Traits of Rehabilitation Clients: The Adapted Inventory of Virtues and Strengths," *Journal of Occupational Rehabilitation* 26, no. 1 (2016): 32–44, https://doi.org/10.1007/s10926-015-9619-9.

factors were significantly correlated with resilience and psychological well-being, and all but the practical wisdom factor were significantly correlated with life satisfaction.

In the above study, these significant correlations provide evidence for the validity of their scale. However, these findings also provide an interesting look at the passage we just discussed from 2 Peter 1. With the AIVS, we could develop our own research study to explore these factors even further and particularly examine correlations with the variable of effectiveness. Of course, we would have to define the construct of effectiveness (or ineffectiveness) further and identify a validated instrument to measure it. From the study we just described, we know that things such as resilience, life satisfaction, and psychological well-being significantly correlate with the factors on the AIVS. This finding is a great start. Where else could you take this line of inquiry? How would you define the construct of *effectiveness*? Are there other factors besides the five in the AIVS that you would be curious about based on the list in 2 Peter?

Some additional variables that I (Paul) have analyzed in this regard are humility, gratitude, and compassion. In my dissertation, I sought to understand the relationships between these virtues, attachment to God, and well-being.[7] I used a path analysis, which is a complex way of analyzing relationships between variables. In short, this analysis looks at mediators and moderators, which are variables that influence or change a correlation between two other variables. Prior to conducting a path analysis, I had to look at the correlations between all the variables because if they were not significantly related at the most basic level, then they certainly wouldn't have shown up in a more complex analysis. In my

---

[7]Paul W. Loosemore, "The Mediating Role of Character Virtues Humility, Gratitude and Compassion Between Relationship with God and Well-Being: A Path Analysis" (PhD diss., Regent University, 2020).

exploration of correlations, relationship with God, humility, gratitude, compassion, well-being, and affective experience were all significantly correlated at a moderate level.

Humility Development Through the Peer-Review Process

Our claim throughout this book has been that the research process has the power to spiritually shape and form us. There is perhaps no better example of this than the peer-review process. You'll notice that we have described scholarly research as "peer-reviewed articles," so what exactly do we mean by that? What is it like as a researcher to try to publish a scholarly article? Here are the common steps to scholarly publication:

1. Complete your research and write in an article format, typically following the outline of literature review, method, results, and discussion.

2. Identify a journal that publishes research along the themes of your study. Looking at your own references list might give you a few ideas. You do have to limit your submission to one journal at a time.

3. Locate the website through which the journal receives submissions and complete all formatting requirements. Usually they require a blind copy of the manuscript so that the author's (or authors') name is not present for a neutral peer review.

4. Upload all documents to complete your submission. Often figures and tables have to be submitted as separate files, and some want a cover letter as well.

5. Wait anywhere from a few weeks to a few months or more while the journal finds peer reviewers who would have knowledge of the subject and can provide critique.

6. Typically, the best response you will get is a "revise and resubmit," in which you read what two to three reviewers have said about your article and revise it accordingly. Once you resubmit, these same reviewers will read your updated article. You usually have to submit a document identifying the changes you made and responding to the reviewers' feedback. Again, you most likely have another few months of waiting for a response.

7. You receive a final response, and your article is accepted and published (or not!). If your article is rejected at any point, have in mind the next journal to which you can submit. Don't let a finished article languish on your desk. Press on and keep revising until you reach publication.

As doctoral students, both of us had our first experiences of submitting articles for publication. I (Kristen) was thrilled when my statistics class projects resulted in not one but two articles that were deemed worthy of pursuing publication. Our professor, Dr. Olya Zaporozhets, and her colleague Dr. Mark Yarhouse had collected data on a Christian sexual-minority population they called "celibate gay Christians." We highly recommend their book from this research study, *Costly Obedience*.[a] My articles had evaluated their data set in a few ways that were not yet represented in their analyses. I completed revisions to take the articles from class projects to scholar-ready and located journals that I thought might be interested in the topic. In my complete ignorance of the peer-review process, I first attempted to seek publication of one of the articles in a secular journal focused on LGBT issues in the field of counseling. I was quite shocked to discover they ripped my article to shreds. Not only did they have no desire to publish it, but they expressed that they hoped the findings would never be published. While they slammed me for having an agenda, they shot back with quite the agenda of their own.

As the months (and years!) went on, I had to submit those two articles to about ten different journals. Unlike the first one, in which the peer reviewers fundamentally rejected the entire premise of the celibate gay Christian population, most of the rejections came with useful feedback. Each time I would make revisions based on their suggestions. Some of the feedback taught me a lot about what makes an article worthy of publication. For example, some of my figures were too zoomed in on the data, which made the differences visually appear very drastic. I learned from the peer-review process that I need to capture a wider range of the scale when presenting findings.[b] I also learned to tone down the language in my discussion section quite a bit. When you are writing your first research articles, it is exciting. Especially if your findings are significant, it can be easy to fall into the trap of coming to grand conclusions: "Clearly these data prove that . . ."

or "This study contributes great knowledge to the body of literature." It is important to learn how to write in a measured and data-focused style. One of the two articles has been published, and at the time of this writing the other one is still sitting on a peer reviewer's desk after a revise-and-resubmit (six years after my statistics class project and five journals later).

To say my humility has grown as a result of the peer-review process would be an understatement. I have learned to look forward to reading the peer reviewers' comments and am now excited to make my articles better. I began with an overconfidence in my work, and time and time again having my flaws pointed out was painful. My enthusiasm for research made me want to publish the next earth-shattering breakthrough. I have come to accept that such studies are extremely rare and are usually the culmination of a lifetime of prior work and research. As I have grown as a researcher, I have developed greater Christlikeness and humility as I see myself as just a tiny drop in an ocean of research. That idea no longer discourages me but instead helps me feel free to chase my curiosity wherever it leads.

[a] Olya Zaporozhets and Mark A. Yarhouse, *Costly Obedience: What We Can Learn from the Celibate Gay Christian Community* (Zondervan, 2019).
[b] The advanced reader may also find useful Edward Tufte's book *The Visual Display of Quantitative Information*.

We can consider the implications of these findings with both a spiritual and a clinical lens. We are quantitatively connecting the dots between having a relationship with God and experiencing positive well-being, which simply provides statistical evidence of a spiritual reality. Connection with God has a positive correlation with well-being. Through the findings of the path analysis, we also know that this connection is strengthened by higher levels of humility, gratitude, and compassion. This means a discipleship process could involve a specific focus on the development of these virtues, and it is likely to support spiritual growth and improved wellness. As counselors and clinicians, we can facilitate client growth in these three areas to help move a person from poorer mental health symptoms into a more thriving state. There is a growing body of research from both Christian and secular researchers on gratitude interventions in particular as a mechanism for posttraumatic growth and mental health improvement. If you have an interest in this topic, we recommend combining the search terms *gratitude* and *mental health* in both your academic databases and general search engines.

What does all this correlation talk mean for us as we seek to understand God and truth? First, we are training our minds to think critically and biblically so that we notice the quantitative principles that are right in front of us. With the same eye that we examined these biblical ideas, we can turn to peer-reviewed research to understand truth and how things in our world are related to one another. Second, we can observe the ways in which God reveals himself to us through an established order of relationships in the world. He has empowered us to act, and he has set out a series of systemic principles through which we can pursue him. Individual variables and actions are related to both individual and collective change. For this reason, our own individual spiritual growth relates deeply with the broader mission and work of the church.

BETWEEN-SUBJECTS COMPARISONS

Moving beyond correlation, we can use quantitative analyses such as *t*-tests and ANOVAs to compare groups. This type of research—known as between-subjects or between-groups—is very valuable in psychological and counseling research to determine the effectiveness of treatments. In this case, group comparisons require an experimental design in which we are controlling for particular variables. We would have a control group and a treatment group, comparing their outcomes. In survey research, we can still use group comparison if we want to determine whether differences exist between demographic groups on validated instruments or survey questions.

As you may have already learned, *t*-tests compare two groups on one variable. If your analysis is more complicated, such as comparing three or more groups on one variable, then you'll need the ANOVA family of analyses (known as F-tests). When you are comparing groups on *m*ultiple variables, you need an M for a MANOVA. If you have *co*variates, you'll use an ANCOVA. With *m*ultiple variables and *co*variates, you'll need a MANCOVA. There are other, more complicated analyses, such as the Wilcoxon Signed-Rank test, if you are dealing with two groups that are not normally distributed. However, it is always important to keep in mind that when comparing groups you want to compare apples to apples, not apples to oranges. If your groups are fundamentally different for reasons you are not seeking to measure, your data will lead you to false conclusions. In the quest for truth, that error will derail you. For this reason, Christian researchers need to lean on virtue and ethics to avoid cutting corners for convenience.

The Bible offers a variety of group comparisons, perhaps most striking of which is the series described in Matthew 25. First, Jesus uses an analogy of bridesmaids (Mt 25:1-13). Of the ten women, five are wise and five are foolish. While this sample size is small (and this is a parable, not a research study), we do have equal groups, which nicely meets the assumptions of a *t*-test. The wise bridesmaids bring lamps along with extra oil when they go to meet the groom. The foolish bridesmaids carry their lamps but fail to bring additional fuel. Because they have to run out to buy more, they miss the groom completely. The groups perform differently.

The second parable begins in Matthew 25:14 as the passage switches to the parable of the talents. The passage starts to read more like a single-case research design, in which the sample size is not large enough for group comparison. Yet the story reads like an experiment as the master gives one servant five talents, another two talents, and another one talent. The first two double their money, but the third operates with a scarcity mindset. He is given the least, and his fear leads him to bury it rather than trying to invest.

By the time we arrive at the final group comparison in this passage (Mt 25:31), the tone is heavy. Jesus describes God's ultimate judgment, in which people are divided into two groups. The differences? The group that is ushered into the kingdom fed and clothed the poor, and the group that is cursed and forced to depart from God are those who did not. This is a sobering idea that hopefully pushes us to see through our own biases and consider our own group membership. Psalm 1 paints this picture as well: the sinner versus the righteous. The variables considered here include social influences, level of delight in God's law, and spiritual prosperity. The psalm tells us that these variables are the differences between those who live in sin and those who pursue God. Hypothetically, a t-test could expose the differences between the sinner and the righteous on the variables discussed in the psalm. This could be hugely instructive and efficacious in a culture such as ours that says, "Show me the facts."

Another biblical illustration of comparison using scientific experimentation can be found in 1 Kings 18. It is the ultimate test: the God of Israel versus the false god Baal. Elijah creates equal conditions to compare God and Baal. The level of detail is striking: two bulls, two altars, loud cries to both deities. Elijah even makes the conditions of the experiment more challenging by adding water to his altar. The control group (Baal) has a dry altar to which they hope their god will bring fire, while the experimental group (Yahweh) has a wet condition. If we were to attempt to replicate this experiment, we would likely arrive at the opposite result. Fire is less likely to start on a wet surface. Of course, this is exactly the point. Only the true God can prevail under those circumstances.

There is tremendous spiritual and practical relevance for the church in group comparison. We can identify ways in which Christian believers vary from nonbelievers in myriad directions. For example, a 2021 study by John Lace and Luke Evans explored differences in IQ between those who were "religious only," "spiritual only," "spiritual and religious," and "neither spiritual nor religious."[8] They also compared groups based on affiliation (i.e., Christian, atheist, agnostic). Perhaps to the dismay of the Christian reader, these researchers found that those who were more religious had a significantly lower mean IQ score than those who were neither spiritual nor religious. These authors used a MANCOVA to compare more than three groups on multiple variables, using the covariates of age, gender, level of education, and household income. As a refresher, using these variables as covariates in a sense mathematically removes them from the equation and treats them as if they were not a factor. All these being equal, Christians had significantly lower IQs than both the atheist group and the agnostic group.

What does such a between-groups comparison tell us as the body of Christ? Some might actually be pleased with the results, as in some conservative Christian circles there has been a historical tendency to warn against too much education. In Matthew 18:1-5, Jesus tells his disciples that they must become like little children to enter the kingdom of God. So perhaps this research study indicates that we are on track, at least in the United States, where the participants were pooled from in the study. However, if you are reading this book,

---

[8]John W. Lace and Luke N. Evans, "The Relationship Between Religiousness/Spirituality and Psychometric Intelligence in the United States," *Journal of Religion & Health* 61, no. 6 (2022): 4516-34, https://doi.org/10.1007/s10943-021-01394-4.

you might feel the opposite and, much like we were, be dismayed by these findings. We are challenged to ask ourselves as researchers and intellectuals, What impact might we have locally and globally on the church to help people to think deeply and critically? Is it possible to do so without moving into agnosticism or atheism? Can faith and intellectual curiosity flourish together? Certainly those questions are foundational to the reason we wanted to write this book.

Let's look at another example of between-groups comparison, this time focused on the differences in a religious versus nonreligious cognitive-behavioral therapy (CBT) treatment approach.[9] These researchers set up a true experiment using a stratified randomized design between three groups: a control group (waitlisted for later treatment), a religious group, and a nonreligious group. Because they wanted participants who were religious to receive a modified CBT treatment that had spiritual components, they could not randomly assign all participants. Instead, they used a stratified approach so that those participants who were more highly religious were randomly assigned to either the treatment or control group, and those who were nonreligious were randomly assigned in a similar fashion. When comparing depression scores between all three groups, these authors found significant differences between each of the treatment groups and the control group but no difference between the two treatment groups. Thus, the CBT treatments worked equally well and were significantly better than no treatment. This study was conducted with Romanian participants, but a similar study was done in the United States as well.[10]

---

[9]Bogdan Tudor Tulbure, Nastasia Sălăgean, Gerhard Andersson, Michelle Pearce, and Harold G. Koenig, "Religious Versus Conventional Internet-Based Cognitive Behavioral Therapy for Depression," *Journal of Religion & Health* 57, no. 5 (2018): 1634-48, https://doi.org/10.1007/s10943-017-0503-0.

[10]Michelle J. Pearce and Harold G. Koenig, "Spiritual Struggles and Religious Cognitive Behavioral Therapy: A Randomized Clinical Trial in Those with Depression and Chronic Medical Illness," *Journal of Psychology & Theology* 44, no. 1 (2016): 3-15.

We could conclude from these between-groups comparisons that integrating religious concepts into CBT is not necessary. Both treatments worked equally well. However, there are a few reasons we would caution against jumping to that conclusion. First, in the above study the researchers placed the religious participants into the religious CBT group and the nonreligious participants into the nonreligious CBT group. We do not know what might have happened if those were reversed. Would the treatment have worked as well had the treatment been a mismatch for the clients' values? Second, in the similar study conducted in the United States by Michelle Pearce and Harold Koenig, those authors expressed concern that their religious CBT was not different enough from their nonreligious CBT. When comparing treatment groups, one must always consider whether the groups are receiving interventions that are different enough to be distinguished clearly. For any group comparison, we run the risk of a type II error (finding no significant difference when a difference actually does exist) if our treatments are too similar.

As we consider the spiritual and clinical implications of between-groups research, we would encourage you to consider the importance and relevance of experimental research in general. In both the church world and the clinical world, we can rely too heavily on anecdotal evidence and poorly constructed surveys that are not validated or statistically analyzed. Once we have formed a theory in our minds based on one or two cases, we may fall victim to confirmation bias and start seeing "evidence" all around us that supports our theory. Quantitative research is not perfect, and all research contains some error, but data-driven and data-validated metrics carry more weight than anecdotal claims and interesting sermon illustrations. Pastors are generally not trained in quantitative data analysis, and unfortunately many clinicians do not have extensive enough training to avoid common pitfalls. Thus, we'd encourage you to keep an eye out for group comparison claims in Christian and/or psychology-based books, blogs, or headlines that don't meet the appropriate standards for quantitative research.

WITHIN-SUBJECTS DESIGNS

Within-subjects research is frequently done alongside between-groups analyses. We referenced one such example in the previous section when talking about differences in control versus treatment groups. Usually you make that type of comparison by administering a pretest and a posttest, and then comparing the groups on the amount of change in a specific variable. Thus, we do not have to view within-subjects designs as entirely separate from between-groups designs. However, there are times in which we might want to focus solely on change over time within an individual without making a group comparison. Here is where we will spend our time in this section of the chapter. Both spiritually and clinically speaking, within-subjects designs are important for measuring growth.

When we consider personal change over time from a Christian perspective, our minds head right to the concept of sanctification. Spiritual growth is the subject of many sermons, as pastors seek to lead their congregations toward greater levels of wholeness and holiness. Certainly a plethora of books has been written on the subjects of sanctification and spiritual growth—this process of being transformed into greater Christlikeness. We sing, "More of you, less of me," to a variety of tunes. But exactly what are the methods by which we change over time, and are they measurable?

Let's turn to Romans, where Paul describes an equation: sin = death. In Romans 4–5, he describes two additional variables: faith and grace. (For those of you advanced stats thinkers, pause to consider how you might set up a path analysis with these variables.

Would you include any others?) By Romans 6:1, Paul writes, "What shall we say then? Are we to continue in sin that grace may abound?" He's calling out some understandable but flawed calculations. It was genuinely confusing to shift from a law mindset to a grace mindset. What are the Roman Christians supposed to do to become closer to God? Even though the law was impossible to keep perfectly, at least they had measurable steps to take.

By Romans 12, Paul offers some directions for spiritual growth, including offering your body to God as a living sacrifice, maintaining humility, serving the church through the use of spiritual gifts, genuinely loving others, rejoicing in suffering, and praying continually. To the Corinthians, Paul describes the growth process in terms of human growth, from infancy to maturity (1 Cor 3). In Ephesians 5–6; Galatians 5–6; and 1 Thessalonians 5, Paul repeats and adds greater meaning to the variables of sanctification. Each of these constructs would have to be defined in much greater depth to measure them, but we could arrive at some form of assessment of each. And indeed, many have tried to do just that.

We will explore some current research on spiritual assessment shortly, but we would be remiss if we did not look at additional examples of within-subject growth found in the Bible. Jesus himself is described in Luke 2:52 as growing on two specific variables: wisdom and stature. What might happen if we try to experiment with those variables? Perhaps we might think we have found a positive correlation here as well: In ideal conditions, as one's height increases, so does one's wisdom. We could imagine giving the kindergarten Sunday school class a pretest that would quantitatively measure the construct of wisdom, and we could also record their height. With a longitudinal design, we could return to these same children as they graduated high school and administer the same tests. One could safely assume that all the children would have grown in stature except in rare circumstances. Perhaps we would hope to assume that they all grew in wisdom as well, even if not at entirely equal rates. Our experiment might cause us to wonder what variables most influence the growth of wisdom in a child's life.

However, such a simplistic study would be likely to result in a type I error in which we believe we have found a significant relationship between height and wisdom when in fact that relationship is far more complex and perhaps not at all linear. This is a prime example of how one research study leads to another and to another and to another. Any single research study provides only a sliver of the information pie and runs the risk of producing error.

Let's consider how a final biblical example of the wisdom of King Solomon contributes to our thinking. We have the opportunity to follow his life from his birth in 2 Samuel 12 to his death in 1 Kings 11, although his childhood is not described. Most scholars seem to agree that Solomon was about twenty when David died and handed over the kingdom in 1 Kings 2. It is at this moment of transition that Solomon asks God for wisdom, translated in the ESV as "an understanding mind" (1 Kings 3:9). He also uses the word *discern*, which gives us further information for defining the construct of wisdom in measurable terms. With this wisdom, he famously built the temple (1 Kings 6) along with a magnificent house for himself and a fleet of ships for the kingdom.

Fast-forward twenty years, and he is still amassing great wealth, astounding the queen of Sheba with his wisdom and knowledge. An unknown amount of time passes, and Solomon turns from the Lord, marrying a vast number of foreign wives and allowing them to bring with them their worship of false idols. He manages to thwart his enemies from overtaking the throne, but God establishes that the kingdom will be taken from Solomon's son's hands. What does all this tell us about measuring wisdom? Certainly it helps us realize that a simple pretest/posttest does not give the whole picture. Had we measured Solomon in a similar way to our earlier Sunday school experiment, we would have seen that his height and wisdom were positively correlated, and both grew from time 1 to time 2. We could have even set up a longitudinal study to measure again twenty years later and we still would have seen positive growth, at least on the variable of wisdom.

Let's think about the conclusions we might have drawn from that set of measurements: Height and wisdom initially grow together, then at some point height levels off and wisdom keeps increasing, and then many years later even as height has no measurable change, wisdom continues to increase. Thus, wisdom must continually increase all the way until death, right? In this case, we came to a conclusion without all the data. Solomon turned from God and showed a decrease in wisdom in the later years of his life.

We use this illustration to encourage you to think carefully about the assumptions you make and the conclusions you draw from a small set of measurements. It is entirely possible to miss important data because it is simply unreasonable to practically collect it. For this reason, in any research study you conduct you should express your conclusions with a measure of tentativeness and caution. As you read research, look for this as well. Anyone claiming to have found dramatic results likely does not have the entire data picture.

To lean into curiosity further, we can explore research on spiritual assessment and how it is used to measure growth and development. One study, titled "You Can't Measure That . . . Can You? How a Catholic Seminary Approaches the Question of Measuring Growth in Human and Spiritual Formation," seems like the perfect place to start.[11] In this article, the authors describe years of scholarly

---

[11]Paul Hoesing and Edward Hogan, "You Can't Measure That . . . Can You?: How a Catholic Seminary Approaches the Question of Measuring Growth in Human and Spiritual Formation,"

work to create an assessment that could be used to measure spiritual formation in a seminary context. Their narrative is an excellent picture of just how much thought and work goes into the development of a scale that can be used for within-subjects research. Using a simple *t*-test, these authors measured significant change from pretest to posttest for several consecutive years, which they display in a table in an appendix. Through this statistical analysis of within-subjects change, they provide evidence of validity for their instrument. We'd like to note that the methods described in their article are simplistic from a quantitative perspective, and we'd love to see them (or others like yourself!) come along and run these questions through a factor analysis to create an improved instrument that could be used in a wider context. However, their model provides a good way for student researchers to think about the typical pretest/posttest design of within-subjects research.

Another example of a spiritual assessment useful for within-subjects research is the Communion with God scale.[12] This scale, developed by Joshua Knabb and Kenneth Wang, is increasingly being used in research, including my (Paul) own dissertation referenced earlier. This scale helps define the construct of *personal relationship with God*, a frequently used term within evangelical circles for the past century. These authors take care to place their construct and assessment tool squarely within this context, pulling their question items directly from the cultural and spiritual framework they are seeking to measure. They began by creating a list of thirty-six questions in twelve categories, each rated on a Likert scale from 1-5. After consultation with outside experts who

---

Journal of Spiritual Formation & Soul Care 14, no. 2 (2021): 254-75, https://doi.org/10.1177/19397909211040518.

[12]Joshua J. Knabb and Kenneth T. Wang, "The Communion with God Scale: Shifting from an *Etic* to *Emic* Perspective to Assess Fellowshipping with the Triune God," *Psychology of Religion and Spirituality* 13, no. 1 (2021): 67-80, https://doi.org/10.1037/rel0000272.

could refine their item wording, they gathered a sample of 219 participants who took their instrument. They used both exploratory and confirmatory factor analysis, a quantitative process that helped them reduce their measure to just twelve items. They used correlational analysis as well by giving the participants other measures that related to their construct, an approach to scale validation we saw in the earlier example of the Adapted Inventory of Virtues and Strengths. Further, their analysis calculated the Cronbach's alpha for their scale to demonstrate reliability (a value above 0.70 is generally regarded as good, and these authors reported a value of 0.95). Their article is an excellent example of a thorough approach to creating and validating an assessment tool.

Because of our interest in the Communion with God scale and measuring change over time, I (Kristen) will be incorporating this scale into my master's-level Christian integration course in the counseling program. I am curious to see whether students' sense of connection with God via this scale can significantly change from the start of the course (pretest) to the end (posttest). Because a large focus of the course is on the spiritual formation of each student, my hypothesis is that the work we do in the course can have a significant impact on the students' relationship with God. However, this is a tall order for a seven-week course. I plan to informally test this for a year or two in all sections of the course prior to launching a wider study.

What interests you most about within-subjects research? Do you find yourself thinking more about your clinical interests and how you could measure change in symptoms over time with the use of appropriate treatment interventions? Or are you more curious about spiritual formation and the idea of measuring spiritual growth in a broader church context? Are there additional variables you would like to measure? Perhaps you even have ideas about developing a scale much like we have seen in these examples. We would encourage you to keep a notebook or electronic file that captures your impulses of curiosity whenever they arise. You could title it "My Research Agenda" and dream big about the quantitative possibilities that God has prepared in advance for you to do (Eph 2:10).

REGRESSION

Our final quantitative analysis to explore is regression, which is all about prediction. If we know x, can we accurately estimate within a range what y will be? It is important to note that correlation is an assumption of regression, meaning that a linear relationship is necessary for a regression analysis. If you imagine a simple line graph in which the line keeps going infinitely, you would have an equation for the slope of the line. Even if we only had a few measured data points, we could predict other data points that could occur on that same slope. That is the heart of what a simple (bivariate) regression accomplishes.

When we ask more complex questions with many variables, we use multiple regression. In this more advanced analysis we are not aiming to create a regression equation, nor are we only interested in significance. Instead, we are interested in effect size, which is measured as adjusted R^2. This number on our regression output tells us the percentage of the variance explained by a particular variable. Essentially, how much of the puzzle picture is filled in with this one predictor? Sometimes, our combined predictors fill in a decent amount of that puzzle picture (about 50 percent explained would be outstanding for one study). The more of the puzzle we can explain with our selected variables, the more we can accurately intervene to change outcomes we can predict.

If we revisit some of our correlation examples, we can play out how regression might inform us. Returning to the concept of poverty, we might imagine that an examination of linear relationships could identify risk factors for poverty—with poor work ethic being one variable of many. Understanding which variables correlate with poverty to a significant degree would allow us to run a regression in order to determine which factors are most predictive of poverty. This statistical process would enable us to identify specific risk factors and prevention strategies to empower people likely to be on a path to poverty. If you are interested in this topic, there are certainly myriad studies to read regarding the predictors of poverty.

We could say the same about the development of virtues, as we had noted from 2 Peter 1 in our section on correlation. What would you hypothesize are the strongest predictors of spiritual maturity based on what we know about significant correlations? If you had to rank variables in the order you believed would provide the best model fit, how would you place these in order: faith, virtue, knowledge, self-control, steadfastness, godliness, and brotherly affection? Once you identified the strongest predictors, what would you do with that information? How might it inform a Sunday school curriculum, a sermon series, or a discipleship process? We ask these questions to challenge you to think more like a researcher and a scholar. Unfortunately, many Christian books, curricula, and programs have been based on gut feelings or anecdotal evidence, which can cause harm when misapplied. We are writing this book in part because we want you to see the connection between thinking like a researcher and affecting the church and the kingdom of God.

Another biblical concept that points us toward the principles of regression is prophecy. Both can relate to prediction, one from a quantitative approach and the other from a spiritual framework. The two are not a perfect parallel, but both help us think about knowing the future. Of course, biblical prophecy foretells certainty, while research attempts to help us be as certain as possible. So, let's consider prophecies that offer a prediction through researcher eyes, and also look at the idea of regression and predictive factors as spiritually useful.

Isaiah is a long and complex book of the Bible, and in it we can look for a few different predictor variables (the ones that lead to an outcome) and criterion variables (the things being predicted). Let's consider the criterion variable of God's judgment. What are some of the predictors of God's judgment that we find in Isaiah? Isaiah 10 gives us a few possible variables: oppression, injustice, and worship of idols. If we could quantify these constructs and measure nations and rulers by these variables, might we be able to predict—both mathematically and spiritually—those who will receive God's wrath?

Lest we become lost and dismayed at the depictions of God's destruction, we continue on to Isaiah 11, which describes the coming Savior. There we can ask: What are the predictor variables that will lead us to the conclusion that we have found the correct Messiah? Again we see variables such as wisdom, understanding, righteousness, and faithfulness. These are the prominent predictors of the Messiah and his coming kingdom. Of course, other details, such as a virgin birth and healing by way of his woundedness, fill in the complete picture. Many missed Jesus as the Messiah because of how they defined predicting variables, replacing God's definitions with their own. They measured a limited set of variables, and their hypotheses were misguided by their own biases. When using regression to predict outcomes, we have to remember that our conclusions are only as good as our construct definitions, our choice of variables to measure, and our ability to account for our own bias.

You may have also encountered the concept of logistic regression, which provides us with odds ratios. For example, a study of older adults from India measured loneliness, religiosity, and life satisfaction. These researchers found that those participants who were lonely and nonreligious were 1.51 times more likely to have low life satisfaction than those who were not lonely. Participants who were lonely but did participate in religious activities were only 37 percent more likely to have low life satisfaction than their nonlonely peers.[13] With logistic regression, we can look at the statistical odds of something occurring and identify prevention strategies. From our example, if being lonely in older adulthood predicts low life satisfaction, then we might think of strategies to increase friendship among that population. We can see that religious practice already plays a role in shifting this predicted outcome, and greater levels of community would seem to help as well.

Taking this concept back to the Bible for an exploration of where we see this playing out, look at the Ten Commandments in Exodus 20. Exodus 20:12 reads, "Honor your father and your mother, that your days may be long in the land that the Lord your God is giving you." Ephesians 6:2 refers to this verse, calling it "the first commandment with a promise." Thinking from the mindset of a quantitative researcher, we might suggest that it is the first commandment with a measurable prediction. If there is a linear correlation between honoring your parents and length of life, then we could run a regression to evaluate the prediction. Using a logistic regression, we would turn the *honoring parents* variable into a binary yes/no (an oversimplification of the construct, to be sure).

---

[13]T. Muhammad et al., "The Association Between Loneliness and Life Satisfaction: Examining Spirituality, Religiosity, and Religious Participation as Moderators," *BMC Geriatrics* 23 (2023): 301, https://bmcgeriatr.biomedcentral.com/articles/10.1186/s12877-023-04017-7.

However, with a valid approach to measuring this variable in a yes/no fashion, we could identify the odds of living longer based on honoring parents. To our knowledge such a study has not been done, and indeed there would be some challenges in measurement. Take a moment and consider how you might develop a research design for this line of inquiry and how it might make an impact if you had significant findings.

Looking at regression in the spiritually integrated clinical literature, a study by Julie Exline and colleagues provides an excellent example.[14] The researchers in this case used regression to look at predictors of growth after spiritual struggle. Note that their title captures their population as well: Christian undergraduates. We point this out because we want you to notice the demographics of the participants in every article you read. Some, such as this one, directly indicate their population in the title. Others do not, and this can lead to a misapplication of research. In this article, the authors describe what they call "spiritual struggle," which is a common effort to work out our faith as described in Philippians 2:12. There is an important kind of wrestling that happens in spiritual formation. But we know that some can lose their faith in the process of this struggle.

Using a type of regression analysis called structural equation modeling, these researchers found that positive religious coping (e.g., viewing God as helpful, using prayer as a way to positively cope with stress), perceptions of direct communication from God, and a sense of closeness to God were all predictive factors that significantly contributed to positive growth outcomes. While we

---

[14]Julie J. Exline, Todd W. Hall, Kenneth I. Pargament, and Valencia A. Harriott, "Predictors of Growth from Spiritual Struggle Among Christian Undergraduates: Religious Coping and Perceptions of Helpful Action by God Are Both Important," *Journal of Positive Psychology* 12, no. 5 (2017): 501-8, https://doi.org/10.1080/17439760.2016.1228007.

cannot apply these findings to every population, we can consider the experiences of Christian college students, who often begin a deeper spiritual struggle as they leave home and hear a more broad range of ideas for the first time. Those who feel close to God perceive his communication to them, and who use positive religious coping strategies are likely to come out of this period of wrestling with a stronger faith than before. Those who see God as judgmental, punishing, silent, or distant may not fare as well spiritually. Some may even need to heal from religious trauma or spiritual abuse in which negative religious thinking has been a bedrock of their theological training or experience. Parents, pastors, and clinicians can all play a role in facilitating growth and healing for these students by helping them connect with ways they have felt close to God throughout their lives and ways they may have heard his voice in the past. Students may benefit from an emphasis on God's love rather than his judgment in the midst of expressing doubts, struggle, or pain. We might suggest that Christian-integrated narrative therapy could be useful if working on a clinical level with college students going through this emotionally challenging journey.

Beyond the spiritual struggles of college students, what does regression tell us about religion/spirituality and creating meaning in life? Eunju Yoon and colleagues used a hierarchical multiple regression to explore this idea.[15] In this study, the researchers looked at mental health factors, including depression and anxiety, and examined the relationships between those, a sense of meaning in life, and religion/spirituality. Their findings challenge us as Christian readers, as they found that an increased sense of

---

[15]Eunju Yoon, Latifat Cabirou, Angela Hoepf, and Michael Knoll, "Interrelations of Religiousness/Spirituality, Meaning in Life, and Mental Health," *Counselling Psychology Quarterly* 34, no. 2 (2021): 219-34, https://doi.org/10.1080/09515070.2020.1712651.

meaning in life was more predictive of reduced depression and anxiety outcomes than deeper religion/spirituality. We would encourage you to dig into this study to look at how they chose to define each of their variables and to draw your own conclusions about their findings.

Depending on one's bias, one could draw a variety of conclusions from the article. Some might use these data as a way to demonstrate that organized religion or connection with a spiritual realm are not as important as having your own personal sense of meaning in life. As Christians, we might not want to sit with that conclusion. However, what else might the data point to? Or what if it does reflect a reality that we need to consider more deeply? What would it mean for pastors and church leaders to do more to connect parishioners with a sense of meaning rather than emphasizing church programming and events? Could there be current church models and trends that could benefit from these research findings? And remember, this is all happening within the social imaginaries and complex factors that shape our self-understanding.

Finally, we want to bring you to a practical example of how regression can help us identify risk factors and at-risk populations that we may want to serve, both as the body of Christ and as clinicians. Studies on adverse childhood experiences (ACEs) are plentiful and date back to the original research on the subject in 1998.[16] Many studies that have examined ACEs offer wonderful examples of the use of regression to understand prevention and intervention strategies. In one such study, researchers analyzed the predictive relationships of ACEs and depression, anxiety, and behavioral

---

[16]Vincent J. Felitti et al., "Relationship of Childhood Abuse and Household Dysfunction to Many of the Leading Causes of Death in Adults," *American Journal of Preventive Medicine* 14, no. 4 (1998): 245-58, www.ajpmonline.org/article/S0749-3797(98)00017-8/fulltext.

problems in children.[17] Using a series of logistic regressions, they found that for children aged zero to five years old, just one additional point on the ACEs scale—one adverse childhood experience more than another child—increased their odds of having depression by 115 percent and their odds of anxiety by 61 percent. These authors did not find that demographic predictors significantly increased the odds of trauma, but factors such as race, sex, and income level did play a role in the development of depression, anxiety, and behavioral problems. For example, females and White participants were more likely to develop depression and anxiety, while males and African Americans had higher odds of behavioral problems. The article presents far more data than we can capture briefly here, but our goal is to illustrate how such a research study can help us identify at-risk children and treat them with evidence-based interventions.

From these examples, we hope that you can begin to see the power of regression for prevention and intervention strategies. These strategies may happen in a church discipleship context, or they may be more clinically focused. In either case, understanding the variables that are most predictive of a given outcome help us strategically narrow in on how we best influence individuals and groups toward a positive end. We like to consider this work as a sort of ushering in of the kingdom of God as we bring the healing and wholeness of heaven to earth. Identifying predictors can provide a clearer picture of those who are at risk for negative symptoms or outcomes, and often these at-risk groups could be considered the marginalized and the "least of these." We define integration of Christian faith and counseling

---

[17]Kaprea F. Johnson, Shonn Cheng, Dana L. Brookover, and Brett Zyromski, "Adverse Childhood Experiences as Context for Youth Assessment and Diagnosis," *Journal of Counseling & Development* 101, no. 2 (2023): 236-47, https://doi.org/10.1002/jcad.12460.

research not only by a fusion of ideas but by a practical living out of our faith via our work. Research provides a powerful strategy by which we can offer ourselves as living sacrifices to God (Rom 12:1-2).

CONCLUSION

We have given you a taste of some common quantitative research concepts and methods of analysis. The aim is to give you tools to observe the Bible and the world in quantitative ways and see how this helps shed light on God's world. In the next chapter, we will similarly explore these ideas with qualitative research. We hope that at times you will use the quantitative lenses to read God's Word a little differently and that you are enticed to intelligently and Christianly evaluate principles and systems that God has established. Too often the natural and supernatural worlds—or even faith and science—are separated and viewed from opposing vantage points.

As we conclude this chapter, pause to ask yourself: Have I separated faith and science in my own mind? Do I see these as overlapping circles in a Venn diagram, distinctly different domains but with commonalities? Or do I see how my imaginary can hold space for quantitative discovery as a part of my life of faith? Your answers to these questions will influence the way you read quantitative research. We hope you'll keep pondering these ideas as you continue to read to increase your self-awareness and understand more about the ways you are approaching research.

DISCUSSION QUESTIONS

1. What is the importance of quantitative research for the church? For the clinical professions?

2. Which aspects of quantitative research excite you? Which feel overwhelming or confusing?
3. Choose one study cited in this chapter that most interests you and read the entire article. What insights did you gain from the findings, both spiritually and clinically?
4. If you are practicing connection to God in the process of research as described in chapter one, how might further development of virtues such as humility, gratitude, and compassion increase your sense of flourishing as a researcher? What are three steps you could take to add these to your faith and your knowledge (2 Pet 1:5-8)?
5. What else are you curious about after reading this chapter?

LEARNING ACTIVITIES

1. In groups of three to four, create your own study based on some of the biblical claims mentioned in this chapter. Write a list of the constructs you would have to define and search for validated instruments that exist related to those constructs. Develop a research proposal with at least two research questions. Describe your method and the analysis you would use to evaluate your findings.
2. Divide the class into five groups: descriptive, correlation, between-groups, within-subjects, and regression. Use your university library to search for an article related to counseling that provides an example of each specific type of quantitative analysis. What were its variables? What population did it study? What were the findings and conclusions? Were there any threats to validity or problems with the study (i.e., limitations)? What else did the article make you curious about? Depending on instructor preference, groups can present their articles to each other formally or informally.

FIVE

Sitting *with* Stories *and* Meaning-Making

DO YOU GET LOST IN STORIES? At times, when I (Paul) am driving in the car with my wife, there is a lull in our conversation and she shifts and exclaims, "You just remind me so much of [a particular person]. He was joking about his feelings, and it's sooo similar to what you just said!" Hand(s) on the wheel, I mumble, "How do you mean?" And then she usually recounts in detail the adventures she heard that morning from her favorite podcaster. She doesn't just listen to the episodes; she dwells in them, she really hears. After a time, it's almost as if she knows the presenters and feels connected to them.

I relate. I can get lost in beautifully written spy novels dripping with complex espionage. I love to know the characters, enter their world. It's almost as if I could respond to them. Most of us have been truly sucked in and lost in a story. Perhaps it hasn't happened to you since you were small. Did you get sucked into Narnia? Hogwarts? The magical lands of Dr. Seuss? Somewhere else?

The key to losing yourself in stories is not just the author's art of prose and linguistics but the willingness to hear and accept the author's voice, the author's reality. Podcasts are fascinating because you get to journey with people in their stories at their pace and follow their interpretations. My wife is a willing participant, but she can't adjust the stories, can't control them, and sometimes she says to me, "I just wish they had talked more about _____", or "It's so interesting how they _____. What would that be like to do!?" She is hungry to know more. She doesn't just ask these questions out of her own desire for satiation or wisdom; it's more than that. She wants to understand the whole story. She can't do much *in* this story, and sometimes that feels limiting. I mean, who hasn't wanted to scream something to a book character before? But what if she could? What if she could speak back, ask her questions, and then provide insight, offer comfort, or joke with them? Her participation might become a gift to more than just herself.

We suggest that qualitative research is a place to participate in stories, a rich participation in the complex, storied lives of others as you seek their good. You get to step into the podcast, into Narnia, into Hogwarts and ask more of the characters. You get to really understand, draw out story lines, and uncover needs. With the character's help, you collaboratively discover and discern ways you might respond, and you can even invite the characters to help you in the responses. Far from passive observation, qualitative research asks you to step into the lives of others to hear them, know them, and ultimately serve them. Wonderfully, we were created for this type of engagement with one another, and in this chapter we will explore how Jesus' life models this engagement. You will discover how to enact your own story-dwelling qualitative research as a response to your curiosity and others' needs.

COUNSELING AS QUALITATIVE RESEARCH

In the last chapter we acknowledged the ambivalence many students and professors feel in regard to math and subsequently quantitative research. This chapter presents the easy-to-sell arts of listening, inviting, learning, and loving the other. Yes, we really see qualitative research this way, and we invite you to journey with us and see why. (Of course, quantitative research also aims to connect God's reality to our flourishing in a manner that loves and serves. It is just a little less obvious at first glance.)

Consider with us what is at the heart of the counseling and psychology work we do with clients. First and foremost, we hear them. You try to really hear this person who is with you, and you want them to feel and know that you hear them. In the process, your mind gathers momentum, and you ask questions to help them tell you their story in its fullness. You respond and reciprocate with expressions, gestures, and more. A careful counselor recognizes the culture and systems that surround the client, taking stock of how this shapes the client's experiences. Yet however carefully you listen, you are always performing interpretive acts, understanding this client's story through your own personal formation and ideas. It is inevitable that we will understand this client in our own way. This is true of all human communication and interaction. The difference here is our intense effort and desire to honor and respect the experience that the other is communicating to us; we do not change it, we do not manipulate it, we do not make presumptions. At its very best, the beginnings of our counseling efforts feel to the client as if someone has seen into their heart and held up a mirror. They feel seen, known, and understood. What a marvelous experience this is.

In essence, this is the heart of qualitative research: to assist, honor, and represent the participants by making their experience known. Do you notice how your counseling skills are setting you up so well to engage in this process? You are already learning to attend to people in this way. Mark Thorpe agrees but adds that this work will shape you too:

> By conducting qualitative research the student optimally develops a psychologically sophisticated understanding of their own worldview and personality,

an intellectual rigor, and trust in the process and an empathic, open, curious and respectful ability to become immersed in the research participant's lived world. Leaving the security of the already known, maintaining an optimal distance from the data and resisting the pull for premature closure, the student learns to tolerate complexity, confusion and ambiguity.[1]

Don't we hope to be clinicians who can remain empathic, open, and respectful, being immersed in our clients' lives without being overtaken by them? And don't we hope to hold the complexity of life without running too soon to security and answers, allowing the client to be understood and supported?

Here we share a concrete example of qualitative research that looks a lot like mature counseling. In the previous chapter, we presented the findings from the Barna Group showing the rise of pastors who considered leaving their positions between 2021 and 2022 and discussed the questions that might arise. Why are more pastors considering leaving? Are they burned out? Do they feel overwhelmed with people's needs? We named that more research is needed to fully answer these questions. During those years, many of us heard stories about pastors struggling with too many tasks, too little help, rising needs during Covid, inflamed social and political relations, factions within churches, and more. Therefore, we have ideas about what is going wrong, and this could limit or bias how we attend to the problem. So, let's slow the process down.

What if you were able to sit with multiple small groups of pastors who were thinking about leaving and really got to hear their hearts? Remaining aware of our biases and worldview, we are open yet separate and tolerate the complexity until we really hear them. Then we might have clearer insight into what is actually happening. Do you see the counseling skills? We set aside our prior ideas and

---

[1]Mark Thorpe, "The Process of Conducting Qualitative Research as an Adjunct to the Development of Therapeutic Abilities in Counselling Psychology," *New Zealand Journal of Psychology* 42, no. 3 (2013): 135.

assumptions just as we do with counseling intakes and assessment. Then we create a safe and trusted environment where the pastors can share, just like we do with informed consent, confidentiality, and relational rapport. Next, we use skills and courage to ask invitational and probing questions for the good of the other, just as with counseling ethics and core skills. Finally, we collect data and record it in a reliable manner we can use later, just as we do with notes and treatment plans.

Imagine that you have set up small group meetings with these pastors, and you ask winsome questions that invite the pastors to share their experience. You gently probe, listen, reflect, and inquire all the way to the bottom of the well—all the way until you really understand what is happening for these pastors. A pastor might say, "I'm just so overwhelmed by people's needs!" and you pursue the bottom of the well by asking, "Tell me more about people's needs and what that looks like in your experience" or, "Tell me how these needs connect to your overwhelm." The key is to catch yourself when you make an assumption or assume you understand and then ask a good question instead. Once we have listened to enough pastors for long enough, we may see a pattern emerge that describes their collective experience.

The researcher's final step is to share the pastors' experiences and needs with others who can attend to them in the specific way they need. In our circles, a normal response to burned-out pastors is to give them a sabbatical (a time away), but does this always help them with their concerns? What if they are exhausted from struggling to manage relational dysfunction that has arisen in their church or are feeling socially isolated? Shouldn't we help them with leadership, discipleship, and other skills? Or what if the issue is that they need more hands for the amount of labor? Curiosity that seeks to understand the lived experiences of the pastors fuels exploratory questions and better understanding, and paves the way toward effective solutions.

QUALITATIVE RESEARCH IN A CHRISTIAN IMAGINARY

We discussed qualitative research in chapter two, stating that its methods and process can be diverse, which can often confuse newcomers. Our hope is to provide some clarity about qualitative research seen from a Christian story. Qualitative research remains an empirical method because it involves data collection, analysis, and interpretation.[2] We sum up this empirical work more poetically as *collaborative acts of observing others and inviting readers into these experiences and their meaning.*

You will notice that this statement emphasizes both understanding the participants (often those with an identified need) and inviting participation from others (those who can help or can initiate change processes). These two elements are usually held together within social-scientific research in which the end goal is to seek human flourishing. Positively, our modern, wealthy, cultural and scientific moment has allowed attention and resources to turn to the heart of the Christian imaginary—flourishing. Yet there are some gaps between our approaches. As we saw earlier, a Christian story provides a bedrock of truth that calls us to live for the good of others and ourselves; however, many people come to similar conclusions through different means. In our cultures many people are aware of social, physical, and relational distress that requires unique contextual responses. The Christian starts their response with a big explanatory framework for distress, and qualitative research can help nuance our understanding of unique issues. We

---

[2]Joseph Ponterotto, "Qualitative Research in Counseling Psychology: A Primer on Research Paradigms and Philosophy of Science," *Journal of Counseling Psychology* 52, no. 2 (2005): 128, https://doi.org/10.1037/0022-0167.52.2.126.

aren't starting from scratch. For example, the rise of loneliness in the modern West has been connected to a rise in smartphone and social media use.³ As Christians we can start to think about this problem, knowing that we were made for a certain kind of other-oriented life.

Even though Christians can engage qualitative research with a bigger framework for human life in mind, the execution of the research looks *very* similar. Our research will follow the same sound scientific practices because the art of hearing the other in an unbiased manner doesn't change. We still collect data and interpret it, just as we saw in our previous chapter on quantitative research. Further, like any good researcher, our values are not permitted to take over the research process, and we carefully track our experience and its potential impact so we can account for this in our interpretations.⁴

However, as Christians we can relate to the qualitative research process in two ways that others may not. First, as we saw in chapter two, our insider (*emic*) position, holding to a Christian story, allows us to overtly engage those (participants) who share this understanding of life with overtly Christian ideas. This means constructing our research questions and methods with explicitly Christian language and ideas. For example, we might ask directly how Christians experience their relationship with Jesus providing hope for change amid struggles with substance abuse. Our questions could overtly use shared Christian ideas and language and allow us to dig deep into their experience.

---

[3] Emily O'Day and Richard Heimberg, "Social Media Use, Social Anxiety, and Loneliness: A Systemic Review," *Computers in Human Behaviors Reports* 3 (2021): 11, https://doi.org/10.1016/j.chbr.2021.100070; Mengwei Ge, Hu Fei-Hong, Jia Yi-Jie, and Tang Wen, "The Relationship Between Loneliness and Internet or Smartphone Addiction Among Adolescents: A Systematic Review and Meta-Analysis," *Psychological Reports* 128, no. 3 (2003): 1, https://doi.org/10.1177/00332941231180119.

[4] Ponterotto, "Qualitative Research in Counseling Psychology," 128, 131.

The second difference the Christian imaginary provides is a different set of priorities for our research agendas. Our imaginary shapes our value system and leads to curiosity about specific issues that we may not otherwise pursue. For instance, I (Paul) care deeply for the human experiences of collaboration, development, and mutual growth. This general curiosity has led me to study the supervisor-supervisee mentoring relationship in counseling and psychology. At first, I did this with general scientific language, but my Christian story shaped how I saw the issue. I wondered how the construct of discipleship might be an older wisdom that could teach Christians about their development in the helping professions. As a result, I began to research mentoring through a consideration of the role Jesus played with his disciples. I was curious to see whether the formative experiences of the disciples would shed light on a Christian approach to mentoring supervision. Indeed, Jesus' example had much to give.

Another example could be exploring the experience of church leadership and congregants in regard to mental health care. Specific Christian language and theology would help any researcher connect to these Christians. For instance, church leaders might think about well-being and mental health differently from the secular sciences. The work looks very similar to secular qualitative research, yet the driving impetus would be different. The Christian story can shape your interests, lead you down different roads of inquiry, and provide common ideas from which to explore people's experience. We just have to learn to name these realities well, as discussed in chapter two.

JESUS AS A MODEL FOR QUALITATIVE INQUIRY

We said that counseling skills are a great advantage to the qualitative researcher. This is true, and yet we are excited to share that

Jesus provides Christians (and others) a stunning model for engaging other people's hearts that can shape our approach to qualitative research. Jesus' early years led him to a deep appreciation and unwavering pursuit of life according to God's design. Let's slow down to wrap our minds around that—Jesus learned as a boy, teenager, and man to see through God's story, to ask questions from within, and to understand flourishing as the provision of his Father. He wasn't just born that way. Jesus saw the day-to-day creatureliness and humanity of life and didn't treat it as anything but spiritual. In Jesus' mind, every feeling, thought, choice, and act occurs in God's world. Jesus knew that some people he engaged were aware of his Father's world and others simply were not.

Jesus asked many questions to open people up. He used qualitative inquiry regularly, not to teach correctness but to stir up people's hearts, to understand what they loved, and to invite them to hold this up for examination. He held up a mirror to them and let them wonder whether their pursuits would sustain them. This was a special kind of provocative and tender invitation. Of course, we do not have the mission or place of Jesus in our research, yet we may curiously investigate life as Jesus did, inviting people to see, to consider, to expose, and even to critique.

Did you ever see the wrist bands that had the letters WWJD (What Would Jesus Do)? We are dating ourselves here in using this example, yet it helps us illustrate how we can follow what Jesus would do in qualitative research. Jesus demonstrates engagement designed to create reflexivity—the skill of self-reflection and awareness—which is critical for both researchers and those looking to flourish.[5] Jesus wasn't really conducting research, but he wasn't

---

[5] Randolph Bowers, Victor Minichiello, and David Plummer, "Qualitative Research in Counseling: A Reflection for Novice Counselor Researchers," *The Qualitative Report* 12, no. 1 (2007): 139, https://nsuworks.nova.edu/cgi/viewcontent.cgi?article=1650&context=tqr.

afraid to do the hard relational work that underpins caring research while looking at the world and its problems through God's kingdom eyes. Jesus developed these skills and virtues just as we will. Let us turn to a few of the skills that Jesus models for researchers who seek to hold to the Christian imaginary in qualitative research.

Authenticity. Jesus is unashamed of who he is and expresses himself accordingly. He lets his Father's mission guide his choices and actions, and models alignment across identity and purpose. Many of us spend years struggling with who we are, how we think, what we stand for, and how we might live these things out in our lives. That is quite normal. A defined identity and mission provides conviction to our pursuit of goals and research questions, and limits what we will and will not do as we engage participants. Our beloved identity as Christian researchers can bolster us amid self-consciousness or confusion that could lead to self-protective actions such as obfuscating, distracting, or just following our gut—all of which can lead to dilution of self-efficacy, clarity, and purpose. We have both experienced times when we forgot our frame and our gut reactions were less than helpful in the research process. It happens, and we can admit it and return to our solid and firm foundation as loved children.

Throughout his ministry Jesus knew who he was and that some would not accept him (Jn 6:64). He knew that some would stumble (see the Pharisees who reject Jesus' testimony and healing in Mt 12:1-32), and some would rejoice (see the Syrophoenician woman's faith in Mk 7:24-30). Nonetheless, he consistently acts to demonstrate and declare who he is and what he is about—declaring his role as the Messiah. Jesus healed when healing was needed and said who he was when such was needed.

Jesus' authenticity arose from the self-assurance that flows from a solid identity, bringing with it a set of values that give rise to purpose. The Father affirms Jesus' identity by declaring that Jesus is his loved Son and that he is pleased with him (Mt 3:17). In response, Jesus later declares that he is working for his Father's name and looks only to his Father's will (Lk 22:42; Jn 5:41). We see in the New Testament that Jesus rests in the Father's presence again and again in prayer. He saturates himself in his identity and purpose all throughout his ministry. As researchers we must do likewise, especially when we feel knocked off-balance by challenges or negative participants.

We have two layers of identity. First, we, like Jesus, are precious children who are very pleasing to our Father. God alone gives us internal stability that we also feel in our intimate Christian connections. He knows we can contribute because that is how he made us. Second, we remind ourselves of what we are about, which is ushering in knowledge and awareness of God's world. We can saturate ourselves in God's view of us through reading, community, prayer, and more. With our identity secure, we can authentically attend to the central premise of our research without hubris and acknowledge our goals, limitations, biases, and needs, and readjust as necessary. This is research that our loving Father will sing over. It isn't always easy, and it takes self-awareness, but in our experience, it is deeply satisfying work.

Compassion. Compassion is the full experience of empathy for another that is turned into motivated action on their behalf.[6] Throughout his life Jesus chose not to look away but to emotionally engage with the present experiences and wider stories of people's lives. He allowed himself to be moved to tears and outrage when he witnessed the plight of those he loved or the folly of his

---

[6]Shane Sinclair et al., "Sympathy, Empathy, and Compassion: A Grounded Theory Study of Palliative Care Patients' Understandings, Experiences, and Preferences," *Palliative Medicine* 31, no. 5 (2016): 445, https://doi.org/10.1177/0269216316663499.

detractors. And in a very human manner, his strong emotions motivated him, time and again, to actions that matched the needs of the other at each moment. Jesus enacts such compassion because he feels deeply and accurately for people (see his weeping with others, Jn 11:35), he understands the wider cultural frame surrounding their needs (see his lamenting the lost crowds and Jerusalem, Lk 19:41), and he doesn't forget their personal needs amid these experiences (see his encouraging one-on-one, Jn 21:15-25). Jesus' compassionate actions left indelible changes; people were really healed, convicted, provoked, soothed, and saved.[7] In essence, Jesus models an other-focused tenderness that moved him to kingdom-oriented actions.

When responding to a particular qualitative research inquiry, we are responding amid the general human condition. Charles Spurgeon describes the human condition of need and despair, and the Christlike response we need, very well:

> When my sins compassed me about like bees, and I thought it was all over with me . . . it was at that moment when Jesus revealed Himself to me. Had He waited a little longer, I had died of despair, but that was no desire of His! On swift wings of love He came and manifested His dear wounded Self to my heart. I looked to Him and was lightened, and my peace flowed like a river! I rejoiced in Him! Yes, He was moved with compassion.[8]

Many people and groups long to be seen, understood, spoken for, and uplifted as Spurgeon describes. Only compassionate researchers are able to hold this human condition, allow themselves to be moved by participants, and maintain the research. Sometimes more questions are needed for deep resonance; sometimes

---

[7] Chidinma Ukeachusim, Ezichi Ituma, and Favour Uroko, "Understanding Compassion in the Gospel of Matthew (Matthew 14:13-21)," *Theology Today* 77, no. 4 (2021): 373, https://doi.org/10.1177/0040573620956712.

[8] Charles Spurgeon, "The Compassion of Jesus," December 24, 1914, Spurgeon Gems, www.spurgeongems.org/sermon/chs3438.pdf.

they feel intrusive. Sometimes coauthoring a story with participants is empowering; sometimes it feels like mistreatment.

The compassionately oriented researcher can attend to their gut responses (the home of compassionate reaction) with conviction and kindness.[9] Similarly, only the convicted researcher will maintain focus in the face of human suffering. Jesus models both of these, and we can follow. It is incredibly hard to maintain a Christian imaginary as your framework for understanding the pain and need of others while also allowing them to communicate with you just how differently they understand their pain. Yet, like Jesus, you can continue in compassionate responses that do not demand more than the context will allow. You will not be preaching but serving participants with the compassion of Christ that you first received yourself.

Attunement. The central theme of Jesus' attunement for us to grasp is that he truly saw and heard the person with whom he was engaged. Jesus doesn't miss a beat—unless he does it intentionally, as it seems when he falls asleep in a boat through the storm (Mt 8:23-27). Jesus' life and ministry focus on revealing the kingdom and calling people to reckon with their understanding of who he is. While researchers have a different focus—their research question—they must not allow this focus to trump attunement. The researcher attends to the participants to collect faithful information rather than bowing to any other agenda. Jesus does this. Having witnessed or spoken to someone, he manages to tune in so that he can tease apart the core of someone's needs from the extra information. Similarly, a good researcher attempts to tune into participants in such a manner that they discern what is happening during data gathering and can reflexively adapt their strategy and presentation to support further clarity and insight.

---

[9]Ukeachusim et al., "Understanding Compassion," 373.

Two very different scenarios expose Jesus' attunement. First, in John 4, Jesus addresses a woman from Samaria, something that was simply not done in that culture. Jesus sees the woman and treats her with dignity, knowing that this would be confusing and provocative. He engages her supernaturally, knowing her relational history, and pursues a dialogue in which her heart and life can be exposed so that she can receive what she truly needs. While Jesus' power is well beyond our pay grade, his example of attending deliberately to the other is not.

Second, in Luke 10:38-42, we see the familiar story of Mary and Martha. Again, Jesus is attuned to the cultural expectations, which in this scenario would concern hosting guests and female service. He chooses not to speak into this until Martha reveals the distress she feels, and Jesus' response exposes her heart. We too are able to read rooms, faces, and words and to make wise discernments. Jesus doesn't hold back, but attunement makes his direct engagement effective. Attunement takes effort and intention but allows us to tailor our words and respond with kind effectiveness.

Questioning. Jesus used a lot of questions in a lot of different ways for a lot of different purposes. Illuminating questions were at the heart of Jesus' teaching method—they are all throughout the Gospels. Through his questions, Jesus "aroused interest, provoked thought, requested information, elicited response, clarified issues, applied truth, and silenced critics. . . . His questioning kept His audiences intensely alert, for it spurred them to recall, reflect, speculate, evaluate, and mediate, while it achieved life-changing results."[10] We make sense of Jesus' continued use of questions by remembering his authenticity, compassion, and attunement. These

---

[10] Zummy Dami, Ferdinant Alexander, and Yanjumseby Manafe, "Jesus' Questions in the Gospel of Matthew: Promoting Critical Thinking Skills," *Christian Education Journal* 18, no. 1 (2020): 93, https://doi.org/10.1177/0739891320971295.

traits combined provided Jesus a disposition that was radically other-centered. Sure, the questions helped people learn and see from another perspective, but ultimately Jesus' "questions reach[ed] into a person to disclose what was already there, perhaps a fact about the person, but uninterpreted ... or even something unrecognized."[11] The goal was to help the other through asking what would prompt them into reflection and sharing. Sometimes true faith in God was found, like the woman who anointed Jesus' feet in her shame. Other times, there was hypocrisy and self-preservation, like the Pharisees and the scribes. Nonetheless, whatever was exposed provided the context for Jesus' next engagement, the next careful question or intervention.

The same is true for qualitative researchers. What is found in the heart of participants is all-important. Wonderfully, participants also learn about their own concerns, perspectives, and limitations as they are lovingly engaged by an interested other. Have you ever had a good friend, pastor, or counselor ask you one of those questions that when you answered you were blown away by what you realized about yourself? I (Paul) still remember being asked, "So, it sounds like you struggle to trust anyone. How does that impact you?" Ouch. I knew it. But I didn't know it in the same way until it was asked. I was grateful for that heart-revealing question.

Jesus used questions skillfully. Houston Heflin discusses Jesus' different use of questions, and we track his ideas.[12] Heflin shows Jesus regularly helped people to make meaning from their experiences with questions such as, "Have you understood all these things?" (Mt 13:51). Then he notes that Jesus helped listeners apply

---

[11] Michael Buckley, *What Do You Seek? The Questions of Jesus as Challenge and Promise* (Eerdmans, 2006), 9.
[12] Houston Heflin, "That's a Good Question: Inquiry as a Pedagogical Strategy of Jesus in Matthew," *Christian Education Journal* 19, no. 1 (2022): 120, https://doi.org/10.1177/07398913211009524.

what they knew with case studies and parables, with a key example being Jesus asking the teachers of the law, "Have you not read . . . ?" (Mt 12:3). Heflin also notes that Jesus helped listeners evaluate, remember, analyze, and ultimately share their experience so that he could continue in conversation with them as they grew in awareness. Finally, Jesus used silence and patience when he sought to uncover the depths of the human heart (Mt 9:28; 13:51; 16:13); he didn't rush but allowed an internal focus and pursued honesty.[13] What a fantastic model for the researcher.

Like Jesus, both researcher and participant learn about current conditions, needs, desires, challenges, and more as they collaboratively work to peel back the layers of personal experience. We can practice the art of questions, as this is a skill like any other, but the heart that guides their use must also be formed. You can do this by remaining vigilant for biases and avoiding questions that are designed to affirm your own ideas. Jesus masterfully inquires of the person about the topic of interest but refuses to exert undue pressure or influence. We can copy by using our knowledge of a subject and then humbly allow participants to show the next steps on the pathway to insight.

Responding. Have you ever noticed that Jesus seems to move encounters and conversations from one place to another? He doesn't just allow people to stay with their first impressions, needs, or complaints. Jesus is interested in people having an experiential encounter or coming to new conclusions. One example of this is how Jesus uses parables such as that of the good Samaritan (Lk 10:25-37). Here Jesus boldly moves the lawyer from thinking about whom he must serve ("Who is my neighbor?") to seeing all who are in need ("When he saw him [the beaten man], he had

---

[13]Heflin, "That's a Good Question," 128.

compassion") as opportunities to love as God does. This inverts the lawyer's thinking from categories of people to love, toward emotionally engaged responding within his life. This is quite a different emphasis.

Similarly, a good researcher wants to move from a research question (the first engagement) to understanding (a developed conversation) and to communicate these new insights to others. In effect, researchers tell accurate stories about participants so that other readers will change or implement new actions. Consider this: You might seek to understand fathers who don't like to engage with their young children. At first, you hear stories about not knowing how to play, thinking play is kid stuff, or even that it's just boring. Authentic, attuned, compassionate, and questioning engagement will get you past this first part of the conversation, and the dads may open up with you. You may give them imagined scenarios and invite them to respond to their experience. Through this you end up hearing about the dads' confusion and insecurities. Dads start telling you that ultimately they don't know how to play and it makes them feel uncomfortable and unmasculine. Probing further, you find that these dads feel shame and self-doubt when letting go of their normal image and don't want their wives to make fun of how they try to play. You realize that they aren't *bad* dads; they are *scared* dads. If this pattern were to bear out over multiple conversations with dads, you'd be supporting a whole generation of families by responding to this information and sharing it in a manner that people could read and respond to.

As we traced Jesus' interactional style, we hope you saw how the organizing theme of these actions is seeking the welfare of our communities. Jeremiah 29:7 says, "Seek the welfare of the city where I have sent you into exile, and pray to the Lord on its behalf, for in its welfare you will find your welfare." This is the model of Jesus for us, to courageously engage participants to help them express the fullness of their experience, and then to respond. For researchers, this means sharing the stories faithfully. Our sharing will come in academic writing, casework, consultation, and other professional avenues, but it still operates within the Christian imaginary. Similarly to Jesus, we can do this well when we are authentic, attuned, compassionate, curious (questioning), and responsive.

Questions and the Heart

I (Paul) used to shrink away from being asked good questions. I didn't know it at the time, but I felt afraid of good questions and the exposure they could bring. I often struggled to trust what people really wanted or intended if I shared. The sad reality is that those who actually wanted to know me or care for me were kept at least one long arm's distance away. In response to my own fear, I also struggled to ask other people meaningful questions that moved beyond "How was your day?"

It seems strange now to remember those days, especially because healing has come through loving questions and kind responses. As I hope you have experienced, to be known is a blessing and feels life giving even if the knower can't fix or change your struggles. It was kind others who lovingly inquired about my inner world and responded to my ever-increasing openness with warmth and receptivity. Yes, it was good, sweet counseling and friendships. The potent truth is that questions did expose me, showed my values, my disposition, my choices. The question weapon is real. But wielded well, the weapon is powerful *for* us rather than *against* us. Jesus asked some who were following him, "What are you seeking?" (Jn 1:38). When the asker is safe and good, our honest answer can reveal much about our pain, attempts to cope, and what we need. When we respond to Jesus' good question, we become aware of what it is we need from the rich store of God's goodness in response.[a] Only when I expose my aloneness am I prepared for the rich intimacy Jesus offers. Only when I expose my insecurity am I prepared to be held by his mighty arms.

I have learned to listen carefully not just for words and their direct meaning but to their collective messages, their omissions, their paradoxes. And further, I have learned to listen to eye movements, shifting bodies, and changes of direction or topic. As I have done this, I have discovered that questions become a way to offer mirrors to others, not to expose but to find, care, and delight. In counseling, supervision, and research, my questions have become an act of searching for the heart. Not perfectly, but intentionally. In the qualitative research interviews I have conducted, it has been a joy to stick close to the research agenda and use successive questions to invite the speaker to expose their own heart in response. I have made many blunders—asking awkward questions that I needed to reshape. Sometimes because I inserted too much of my own perspective. Sometimes because I broke attunement and lost the speaker. Sometimes because I thought I knew where this person would go next. Learning to use open and exploratory questions is a skill you develop over time.

I have found that when the human heart really opens up, you often realize your question wasn't quite right. And this is a good thing. We can celebrate how the back-and-forth interplay allows us to reshape our questions as we discover the heart of the other and what is truly experienced and needed. Now I like being asked good questions. How about you?

[a] Ronald Raab, "What Are You Looking For?," The Priest, July 11, 2024, https://thepriest.com/2023/12/15/what-are-you-looking-for/.

SYNTHESIS AND MEANING-MAKING IN THE KINGDOM

Each qualitative research method synthesizes data in conjunction with participants so that meaning emerges. A common method that brings meaning, called *coding*, focuses on grouping similar snippets of information that arise across dialogues and coding them into groups. As groups emerge, patterns can be discerned amid the voices that show meaning. Another meaning-making method is the process of helping individual participants to tell their stories in full, thereby helping participants expose and highlight their own experience and meaning.

These methods are not new inventions. The Christian world has a long history of helping others make meaning. The historic Roman, Jewish, and other cultures in which Jesus acted used oral traditions in the process of making meaning.[14] Historically, many cultures used storytelling to pass on information and history that provided cohesion. Throughout these stories, repetition, patterns, key phrases, and other devices that enhance memory and catch attention are common. For our biblical ancestors, when they repeated the word *holy*, it was modified to mean "even more holy." Or, by naming their forefathers, they imported the associated references and lessons of these people's lives. For thousands of years Christians have accurately discerned meaning through patient, dialogical experience against the glowing backdrop of God's Word.

Wonderfully, qualitative research uses the same processes of human communication and listens for themes, patterns, and other methods of identifying meaning. Even literature reviews that filter prior information attempt to capture the stories of our research ancestors, if you will. They bring our past into the present, allowing us to hold new encounters within the glow of the old. With the legacy and process of discerning meaning in mind, we turn to consider specific qualitative methodologies that seek meaning in the context of the Christian imaginary.

QUALITATIVE RESEARCH METHODOLOGIES IN CHRISTIAN CONTEXT

We have chosen to discuss six qualitative methods (or philosophies) that are commonly used by secular and Christian researchers. Qualitative methods often overlap, but we hope to show you how each method seeks to provide answers to research questions that meet human needs. We weave this together with a consideration of how each method dovetails or can be used with a

---

[14]Robert Culley, "Oral Tradition and Biblical Studies," *Oral Tradition* 1, no. 1 (1986): 30-65, https://mospace.umsystem.edu/xmlui/bitstream/handle/10355/63963/OralTradition1-1-Culley.pdf?sequence=1.

biblical perspective of people. We have used a strategic range of studies and biblical examples to demonstrate to you some of the nuances of these methods and spark your curiosity for the wide-open playground before you.

Narrative. Narrative research fills the heart of the natural storyteller. You may intuitively sense that the stories we tell and live help us organize our inner world, make sense of the outside world, and explain how we experience and adapt to events.[15] That is precisely narrative research. For each participant, the full narrative arc of their story acts as a frame of reference for them as they approach upcoming experiences. Stories of overcoming or of perpetual turmoil prepare us. Understanding and engaging these narrative arcs creates the perfect opportunity to engage people as they attempt new actions. We can help them see how choices fit or conflict with the arc. This method of research aligns closely with the story-driven culture of the Bible. We have already referenced Christianity in this way, noting the major story arc of creation, fall, redemption, and consummation. Living amid the fall with sin, pain, and division, Christians hold to the story arc of hope in Christ's return, founded on Christ's work at the cross. This story changes how we live: We worship, we pray, we expect, we hope.

Jesus was a story expert who understood their power and would likely agree with the statement, "It is the enveloping and constituting function of stories that is especially important to sense more fully. We are, each of us, locations where the stories of our place and time become partially tellable."[16] Our stories envelop and make us. The Pharisees lived and told stories of required obedience,

---

[15] Philip Brown, "Narrative: An Ontology, Epistemology, and Methodology for Pro-Environmental Psychology Research," *Energy Research and Social Science* 31 (2017): 218-19, https://doi.org/10.1016/j.erss.2017.06.006.

[16] Miller Mair, "Psychology as Storytelling," *International Journal of Personal Construct Psychology* 1, no. 2 (1988), 125-37, https://doi.org/10.1080/10720538808412771.

strict laws, and hierarchy (e.g., Lk 18:9-12), making it impossible to accept Jesus. Indeed, the disciples struggled to follow Jesus' new story line, constantly asking him questions and getting confused about what God was doing (e.g., Mt 16:21-23). Imagine the Messiah, your dear friend, telling you over and over that he must die to save you. What a confusing twist in your story arc.

Christian faith requires us to adopt a new story arc, which is why many are so confused. The Christian imaginary is a powerful story that frames all of life, and this is why it is so challenging to nontheistic researchers. Christian researchers hold this giant story as the larger frame for the focused stories of participants within. We expect a great range of stories to fit within the Christian grand story, yet some stories work counter to the grand story, and we suggest this is a cause of much suffering. Jesus teaches this on many occasions, calling people back to himself (e.g., Mt 5–7; Lk 6:27-28; Jn 14:6). As Christian researchers, we hear participants' individual stories occurring within the grand human story. We must remember that true flourishing is bound by how God made things, but huge diversity remains due to factors such as culture and preference.

We share an example from modern narrative research that understands the bigger Christian story as a guiding assumption. The research had the Christian assumption that marriage is important and we do well to support and protect it. This shaped the research but did not dictate the outcomes. The researchers wanted to understand how Christian psychology graduate education affected marriage, and as a result they offer recommendations for support.[17] To unravel this issue, they interviewed male and female spouses of current students to allow participants to *tell their story and expose*

---

[17]Mikala Legako and Randall Sorenson, "Christian Psychology Graduate School's Impact on Marriage: Nonstudent Spouses Speak," *Journal of Psychology and Theology* 28, no. 3 (2000), 212-20, https://doi.org/10.1177/009164710002800304.

what was central or meaningful to them. The researchers used extensive quotations to demonstrate that participants found that extended study strained their relationship, that their spouses had become more emotionally expressive, and that they had seen their spouses wane in their commitment to God.

Critically, participants assumed their view of the integration of psychology and theology, despite its simplicity, to be no different from their spouses who were being trained in this discipline. In response to these stories, the researchers recommended that incoming families and spouses be provided information to understand the common impact of graduate study, be invited to support groups or conversations, and be given an orientation to integration and how it affects both professional and ministry spheres. This study clearly helped future students and their families and did so by sharing stories while valuing the broader Christian imaginary. Perhaps your future study might investigate and support single Christian students and how they are affected by listening to their stories?

Let's examine a second study that started within the Christian imaginary. The researcher wanted to explore how students at a faith-based university experience a sense of calling because this is a powerful Christian idea that affects career, satisfaction, and purpose.[18] The researcher interviewed eight students and found their story arcs filled with statements about direction, meaning, and confusion. This all makes sense given the developmental stage of these participants, yet the striking contribution from this study is that the researcher realized he did not hear much about positive steps the universities were taking to facilitate a sense of calling. In response to participant stories, he suggested universities could

---

[18]James Coil, "A Narrative Study of Calling in Christian University Sophomores" (PhD diss., Azusa Pacific University, 2016), 287.

integrate deliberate practices, such as using the language of calling in classes and cocurricular activities, and expanding conceptions of academic advising to include issues of calling and self-reflection. The participants' stories indicated that they experience university as training for a calling but not a partner in learning to understand self in relation to calling. These are more critical insights that are helping to support Christian university students as they transition to work and career.

Really hearing people's stories allowed Jesus to engage them, honor them, and invite them to new action and choices that supported their flourishing. We too can draw out people's stories to understand how their story arc prepares them to react and interpret their lives. From here, we can help honor their customs, experiences, culture, and desires, and move toward new experiences that could affect their lives within God's big story. Whose story are you curious to hear so that you can thoroughly understand their experience and support them toward flourishing?

Phenomenology. At its core, phenomenology is an approach to people that suggests you can study someone's *experience* of any occurrence closely enough to begin to *make meaning out of how they experience the occurrence.*[19] The central premise of this method is that when you learn how someone interprets and experiences something specific, the actions, choices, struggles, and needs they have in response become increasingly clear. We attempt to learn how a person *experiences* an event in a different way from others. The beauty of this method is that you attend so closely to their experience that you learn what it is like to be in their shoes, how they make sense of their world, and therefore what type of

---

[19]Sadruddin Qutoshi, "Phenomenology: A Philosophy and Method of Inquiry," *Journal of Education and Educational Development* 5, no. 1 (2018): 215-17, https://files.eric.ed.gov/fulltext/EJ1180603.pdf.

intervention or support would really fit. This stops us importing our solutions where they will not fit.

Here is an example of what we mean. You probably have a good read on how your parent(s) make meaning during Christmas. Therefore, if you were to let them know you want to skip the next Christmas vacation, it might mean for some parents that you are individuating (and they celebrate you while missing you), but other parents are offended (because they interpret this act as dismissal or something worse). They need different responses because they are parents *with different experiences.*

God is keenly interested in how people make sense of the world and has a front-row seat watching all the data leading to our conclusions. He got to see the tower of Babel (which he wasn't a fan of), he saw the Israelites forget his provision and turn to a golden calf (seems crazy to us too), and he watches as we grapple in our cultural moment with growing entitlement and individuality, leading to fractured communities where many sense that church just doesn't fit anymore. God must be the best phenomenologist because he sees it all and can hold his experience separate. In response, God sent his Son to provide a new way to make meaning of this world by giving us a new experience—we are invited back to himself repeatedly with grace. The local church is involved with contextualizing God's invitation to himself to those who live with a set of experiences and conclusions that can often feel at odds with the kingdom. For example, many Christian women grapple with the idea of calling and how to reconcile both parenting and work. There are often cultural pressures that add distress to any attempt to balance a Christian view of work and family.

A wonderful phenomenological study stepped into this issue to explore what calling means to these women and understand how it affected their lived experience.[20] The researchers interviewed eleven working Christian mothers and coded their responses line by line, then grouped similar content and put words to the themes they discovered through extensive reflective conversation. They found the women resonated with the idea of *calling* as a term for paid employment, but motherhood was experienced as a passion and love. It became clear that women are often swayed by support from intimate others, and it is common for working women to sacrifice goods from their own lives (friendships, rest, etc.) to accommodate the demands of children and work. In sum, the lived experience of honoring both calling and parenting was found to be rewarding, taxing, and a privilege these women urge others not to take lightly.

If Christian institutions and churches take note of these findings, they may prepare to support women with new experiences. Or counselors may be oriented to the complexities these women face and help them adjust their actions and the conclusions they come to around motherhood, stress, and support. Can you start to see how this understanding of women's *experiences* primes us to assist them to flourish in the kingdom?

A different study examined the need for student mental health support in Christian schools by finding out how different groups made sense of this issue.[21] It is a fine example of responding to the complex questions arising in our cultural moment, such as those presented by rising teen mental health diagnoses, concerns around declining distress tolerance skills, and debates about banning smartphones or turning to homeschooling. The authors of the

---

[20] Tina Sellers, Kris Thomas, Jennifer Batts, and Cami Ostman, "Women Called: A Qualitative Study of Christian Women Dually Called to Motherhood and Career," *Journal of Psychology and Theology* 33, no. 3 (2005): 198-209, https://doi.org/10.1177/009164710503300305.

[21] Adam Wilson et al., "Student Mental Health Support in Private Christian Schools: Perspectives and Needs," *Journal of Psychology and Christianity* 42, no. 3 (2023): 187-207.

research demonstrate awareness that Christian schools often struggle to unify their theological foundation with an integrated understanding of mental health, suggesting that support in this area is warranted.

To discern the *lived experience* of educators, parents, and students, each group was included in focus groups within the study. Three key findings emerged. First, the students had "engagement fatigue" from high internalized expectations (perfectionism), social pressure, and perceptions of always being monitored by Christian others and on social media. Second, educators described stress and near burnout due to overengagement with student needs, believing that as Christians they were to keep sacrificing but struggling to know the limits. Third, educators and parents experienced confusion from different definitions of mental health, with each person left to interpret this complex idea. From these three findings in context, you may already be thinking through implications and possible interventions that could support the schools, the parents, and the students toward new experiences of flourishing.

This example shows how the researchers honored the Christian story that calls us to shepherd our children toward maturity by helping them pursue wisdom. Without this research, educators, parents, and students may all attempt this shepherding according to their own bias rather than accurate knowledge of *experience*.

Our lived experience and the meaning we extrapolate from it fundamentally change how we seek to flourish. A Christian imaginary has much to say about flourishing, and if we can hear the gaps and overlap between participant experience and what we know leads to flourishing, we may be better positioned to provide contextually accurate support. Can you think of any situations in which people live through distressing experiences and we could support their flourishing if we understood the meaning they made from such situations?

Ethnography. This method is similar is some ways to phenomenology but emphasizes the impact of diversity in God's world and honoring contextual experience. Ethnography "examines behavior that takes place within specific social situations, including behavior that is shaped and constrained by these situations, plus people's understanding and interpretation of their experiences."[22] From the outside, we can often make educated guesses about the nuance and impact of community behaviors but will inevitably have limited understanding. Ethnography emphasizes how our not knowing accounts for much of the cultural ignorance and offense we encounter in our lives. We see this over and over again throughout Scripture. The Pharisees and scribes cannot fathom the actions of Jesus and the disciples: "Why do your disciples not walk according to the tradition of the elders, but eat with defiled hands?" (Mk 7:5). Jesus responds by teaching them that they do not understand the specifics of the culture he has brought—it is no longer what happens to you on the outside that is of concern in his kingdom (Mk 7:14-23). The Pharisees and scribes have yet to walk closely with Jesus to understand the meaning and purpose of his actions in Jesus' culture; instead, they judge. How often do we do this as clinicians or friends? Have you been in a context where your intervention or input simply missed the context?

God has a head start on the human ethnographer because he can discern every motivation and intention. But imagine if you knew the intricate interplay of the relational, social, financial, familial, and political world of the people who confuse you the most. What if you could see just how all the thoughts, emotions, and

---

[22]William Wilson and Anmol Chaddha, "The Role of Theory in Ethnographic Research," *Ethnography* 10, no. 4 (2010): 549, https://doi.org/10.1177/1466138109347009.

actions linked together and made sense in their relations? Jesus invites us to bring all our complexity to him and receive his understanding and compassion. You are invited to "[cast] all your anxieties on him, because he cares for you" (1 Pet 5:7), and then to look to God's bigger story rather than your own (Mt 6:10). We speak to God to show him right where we are, how lost and confused, and then we invite him to show us the bigger picture, to lift our eyes to him as the one who can help. Ethnography at its best is a glimpse of God's goodness in stooping so close to see all the nuance of this particular person in this particular place and allowing those cares to matter and influence actions.

Two ethnographic studies demonstrate the art of seeing others closely in line with kingdom priorities and seeking to learn from them and bless them. The first study considers the impact of call-and-response during Christian worship in the Black church.[23] Call-and-response is a powerful dialogical and communal act communicating between congregants and ministers: "Black preachers who do not get congregational responses (e.g. Amen, Das right, you sho' 'nuff preachin'), will feel a sense of separation from the audience. Either they have 'lost' the congregation by speaking 'above their heads' or by boring them."[24] Call-and-response encourages emotional and cognitive engagement in a manner quite different from many White churches, which could lead to confusion and judgment. The researchers used participant observation in two congregational settings for one and a half years and examined the data with comparative analysis. The core findings illuminated the important role of "nonvocal calls"

---

[23]Gillian Richards-Greaves, "'Say Hallelujah, Somebody' and 'I Will Call upon the Lord': An Examination of Call-and-Response in the Black Church," *The Western Journal of Black Studies* 40, no. 3 (2016): 192-204.

[24]Richards-Greaves, "'Say Hallelujah, Somebody,'" 197.

(actions that garnered congregational engagement) *in that specific context* to support the collaborative rhythm of worship and urge the minister to respond. In short, the researchers suggest call-and-response is a complex dialectical process *in Black churches* that focused on seeking out God himself.

The study is a wonderful example of helping those unfamiliar with the cultural and spiritual rhythms of the Black church gain insight that would change any approach to issues of community, flourishing, and spirituality. After all, wouldn't we expect cultural plurality to generate plurality of worship? This reminds us of Revelation, where we see the glory of each culture being brought into the city of God (Rev 21:24). We do well to ask what we can learn from the worship described here. What are they expressing of God's creative beauty that we might miss? Without ethnographic insight, we are likely to miss the beauty of culture and seek safety in similarity and isolation, which is certainly not the ethic of the kingdom of God.

A second ethnographic study engages the confusion that can surround Christian conversion.[25] This study invites readers to remember the dramatic conversion of Saul on the Damascus road, which has often seemed at odds with slowly evolving intellectual or moral shifts commonly described in conversion. The conversion experience is defined by *the context and culture within which it occurs*, even though the Bible describes it as a general phenomenon. We learn cultural ideas about what constitutes an appropriate conversion, which can affect how we relate to and treat other Christians. For example, you have likely heard of a more deviant or cultlike practice that described conversion, and you felt suspicious.

---

[25]Pamela Lee, "Christian Conversion Stories of African American Women: A Qualitative Analysis," *Journal of Psychology and Christianity* 27, no. 3 (2008): 238, www.proquest.com/scholarly-journals/christian-conversion-stories-african-american/docview/237249374/se-2.

But where is the line? How can we know when someone has experienced Christian conversion? How can we support and love Christians who come to faith in various cultures with different expectations of self-expression and language around spirituality? It takes a high degree of humility and acceptance of the other's experience to hear about their conversion without theologically analyzing it for veracity because of our expectations.

This study sought to broaden people's expectations of African American women's experiences of conversion so that they may know how to walk alongside them without the negative impact of cultural and spiritual bias. The authors demonstrate that the African American women in their study were influenced in their understanding of conversion by important church-based figures (pastors and family) and believed these were the people from whom we learn what conversion means. Second, these women all understood conversion as a process, starting with an inward change that is evidenced over time by changed character and behaviors. These women felt no shame about their process and no compunction to be converted like the apostle Paul. These findings alter how we think and speak about discipleship and sanctification in these cultural contexts.

A Christian imaginary that asserts a deep desire to honor culture and seek the benefit of others has much room for ethnographic study. It always feels good to be understood, known, and subsequently treated with dignity. This should impress on us to listen amid cultural diversity without the knee-jerk and inhibiting reaction to make everyone like us. Are there any situations in which people express their Christian life differently from you in which understanding the story behind their lives would change how you might engage them?

Grounded theory. This method also seeks to unravel the meaning of people's interactions, social actions, and experiences, but with *the intention of developing a theory* from the data.[26] This is a fantastic method to understand *processes* and practices you didn't before. Researchers start with individual cases and develop conceptual categories into which more data can fit. They then synthesize and link concepts *to explain the data and the patterns within*.[27] We find ourselves doing small versions of this all throughout life. For example, when we work with clients in a therapeutic context, they tell us about their experiences, and we categorize them in our minds using the client's frame of reference. As we engage more clients, similar patterns may emerge, despite each client labeling them differently. As we link categories and experiences together from multiple clients in similar predicaments, we might see bigger patterns at work. Alternatively, remember when you started your last job. At first you gathered information about how people talked, engaged, and got things done. You started to use the job's language, culture, rules, and social nuances to piece together a *theory* of how to work at your job successfully.

Scripture is very concerned with how human processes work. Many of Jesus' teachings describe how things in our lived experience connect to one another, often in sequence and often with important outcomes. For example, Jesus exposes the greed and self-indulgence of the Pharisees and scribes, having watched them perform in front of the people rather than honestly repenting of their sin (Mt 23). Jesus illuminates how their economy of power operates on deception and misperception. The rich young ruler in Matthew 19:16-30 is also exposed. Jesus reveals how wealth, and

---

[26]Kathy Charmaz, "Grounded Theory," in *Rethinking Methods in Psychology*, ed. Jonathan Smith, Rom Harre, and Luk Van Langenhove (Sage, 1996), 28.
[27]Charmaz, "Grounded Theory," 29.

not actually obedience to God, is what provides this young man security.

When we think we have learned why we behave the way we do, we can investigate it alongside the lives of others and see whether there are patterns to human life in the fall. No doubt there are. Of course, Jesus the Creator knows and sees the workings of the human heart. In our limited and fallible state we are required to conduct careful investigation to discover patterns. Holding tight to the Christian imaginary provides us a foundation for how to understand human experience and informs our theorizing and starting point. A Christian grounded theory both respects God's design and accepts that the complexity of the fall and cultural context will muddy what we learn about human processes.

Do you remember the study we discussed under phenomenology that wanted to understand working Christian mothers' experiences? There was a sister study that used a grounded-theory method. We think this is a great example because you can see how the two studies co-inform our understanding. The sister study focused on *how* (*process*) these mothers reconciled their experiential conflict between work (calling) and motherhood, and moved to a place of accepting the cost of pursuing both.[28] The researchers carefully analyzed interviews in which the construct of work as calling emerged. The mothers described coming to terms with work as something more than itself. For them, work was embedded in certitude about its viability and goodness; felt to provide collaboration with God, which boosted self-efficacy; and nested in a larger context that provided relief from guilt and relativized failures. Ultimately the researchers saw that these working mothers *had*

---

[28]Kerris Oates, Elizabeth Hall, and Tamara Anderson, "Calling and Conflict: A Qualitative Exploration of Interrole Conflict and the Sanctification of Work in Christian Mothers in Academia," *Journal of Psychology and Theology* 33, no. 3 (2005): 210-23, https://doiorg/10.1177/009164710503300306.

sanctified their work by understanding it as a calling (did you catch that process?). We learn that to help working women who experience the tension and distress of dual roles, we might engage them in a *process* of understanding the nuances and contours of contextualizing work as a calling done before God. Discovering this process and assisting others in it shows how grounded theory can aid in Christian flourishing.

A second grounded-theory study shows how Christian mental health professionals *work through* the dissonance that often arises when they begin to work with members of the LGBT community.[29] (We selected this dissertation research because it demonstrates the contribution of new researchers!) The researcher found that Christian mental health professionals experience distress from the fear of rejection by either Christians or LGBT clients due to their value positions. Mental health professionals navigated this distress by expanding relational support and engagement with God and others, and they did so to the degree needed to still feel secure while discerning their working stance. Importantly, the mental health professional's final position (either affirming LGBT persons and behaviors or affirming LGBT persons but not behaviors) didn't change the mental health professional's process. We can see that it is likely to help mental health professionals in training to cultivate rich relationships that can tolerate and assist in their questioning and reconciling of beliefs, ethics, values, and actions. This theory is not surprising against the backdrop of the Christian life, in which distress is often met by a secure foundation in God and participation in a rich community. The psalmists often cry out to God for acceptance, support, mercy, and help (e.g., Ps 25), while

---

[29]Gena Minnix, "Reconciling LGBT Affirmation with Christian Beliefs Among Mental Health Professionals: A Grounded Theory" (PhD diss., St. Mary's University, 2015), 344.

the people of Israel and the early church are regularly seen attending to one another's needs (e.g., Acts 2:44-46).

Grounded theory is a wonderful tool to help us peer into the complex process of human life. From a Christian perspective, grounded theory will never find truths beyond the grand narrative of Scripture, but it will help us discern the human experience of turmoil, attempts to adapt, and the pathways through which people thrive. Are there events and experiences in which you see people enduring in a way that surprises or confuses you? Can you imagine peering closely to see the ways in which these people are attempting to flourish?

Case study. This approach can vary dramatically but centrally investigates an individual, group, organization, or event (the case), within a context, so that we *understand the case's structure or needs*.[30] The diversity of case study research is provided by its purpose, which makes it highly malleable, and you can even use different methods (such as ethnography) within your case study. If conducted with care, case studies can provide incredibly *detailed and accurate data to assist in understanding and intervention*. This makes case studies a rich approach to investigating the vast array of situations we might find in this complex world. To complete our Genesis call to cultivate, fill, and tend to the earth, we often need to understand complex issues and discern paths forward. In these instances, we get out the microscope and look at participants and their context carefully.

A current case worthy of attention is the high degree of poverty and social need in some southern rural committees. The church is

---

[30] Adrijana Starman, "The Case Study as a Type of Qualitative Research," *Journal of Contemporary Educational Studies* 64, no. 1 (2013), www.researchgate.net/profile/A-Biba-Rebolj-2/publication/265682891_The_case_study_as_a_type_of_qualitative_research/links/54183f560cf25ebee988104c/The-case-study-as-a-type-of-qualitative-research.pdf.

often on the front lines because of its proximity and social mission. A fantastic case study sought to understand the response of the Brown Baptist Church in Southaven, Mississippi, to the range of social problems in its Black community.[31] To achieve their purpose, the researchers cleverly integrated rapid-ethnographic methods to gather information in a culturally attentive manner in a short amount of time. This approach helped build trust to accurately represent the case's cultural context through multiple avenues of data collection.

The findings showed how the church had twenty-one social services/ministries across education, health, development, and community outreach. One ministry connected local people to health care and determined eligibility for low-cost insurance programs. The researchers shared the case of this church, concluding the impact of their efforts could not be overstated, and called the church an exemplary model of community service. The study does well to expose both the needs of the community and the interplay possible between church and state in response. This type of case study research is truly an example of utilizing our education and opportunity to serve and advocate by sharing detailed stories.

We could provide many other examples of case study research, but instead we invite you to dream of opportunities that case studies provide to support the implementation of Christian values in our communities. Here are a couple of suggestions, and we invite you to imagine your own as you read. First, have you struggled to read Scripture in community? Can you imagine how this might have shaped you if you had? Perhaps one line of research would be *considering youth challenges to studying Scripture in middle school youth groups*. To complete this research, we could deep-dive into the case of a specific youth group that has managed

---

[31] Jerry Watson and Desiree Stepteau-Watson, "Troubled Waters: The Black Church in Mississippi, A Single Subject Case Study," *Social Work and Christianity* 42, no. 3 (2015): 369-84.

to get students to regularly engage Scripture. If we could understand the complexities of this often-fraught practice, then we might be prepared to support a generation to love being in the Word.

Or take another idea. I (Paul) work at Covenant Theological Seminary and teach counseling students. We train our students in theology alongside counseling practice because we believe it transforms their view of people, pain, and flourishing. What if we studied *the impact of a Covenant Theological Seminary theology education on graduating counselors' actions*? We could study one counseling internship cohort as our case, using multiple methods to gather data about their experience. What might we find? If we could capture and share the positive impacts, we might bolster schools' and students' desires to move toward more theologically informed training despite accreditation and financial pressures.

Imagine with us how God would look at case studies that seek to understand his people who are struggling under the burden of the fall. We think he would be well pleased with the loving response to serve our neighbor and seek the welfare of the city in which we live. Qualitative research may still feel overwhelming, and that is OK. Jesus invited the disciples to follow him as he met, taught, and healed all those with whom he came into contact. This overwhelmed his disciples, but they learned to rely on Jesus and the Spirit. Likewise, we can follow and begin to listen to stories framed in a Christian imaginary. Research isn't a side gig for academics but an opportunity to love our neighbor that happens through the tools of social sciences.

Action research. We come to the most active of all the qualitative methods. Originating with Kurt Lewin's desire to see minority and disadvantaged groups raise their self-esteem and seek their own flourishing, action research focuses on *working alongside participants to generate knowledge and enact solutions* *in social contexts.*³² This research process is cyclical. Those who experience a problem are invited to discuss it and collectively discern strategies for action they will attempt. We can help them review and adjust their strategies based on current experiences of their problem. This qualitative process aligns wonderfully with God's design for people that they investigate, decide, act, and move toward flourishing. The biblical themes of upholding personal dignity, enjoying agency, and using gifts are all present. A key difference from other research methods is that the participants become empowered as their own change agents through an active process.

The study we discussed previously on student mental health support in Christian schools provides an example of action research.³³ We return to this study because the method began as a phenomenology, *describing the lived experience* of the participants, but then moved into action research. We thought it helpful to show you just how practical this type of qualitative engagement can be. To recap, students were struggling with mental health, and the school didn't know how to respond. The researchers helped participant groups (teachers, parents, students) shape the requirements of the study, with particular attention on what they needed to learn from one another. They then helped the groups express their experience and shared these findings with the whole group. The effect was to provide problem clarity and awareness of overlapping needs and ideas for changes.

As common ground emerged, the researchers stated, "This research positively influenced the school culture, where the school pivoted from reactive toward preventative mental health care for the

---

³²Clem Adelman, "Kurt Lewin and the Origins of Action Research," *Educational Action Research* 1, no. 1 (1993): 7-9, https://doi.org/10.1080/0965079930010102.
³³Wilson et al., "Student Mental Health Support," 191-93.

students," and new policies were employed.[34] You can imagine lower rates of serious socio-emotional distress within this adapting school. When our communities work together, the stress on all parties is decreased. The Christian imaginary glows in this example. The body, with each part playing its role, brings flourishing for the whole.

Action research is an exciting tool in the fields of counseling and psychology. We see opportunities for clinicians to allow action research to expand their vision for engagement, while remembering that their clinical skills provide the practical foundation for the work. Mental health providers are well suited for engaging different social groups and helping them change their own experiences. One of the greatest challenges we perceive in this current culture is the privatization and commercialization of personal struggles. Despite the necessity and value of counseling care, we often take our problems privately to a paid service provider, who helps us consider individual change. Action research (and similar methods) invite us to similar growth but offer the benefits of enhanced communal understanding, communication, and colaborers.

Jesus himself sought change in the public sphere. He taught and conversed before many, seeking to illuminate awareness and insight, and he invited his hearers to change amid community. What are the cultural contexts in which you could help others speak plainly and seek flourishing together? For me (Paul), an immediate opportunity presents itself in the academic institution within which I work that seeks to foster flourishing for ministry and counseling students. How might I partner with students to help them make the most of learning and formative experiences? We don't always need to go after the big and the grand; rather, we can open our eyes to see the needs of the contexts and communities in which we are placed.

---

[34]Wilson et al., "Student Mental Health Support," 200.

The Challenge of Selecting a Qualitative Method

I (Paul) often feel insecurity as I begin a new research journey because I tend to wonder whether I'm going to miss something critical and select a method that doesn't help toward the goal. No matter how many times I do this process or circle back around in each project, I still feel it. I have realized this happens because I really care about the people that a research project is intended to serve and I don't want to miss them. While this is a good heart orientation, it is a painful process. Have you ever attempted to discover something? How did you pick where to start (even if it was spying on a sibling or friend)?

Selecting quantitative research methods has always come more easily for me. Something about logically defining relationships between variables just seems more streamlined and simpler. But selecting the process to mine people's hearts and share about their needs feels a little more amorphous at times. Would it be best to share their version of their own story? Or present their case as I've understood it? Or make clear the meaning and experience the participants have of this phenomena? Well, each could help.... That's the conundrum. Over time I have started to return to the population I am studying and ask them some version of the following question: "What is your most pressing need or desire in relation to this issue?" This has helped focus my research interest and led to revised questions. It is nice to accept that I might have located a problem, but I am not alone in trying to solve it.

For instance, I wanted to help my counseling students with their ability to conceptualize client cases—not least because they kept asking for help. I began by assuming I should try to figure out where my students felt lost and got agitated during conceptualizing. This led me to think a phenomenological study would help, as it would expose the students' lived experiences and reveal the gaps or problems to be solved. I took this idea back to one of my very sharp students, who immediately said, "Um, wouldn't it make more sense to see how our class goes about conceptualizing so you could help us in our process? We might all have different gaps that make us anxious." The penny dropped. Of course. They needed help expressing their conceptualization *process* and receiving support where it failed them. I admit, I felt like a lousy teacher and supervisor—shouldn't this have been obvious?

When I had rallied from shame, it became clear that pursuing a grounded-theory study made more sense. If I helped my students express their process of conceptualization using the conceptual mapping task I planned to use, then I might be able to synthesize the data, understand their approach, and provide support in the gaps. The class would, in effect, simply show their own need. Brilliant! In reality, it was fine, we got some good data, and now I help teach the students more effectively. Your target population often has more insight into their needs than you do.

Setting up a research process in response to a problem you identify can be confusing. However, we have some thoughts that can help you consider how to approach a qualitative inquiry (and maybe feel less anxiety or shame):

1. Ask yourself, Can I clearly state the concern that I am looking to address, and if not, what do I need to learn to refine my statement?
2. Offer your thoughts and plans to the target population and be open to their feedback. You might be surprised.
3. Return to straightforward definitions of each qualitative method and see which one most effectively and simply addresses the concern and needs of the target population.
4. Remember that you can combine methods and carefully adapt your approach to your particular context. This is far more likely to achieve the goal of the research and provide valid and reliable data. Get help from a research mentor as you need it.
5. Be open to reflexive revisions during your research process that honor what is emerging from your participants.
6. Accept that you will make mistakes and feel insecure at times.

CONCLUSION

This chapter began by exploring how we approach qualitative research and looked at diverse methods the curious researcher may use to discover meaning in people's stories. Many texts will help you nuance the differences in precise methods, but we hope you have gotten a taste of how you can explore. To use these methods successfully, we invite participants to share their stories and their hearts with us. Few people will do so before they feel comfortable. We can use informed consent and controlling for validity to establish a trustworthy relationship and bolster this by following Jesus' example of authenticity, compassion, attunement, questioning, and responding. This humble approach will increase the researcher's ability to pursue meaning-making that holds a Christian imaginary as the context of human flourishing.

We urge you to seek an honest and grace-filled Christian community as a fantastic place to grow in self-reflection, awareness, and humility. There, you will be able to acknowledge your limits and be encouraged to reengage, revive your curiosity, and play again. Here are some helpful questions to consider: Am I willing to hear and learn from others about this topic? Do I acknowledge that I may not know the most effective methods and could learn from a mentor? Will I follow and explore what participants are showing? Can I tolerate and accept emerging responses that I do not expect or like? Am I prepared to share the experience of the other widely even if I do not feel comfortable with it for some reason?

Tips for Developing Meaning-Making Questions

While we want this book to challenge your thinking and deepen your perspective, we also want to provide practical tools as you engage in research. When preparing for qualitative research, you can expect to start by identifying your research questions and methodology. Next, it is common to write your semistructured interview or open-ended survey questions. When writing questions, it is especially important to maintain an awareness of potential bias due to the subjective nature of qualitative study. Do you remember our discussion of this from chapter three? How we ask questions of our participants can slant how they answer them, just like leading questions in a courtroom. This practice is generally frowned on. The goal of research is never to get our participants to say what we want them to say, which can happen if our questions are too narrow.

Before you write your questions (even if they seem *so wise* at first), start by asking yourself, What would be the best possible outcome of my study? Your answer to that question will reveal possible biases embedded in your hopes for your results. We cannot approach research with an axe to grind or a point to prove. We must step back, go beyond bracketing, as we talked about earlier, and work through our motivations. Emotionally, you must bring yourself to a place where your biggest desire for your research is to reveal or create new ideas that are truly representative of your population. Ideally, our assumptions are challenged when we do good research. With that in mind, here are some practical tips for writing your questions:

1. Each question should allow answers to go in a variety of directions. Narrow questions lead to narrow answers. Here are some examples of narrow or leading questions:
   - Why do you think cognitive-behavioral therapy works so well?
   - What contributes to a trend of abusive pastors in churches?
   - What has been your lived experience of being stigmatized for having depression as a Christian?

   Instead, try questions like these (each a reframe of the ones above):
   - What forms of therapy are most effective, and why?
   - What are some common trends you have observed in the church recently?
   - What has been your lived experience of having depression as a Christian?

2. Your questions should use words that have plain meaning. Overly technical words or constructs without clear definition will confuse participants. For instance, this question might be hard to interpret: *As a counselor, how have you led your clients in insight-oriented work?* There are a variety of theoretical frameworks that could connect to the idea of developing insight. Instead, try something like this: *As a counselor, how do you define insight-oriented work? Share some examples of how you have engaged in this with your clients.*

3. Your questions should match the goals of your chosen methodology. If you have chosen to do a phenomenological study, your questions

should all point to someone's lived experience of a specific phenomenon. If you selected grounded theory, your questions should seek to discover the participant's process or motivations. A case study should involve a semistructured interview that allows for participants to give specific details of an intervention, program, or pathology.

4. Finally, you should decide in advance what your coding or analysis process will be. An inductive process will start with an open idea and very little in the way of hypothesis, allowing themes in the data to emerge during the research process. In contrast, a deductive analysis already has a theoretical framework in mind, and the data provide insight or support to that theory. Inductive analysis will require open-ended and broad questions, while deductive analysis (such as grounded theory or case study) will ask questions to understand the details that are currently unclear.

If you are doing semistructured interviews, you will have the opportunity to clarify any statements from the participants. However, when you have multiple researchers on a team asking questions, you need to carefully plan how you will ask for clarifying information. It is usually a good idea to have prewritten subprompts that all researchers will use to extract more data when needed on a given question. With open-ended surveys, you will not have the opportunity to ask follow-up questions. This limitation makes the wording of your questions even more important. You can also triangulate the data by adding a few Likert-scale questions and see how the quantitative and qualitative data align. And, of course, throughout the analysis process ensure trustworthiness by using strategies such as team debriefing of independent analyses, maintaining an audit trail and/or reflexive journal, and having an outside auditor review your data and conclusions. All these tools will help the integrity and meaning-making process in your study.

DISCUSSION QUESTIONS

1. How do you understand a Christian imaginary to create a framework for qualitative research that seeks to discover people's lived experiences?

2. What important role can you see for qualitative research in your church or a clinical context?
3. Which qualitative method discussed above grabs your attention and curiosity? Why do you think this is?
4. If you were to engage qualitative research at this time, what personal and professional concerns or fears come to mind? Where could you find help or support?
5. How might action research be used as a tool to enhance church ministry and congregational participation?
6. How can you see virtue development preparing you for the work of qualitative inquiry?
7. If you ask yourself the virtue questions from the final section of this chapter, what stands out to you, and what will you do with this self-awareness?

LEARNING ACTIVITIES

1. Create your own qualitative inquiry in response to this chapter. What specific issues and experiences in the lives of hurting people do you wish to understand? Write a list of the specific concerns and questions you have for this population and situation. Develop a research proposal with a beginning research question that might evolve as you engage your population. Describe the method you would use to present your findings.
2. Choose one study cited in this chapter that most interests you and read the entire article. What insights did you gain from the research findings both spiritually and clinically? How could you share these insights with a wider audience in a manner they would understand?

SIX

Applying Research Through Wise Clinical Practice

As we reach the final chapter of this book and walk from the research classroom into the counseling office, we do not remove our researcher hat and swap it for a clinical one. Rather, we bring everything that contributes to flourishing in research into the counseling space to enhance therapeutic practice. The curiosity that drove the research process and the spiritual formation that occurred as a result help develop the wise counselor-researcher. We might borrow the Venn diagram from Marsha Linehan's dialectical behavior therapy and imagine that our rational selves and our emotional selves intersect, together creating the "wise mind."[1] Here we place our researcher selves on one side, our rational minds stimulated by the pursuit of curiosity. In the other circle, our counselor selves represent the emotion-driven compassion that leads us to sit across from another human being in the midst of their pain and suffering. The overlap of these two circles is where we find ourselves as counselor-researchers who embody wisdom.

As Christians, however, we know that there is something beyond the simple wisdom that comes at this overlap of rational research and compassionate counseling. Imagine that our Venn

---

[1] Marsha Linehan, *DBT Skills Training Manual*, 2nd ed. (Guilford, 2014).

diagram has a three-dimensional depth so that as we enter into wisdom at that intersection, we tap into something deep and vast. What if we were to follow the example of Solomon (2 Chron 1:7-13) and James (Jas 1:5), praying that God grants us wisdom rooted in knowledge and compassion but deepened by the work of the Spirit in and through us? What might we then bring into the therapy room that connects us to God, ourselves, those across from us, and all those who have gone before us? In our pursuit of flourishing as Christians, counselors, and researchers, we need not settle for the fruits of good earthly labor but rather hunger and thirst for a Spirit-filled ancient wisdom that guides us into all truth.

We will finish this chapter and this book by examining how to bring the fullness of a Christian counselor-researcher identity into the therapy room. We will revisit the themes of the book to provide structure for this exploration. What does it mean to embody curiosity, seek truth, embrace diversity, quantify outcomes, and make meaning as we sit across from others? How do we remain on the endless journey to allow the Spirit to shape our character and virtue as we do our work? How do we connect with both ancient and modern wisdom as we build our dwelling in the garden of shalom described in chapter one? We will conclude by reviewing the integration literature to learn from those who have studied evidence-based clinical practice and offer practical ideas for you to remain fully engaged in consuming, producing, and implementing research in your clinical practice.

TRAITS OF THE CHRISTIAN COUNSELOR-RESEARCHER

The Christian counselor-researcher is one who is personally, professionally, and spiritually seeking to go deeper as a way of being. As we seek to know and to help, we appreciate our smallness and how little we actually know. We strain to see the overlay of the supernatural on the physical and then turn our perspective again to see that physical reality acts as an overlay to the supernatural. In a continued effort at clarity, we may decide to abandon the word *overlay* and see that there is an intricate and inseparable weave of the physical and spiritual that too often have been ripped apart by scientific inquiry conducted in a religious vacuum. Defining and redefining our understanding of reality is our life's work, and indeed the work of the Spirit in us as he sharpens our eyes to see and enlightens our hearts to experience life through a Christian imaginary. To fully give ourselves to this spiritual formation process, we must engage in an effort to develop the traits that will keep us at the center of that journey. Let's explore together these various aspects of who we must be and become as Christian counselor-researchers.

Embodying curiosity. To begin, we recall a common guiding phrase for mental health clinicians: Be kind and curious. The very same curiosity within us that we used in our researcher sandbox in chapter one now sits across from another human. It drives the exploration of individuals, couples, and family systems as we peel back layer by layer. In trauma-informed work, we use this curiosity to ask, "What happened to you?" instead of "What's wrong with you?"[2] This is a demonstration of a gentler approach to curiosity when we peer into another person's life. Research by itself can sometimes be as simple as playing in the sand. We dig and dig until something of interest emerges. In the counseling room, there is a greater level of sensitivity and finesse required. We do not sit with another just for the sheer curiosity of hearing their life story.

---

[2]"What Is Trauma-Informed Care?," Trauma-Informed Care Implementation Resource Center, July 7, 2022, www.traumainformedcare.chcs.org/what-is-trauma-informed-care/.

Instead, our curiosity must be driven by compassion. We are curious only to the degree that our doing so helps the client.

The Christian counselor-researcher embodies curiosity while practicing the virtues of kindness and gentleness to apply scientific and spiritual evidence to their clinical work. Deeply rooted and grounded in ongoing study of the research literature, we use methods and approaches that have been shown to work. We maintain curiosity as we apply those strategies, ever eager to identify ways in which new evidence will emerge as we take a theoretical concept and contextualize it amid the contours of an individual's life.

Take breathing or relaxation exercises as an example. One helpful meta-analysis described the large body of research done on breathwork as a positive clinical intervention for reducing anxiety, while another meta-analysis similarly evaluated research on relaxation exercises for those experiencing chronic pain and found overwhelming evidence of effectiveness.[3] Without embodying curiosity, we would take that knowledge and stamp these interventions as "evidenced-based." Thus, we think these approaches will work with our clients because the research says they should.

However, in my (Kristen's) clinical practice, I have encountered two or three clients with anxiety and chronic pain who find their symptoms worsen when attempting breathing or relaxation exercises. Although it is possible that these clients would benefit from ongoing practice and development of these skills, they did not wish to repeat the exercises. Rather than determine that a client is

---

[3]Blerida Banushi et al., "Breathwork Interventions for Adults with Clinically Diagnosed Anxiety Disorders: A Scoping Review," *Brain Sciences* 13, no. 2 (2023): 256, https://doi.org/10.3390/brainsci 13020256; Sara Magelssen Vambheim et al., "Relaxation Techniques as an Intervention for Chronic Pain: A Systematic Review of Randomized Controlled Trials," *Heliyon* 7, no. 8 (2021): e07837, https://doi.org/10.1016/j.heliyon.2021.e07837.

resistant, the curious Christian counselor-researcher asks why this evidence-based approach is not working for a particular client or set of clients in this way and at this time. Our doing so may change the therapy and subsequently inform new research and further innovation in the counseling field as we become curious whether there are other, similar cases that may make up a different subpopulation. Perhaps what is true for these clients has not yet shown up in the literature? Our kind curiosity believes our clients and their stories, keeps asking why, and allows this process to drive us to read and produce new research studies to enhance clinical care.

Truth seeking. Christian counselor-researchers are on a quest for truth. In chapter two, we explored the idea of the social imaginary and how that influences the very things we seek to know. We make assumptions and see the world through our bias, which means we must first and foremost be characterized by our humility. Terms such as *quest* and *truth seeking* might paint a picture of some type of knight or warrior about to conquer some unknown land. In light of the nature of historical conquests, we wish to avoid any version of colonizing truth even as we seek to hold on to the idea that there is a Truth with a capital *T*. Encountering God's absolute Truth is far different from using research or the therapy room to solidify our self-confirming, biased "rightness." Whether we conceptualize coming to know as a discovery of Truth or as a process of meaning-making constructed by humans who were given this ability by God himself, our own smallness in the matter is essential to grasp.

In a full spirit of humility, our curiosity leads us into a process of attempting to know. In the therapy room, truth can seem subjective as we focus on hearing the lived experiences of another. Is something true because a client perceives it to be true, or might we need to evaluate their perceptions of reality? Who has the power in the relationship to assess and determine truth? And for what purposes is truth sought? Let us suggest that knowing takes on an entirely different tone here when it comes to the therapeutic relationship. Biblical concepts of knowing can include compassion, intimacy, and deep trust.[4] Not only do we seek to know and trust God in an intimate way, but he longs for intimacy with us as well.[5] We see this in verses such as Psalm 9:10, "And those who know your name put their trust in you, for you, O LORD, have not forsaken those who seek you," and Psalm 103:14, "For he knows our frame; he remembers that we are dust." This idea is also present throughout Psalm 139, as the reality of *yada* is woven back and forth between God's knowing of the deepest places in our hearts and our knowing of his marvelous works. On a more sobering note, we see this concept used in Matthew 7:23 to signify that God will banish those who did not know (*ginōskō*) him from his presence. Jesus says in John 8:32 that those who know (*ginōskō*) the truth will be set free by it. As truth seekers, we are humble in our pursuit of knowing God in an intimate manner, and we extend this deep personal knowing to our clients as well.

In summary, Christian counselor-researchers are not looking for some detached version of knowing facts; rather, we seek to foster an authentic human relationship stemming directly from God's authentic relationship with us. As we imitate the humility, authenticity, and love of Christ with our clients, we make space for truth to rise into the light. Curiosity leads to exploration, which leads to expression and later insight. The Spirit works to craft that insight into wisdom and even healing. The natural processes of brain repair established by the Creator are the ultimate outcome of the

---

[4] John W. Ritenbaugh, "What the Bible Says About Yada," n.d., www.bibletools.org/index.cfm/fuseaction/Topical.show/RTD/cgg/ID/11198/Yada.htm.

[5] Marisa Fritzemeier, "'Yada': Cultivating Intimacy with God—Curt Landry Ministries," Curt Landry.com (blog), January 26, 2024, www.curtlandry.com/yada-cultivating-intimacy-with-god/.

therapeutic process. While we are coparticipants and guides in this process, we acknowledge that God determines Truth and brings about healing. As we offer ourselves as living sacrifices in acceptable worship (Rom 12:1)—doing so in spirit and in truth (Jn 4:23-24)—he completes the act of healing in our clients' lives.

Embracing diversity. The idea of knowing our clients as an imitation of Christ and an act of worship can lead us to imagine ourselves in the conversation about the good Samaritan in Luke 10:25-37. We are loving God and loving neighbor in the therapeutic approach we described above. Much of the time, that feels easy. But we acknowledged in chapter three that sometimes it is challenging when we encounter others who are different from ourselves. Thus, we ask along with the man who questioned Jesus in Luke 10:29, "And who is my neighbor?" That question inherently seeks to narrow down the population to a smaller subset, perhaps one that feels more manageable or realistic. Jesus instead broadens the definition and challenges us to think bigger about the concept of neighbor and extend mercy beyond what feels comfortable. We too, following Jesus' example as well as the ethical mandates of our profession, embrace diversity to experience a fuller expression of curiosity and assist others in their journey toward truth and flourishing.

Just as we explored how to mitigate inherent bias in the research process in chapter three, we now apply those same principles to the reality of clinical practice. Well-meaning White Christian counselors might feel willing to embrace diversity in their hearts, all the while setting up shop in a wealthy suburb with few non-White residents, declining to take insurance, and marketing in a language that appeals only to a narrow population. While not inherently wrong, these may be examples of operating from privilege. Other examples might include referring sexual minorities to other practices rather than serving them well, or imposing one's own beliefs on Christian clients who are theologically more conservative or liberal than your own perspective. Embracing diversity will require inherent personal sacrifices and a delight in recognizing those different from us as brothers and sisters in need of care. Unfortunately, if this were easy we would not need to address it as a unique trait.

What happens when we make the choices necessary to embrace diversity as Christian counselor-researchers? Where will our curiosity and truth seeking take us if we step out of our guarded world and limited perspectives to sit with others who do not think, act, or live as we do? Pause for a moment to consider your own answers to these questions. What emotions rise up in you when you think about the active steps you could take to embrace diversity, such as changing your practice plans or diligently cultivating a love for difference? Where have you rejected diversity for the sake of emotional safety or expedience? As we write, we feel the challenge with you. To be Christian counselor-researchers who are in a continual and deep growth process, we have to ask and ask and ask such questions. We have to acknowledge and repent and submit to our global neighbors out of reverence for Christ (Eph 5:21). We have to commit to following Christ in seeing all as our neighbor, even when he does not explain in advance where this will take us or how it will affect us.

In addition to the issues of accessibility of our services or imposing beliefs on clients, we must consider how we embrace diversity session by session and hour by hour. First, we are diligent and cautious about the application of research in the counseling room, taking into account the population for which interventions or clinical strategies have been tested. Every time we read articles or learn evidence-based practices, we must ask, Who are the clients for whom this has been effective? By asking such a question, it forces us back into new research questions as we sit with clients underrepresented in research. In an embrace of diversity, we may reach new levels of innovation in the field because we refuse to settle for the assumptions that have long plagued social-scientific research.

Sitting across from a diverse tapestry of clients even within a single day or week also means that we do not adopt cookie-cutter approaches to therapy. No intervention in our toolbox can be contextualized effectively without careful consideration of the cultural dimensions of the person at hand. Each client is treated as a unique individual for whom we have taken the time to consider effective strategies for growth, change, and healing. We view people not by a label or diagnosis—though we are careful to accurately assess and document such—but rather by the dimensions and stories that define their personhood. This becomes possible when we acknowledge our various identities and delineate between the "I" and the "Thou," the "me" and the "them" as we engage in collaborative and mutual clinical relationships.[6]

Finally, embracing diversity means that the Christian counselor-researcher creates space for empowerment, voice, and choice for clients.[7] While as culturally competent clinicians we do not awkwardly ask our clients to teach us about themselves, we do practice the biblical kind of knowing them as we curiously engage their lives. When our clients are empowered to use their voice and make choices for themselves, we learn from them as we observe their approaches to doing so. This practice can certainly result in uncomfortable values conflicts for us as we sit with clients who voice things we do not agree with or make choices we might personally

---

[6]Martin Buber, *I and Thou* (Martino Fine Books, 2010).
[7]SAMHSA's Trauma and Justice Strategic Initiative, *SAMHSA's Concept of Trauma and Guidance for a Trauma-Informed Approach* (Substance Abuse and Mental Health Services Administration, 2014), https://library.samhsa.gov/sites/default/files/sma14-4884.pdf.

deem bad or sinful. And to be clear, we don't just sit—we actively support our clients. We encourage them, we help them, we explore their experience and their need. Mark McMinn expressed his own struggle in these moments, wondering whether he was just making "happier sinners" in his clinical work.[8]

In our conversations with our students at Christian institutions on this issue, and through Megan Anna Neff and McMinn's work on the subject, we have come to embrace the advantage of postmodern thinking that enables us to hold multiple truths in tension at the same time. We can hold our own moral view while also granting our clients the same grace God has given us. In embracing diversity and the counselor-researcher role, we relinquish the need to control the process. We release a sense of moral superiority or responsibility over the choices of our clients. We allow them to penetrate our biases, push the boundaries of our thinking, and reveal to us how God is active in their lives.

It is true that we may at times challenge our clients' assumptions or decision-making to help move them into greater flourishing, with a grounded self-awareness and an avoidance of imposing beliefs. With each intervention and clinical choice, we seek to ensure that our actions are rooted in research conducted with a diverse sample and applicable to the client in front of us. We recognize the potential for abuses of power or deciding ourselves what is right for the client, even as we sit with firmly held beliefs about what God has established for human flourishing. This is all possible amid a Christian imaginary that recognizes that God has ordered his creation and human experience. As we will see later in this chapter, the intersection of psychological research and biblical

---

[8]Megan Anna Neff and Mark McMinn, *Embodying Integration: A Fresh Look at Christianity in the Therapy Room* (InterVarsity Press, 2020), 198.

wisdom helps us operate with both evidence-based and biblically sound principles.

Quantifying outcomes. With a specific interest in measuring the outcomes of our work, Christian counselor-researchers do well to conduct assessments at regular intervals in their clinical practice. Quite often, we have seen agencies and counseling practices begin with a thorough assessment protocol at intake but never return to those measurements, or others, again. This approach to assessment turns a powerful tool into a limited box to check—one and done. Of course, there are important challenges with ongoing outcomes measurement in clinical practice, not least of which is the lack of direct insurance reimbursement for any type of lengthy assessment outside a therapy session. We are not suggesting that Christian counselor-researchers spent significant amounts of time outside session collecting data on client outcomes; in fact, we would recommend the opposite. Finding efficient ways to collect data from clients on a biweekly or monthly basis is a powerful option for faithfully tracking client progress and supporting their flourishing amid a busy clinical practice.

Stephen Greggo in his book *Assessment for Counseling in Christian Perspective* provides a wonderful guide for Christian counselor-researchers to consider the process of assessment through the lens of compassion, virtue, and hospitality.[9] Indeed, we affirm that quantifying outcomes and engaging in assessment with clients can be a deeply rooted spiritual practice motivated by our desire to know (*yada*) our clients and provide the best care possible. Without assessment and evaluation of outcomes, we cannot fully determine whether our clinical approaches are working. When quantitative measurement demonstrates limited

---

[9]Stephen P. Greggo, *Assessment for Counseling in Christian Perspective* (InterVarsity Press, 2019).

change as a result of our efforts to help, we embrace humility and curiosity to seek to understand why. We seek to learn from these data points, adjusting and adapting to improve client outcomes. Data gathering can also include rich dialogue and more subjective measures. As counselor-researchers grow in skill and confidence, they can develop a highly client-centered assessment that is enjoyed and welcomed by clients. If this idea is new to you, we invite you to think carefully about how you might learn more about assessment that works in collaboration with your clients.

For the Christian counselor-researcher, assessment is not only a client-by-client process. We are also interested in stepping back to see a bigger picture—a tapestry of our broader work with all clients in the context of our communities. Needs assessments and program evaluations are necessary here, giving us data-driven clarity on the needs around us and the overall effectiveness of our services that attempt to meet those needs. In our experience, we have seen few clinicians who conduct needs assessments prior to establishing their practices. When we have seen larger agencies conduct program evaluations, it is typically for the purpose of obtaining grants rather than for a purely client-centered motivation. What would it look like for Christian counselor-researchers to set the tone and lead the way on data-driven practice? To ask questions and conduct formal and informal research prior to determining the type of services we will offer? To submit ourselves to an ongoing feedback loop of program evaluation in an effort to provide the best possible quality of care? Consider how you feel about these ideas. Doesn't it challenge our humility? The upside is huge. We can get to know our neighbors, understand their needs, and meet them with the right offerings at the right time.

We encourage you to further explore needs-assessment tools and program-evaluation models in order to consider how you can build these into your current or future practice. For resources on conducting a community needs assessment, explore the tools provided on the website for the National Council for Mental Wellbeing.[10] Courtney Hughes, Ethan Spana, and Deanna Cada also offer an example of a community-based needs assessment that can be replicated in other locations.[11] To develop your knowledge and skills for program evaluation, we recommend reviewing the work of Randall Astromovich and Kelly Coker, who developed the accountability bridge model for social-service providers.[12] In addition, there are qualitative and logic models of program evaluation that can be used in counseling settings.[13] Of course, this is not an exhaustive list of resources, and we invite you to allow your curiosity to lead you to find additional tools.

Meaning-making. The final trait of the Christian counselor-researcher that we will explore together is that of meaning-making. In chapter five, we described the process of constructing and discovering meaning through qualitative research. Most mental health clinicians resonate quickly with qualitative research because the skills used easily overlap with clinical interviewing skills. In the research process we are often engaging in meaning-making for the purpose of understanding a phenomenon, describing the details of a case study, or forming a theory based on the interpretation of

---

[10]National Council for Mental Wellbeing, "CCBHC Community Needs Assessment Toolkit," February 5, 2024, www.thenationalcouncil.org/resources/ccbhc-community-needs-assessment-toolkit/.

[11]M. Courtney Hughes, Ethan Spana, and Deanna Cada, "Developing a Needs Assessment Process to Address Gaps in a Local System of Care," *Community Mental Health Journal* 58, no. 7 (2022): 1329-37, https://doi.org/10.1007/s10597-022-00940-y.

[12]Randall L. Astramovich and J. Kelly Coker, "Program Evaluation: The Accountability Bridge Model for Counselors," *Journal of Counseling & Development* 85, no. 2 (2007): 162-72, https://doi.org/10.1002/j.1556-6678.2007.tb00459.x.

[13]Thomas M. Murphy, Catherine Y. Chang, and Franco Dispenza, "Qualitative Clinical Mental Health Program Evaluation: Models and Implications for Counseling Practitioners and Educators," *Journal of Mental Health Counseling* 40, no. 1 (2018): 1-13, https://doi.org/10.17744/mehc.40.1.01.

qualitative data across many semistructured interviews. Practicing research that seeks participant meaning provides us a learning laboratory to practice and refine these critical clinical skills. This is necessary because we have found in our clinical work that the meaning-making journey changes with each client as we collaborate with them in the restorative process of helping them come to terms with their life experiences. Just like our research participants, we help our clients develop and articulate the stories they embody as they live amid pain, suffering, anxiety, depression, or traumatic events. Some of these clients also begin to tell these stories to others in a manner that truly blesses them and moves them toward flourishing (as some of our own clients do through ongoing advocacy work and writing to this day).

We recognize and emphasize the importance of meaning-making for the client's process of healing, but that is the more obvious result of this trait in Christian counselor-researchers. There is a second, more subtle byproduct of this meaning-making that weaves together the threads of curiosity, truth seeking, diversity, and assessment that we have highlighted here: your own personal, professional, and spiritual transformation. I (Kristen) have often joked with my clients that counselors sign up for being in hours of daily therapy for life. My engagement in the process of therapy and meaning-making with my clients has changed me, perhaps far more than my services have changed any individual client. We resonate with John Coe and Todd Hall's transformational view of Christian counseling, and we see meaning-making and discovery as central to the spiritual transformation of the counselor-researcher.[14]

---

[14]John H. Coe and Todd W. Hall, *Psychology in the Spirit: Contours of a Transformational Psychology* (IVP Academic, 2010).

As clinicians, we are not exempt from the existential questions that life raises. Rather, we are more likely to remain aware of them as they are often brought to our attention through our clients. Sitting with suffering, exploring the problem of evil, facing death anxiety, identifying a lack of belonging, and wrestling with other existential crises are all in a day's work. Our meaning-making with clients cannot be our first consideration of these ideas. Rather, we have to prepare ourselves through the process of learning and self-examination to be fully present with our clients as they ask deep questions of life. Research and study are essential to prepare for a career filled with daily meaning-making so that we can tolerate, attend to, and slowly ponder a broad range of experiences with our clients. If we have not investigated, tested, and experienced meaning-making processes, we are likely to lead our clients in circles or find the process of meaning-making overwhelming, as many of our clients do. Finally, solid research and evidence-based practice grounds us and reminds us of our role in meaning-making as we accompany our clients.

The characteristics we have described drive us to continually construct, deconstruct, and reconstruct our interpretations and meaning as we allow our clients and the Spirit to change us. Many counselors, even Christians, do not seek to engage in such a process. Some become stuck in therapeutic ruts, and others are simply satisfied with using the knowledge they have gained in their educational programs and supervisory experiences. We invite you to join the exciting process of becoming a Christian counselor-researcher, embodying the fullness of all these traits we have described in order to innovate, grow, and change your practice. In doing so, you will be formed, mature as a leader in the field, and develop into an excellent clinician.

ANCIENT WISDOM AND THE GARDEN OF SHALOM

With all of these traits in mind, we want to return with you to the garden of shalom we explored in chapter one. This garden was a place designed for flourishing, and we discussed the five areas of flourishing: happiness and life satisfaction, mental and physical health, meaning and purpose, character and virtue, and close social relationships.[15] Throughout this book, we have sought to identify the ways in which the research process is entwined with spiritual formation and professional fulfillment. Now, as Christian counselor-researchers in our therapy rooms, we have the opportunity to invite others—our clients—into the sandbox where we can dig together. As we embody the wise mind, supported and expanded by the work of the Spirit, we can flourish as we contextualize our knowledge for the compassionate care of others.

One article exploring the difference between wisdom and knowledge states, "Wisdom takes knowledge and applies it with discernment based on experience, evaluation, and lessons learned."[16] When we sit in the counselor's chair, we have the opportunity to turn the knowledge we have gained through research into life-transforming action. We also have a connection to a spiritual wisdom far more timeless, a wisdom owned and released by Yahweh himself. We see a biblical idea of wisdom personified in the female form in Proverbs 1:20-33. Biblical wisdom represents a higher form of thinking that is neither created by nor possessed by individuals. There is a way in which we as individuals can access, use, or apply wisdom, but we are not owners. In the biblical

---

[15]D. Węziak-Białowolska, E. McNeely, and T. J. VanderWeele, "Human Flourishing in Cross Cultural Settings: Evidence from the US, China, Sri Lanka, Cambodia and Mexico," *Frontiers in Psychology* 10 (2019): 1-13, https://doi.org/10.3389/fpsyg.2019.01269.

[16]"'Wisdom' vs. 'Knowledge': What's the Difference?," Dictionary.com, August 23, 2022, www.dictionary.com/e/wisdom-vs-knowledge/.

understanding, God is described as the one who possesses wisdom and dispenses it to us by way of covenantal relationship.[17]

Job 28 presents a poetic exploration of wisdom. Let's consider Job 28:20-28:

> From where, then, does wisdom come?
>   And where is the place of understanding?
> It is hidden from the eyes of all living
>   and concealed from the birds of the air.
> Abaddon and Death say,
>   "We have heard a rumor of it with our ears."
> God understands the way to it,
>   and he knows its place.
> For he looks to the ends of the earth
>   and sees everything under the heavens.
> When he gave to the wind its weight
>   and apportioned the waters by measure,
> when he made a decree for the rain
>   and a way for the lightning of the thunder,
> then he saw it and declared it;
>   he established it, and searched it out.
> And he said to man,
> "Behold, the fear of the Lord, that is wisdom,
>   and to turn away from evil is understanding."

We see from this text Job's hunger for wisdom. In the midst of personal crisis—a circumstance for which today we would certainly recommend professional counseling—Job is desperate for wisdom. Humans, animals, and birds alike cannot find it. Abaddon (referring to destruction or Sheol) and Death are personified here, and their only connection to wisdom is by way of rumors. Job writes that God alone "understands the way" to wisdom, and even more than that, he "saw it and declared it; he established it, and

---

[17]Tremper Longman III and Peter Enns, *Dictionary of the Old Testament: Wisdom, Poetry and Writings* (InterVarsity Press, 2008), 860.

searched it out." Thus, a fear of the Creator God is the only access we have to unlocking the door of wisdom. Job's friends had represented the best of earthly wisdom and had fallen painfully short, and Job 28 is a transitional moment that paints a contrast of the sages of the ancient world with God himself.[18]

What are we as Christian counselor-researchers to make of this text and other Wisdom literature in the Bible that makes similar points? In the history of the integration debate, some biblical counseling advocates have suggested that secular psychology is most akin to earthly wisdom or worldly philosophies.[19] These won't come close to the power of Scripture and the wisdom God has to offer. Are we better off rejecting psychology and counseling research, forsaking the limited pursuits of earthly knowledge for a higher path? Will our clients, hungry for wisdom in the midst of crises, be better helped by our use of Scripture above evidence-based practices such as third-wave cognitive-behavioral therapy or eye movement desensitization and reprocessing (EMDR)?

We highly recommend a thorough read of *Psychology and Christianity: Five Views*, and we would encourage you to read more by Eric Johnson on Christian wisdom theory as well.[20] Coe and Hall directly answer the preceding questions in their chapter of the book, describing the process by which the wise Christian counselor-researcher observes and discerns truth. They write:

> The Old Testament Wisdom literature provides a biblical model for gaining prescriptions for wisdom from doing science in the broadest and best sense of the word. That is, the Old Testament wise man (a sage) insists that it is possible to discern prescriptions or wisdom for living from observing and

---

[18]Longman and Enns, *Dictionary of the Old Testament*, 338.
[19]David Powlison, *The Biblical Counseling Movement: History and Context* (New Growth, 2010).
[20]Eric L. Johnson, "Gaining Understanding Through Five Views," in *Psychology and Christianity: Five Views*, ed. Eric L. Johnson (IVP Academic, 2010), 293.

reflecting on creation and human persons in their complex situations in real life.[21]

Their assertion, which we affirm here as well, is that we begin in wisdom with a fear of the Lord and continue on in wisdom by our observation and study of the world around us. Or, said differently, we allow the truth of God to lead us into a Christian imaginary–seeing the world through God's eyes. Through this process, we develop greater depth of knowledge and appreciation for the Creator himself and the natural order of his world. As this occurs, we engage with research conducted by both believers and nonbelievers alike, viewing all our understanding as God-given and reflective of some aspect of his created order. The knowledge that we have through research is a gift, one that we are able to contextualize in an applied form with our clients. As they hunger for wisdom in our offices, we can offer them the fullest portion of all God has bestowed.

Engaging in evidence-based practice is a bold, faith-filled statement that you are intentionally connected to a larger world that is both physical and spiritual. Doing this work is a direct way in which we live out our Christian mission. We take part in a restorative process to eliminate bias in research and clinical practice—doing justice. We apply our knowledge wisely for the good of others—loving kindness. We rely on others to inform our actions and believe in a process outside ourselves—walking humbly (Mic 6:8). This is what God requires of the Christian counselor-researcher.

If we want to fully flourish and partake in bringing shalom, we need to embody this wise mind that allows us to fulfill our God-given callings. We will be neither happy nor mentally well if we carry the weight of our practice on our own shoulders. We will not develop in character and virtue if we do not employ justice,

---

[21]John H. Coe and Todd W. Hall, "A Transformational Psychology View," in Johnson, *Psychology and Christianity*, 208.

kindness, and humility in our work as we submit ourselves to God and his truth held in the vast body of research as a daily practice. Staying connected to the field of counseling and our colleagues, we will increase our felt sense of meaning and purpose, which will bolster us on the sometimes rocky journey. How wonderful it is to imagine our clients served not just by us individually but by a "so great a cloud of witnesses" (Heb 12:1) from both our spiritual and scientific ancestors, who all fall under the lordship of Christ.[22]

With this as our foundation, we will now turn to practical examples of Christian counselor-researchers creating and applying evidence-based practices in their work.

The Research Literature and the Collective Unconscious

Carl Jung writes, "The collective unconscious is a part of the psyche which can be negatively distinguished from a personal unconscious by the fact that it does not, like the latter, owe its existence to personal experience and consequently is not a personal acquisition."[a] There are certain instincts and even spiritual realities we all share, seemingly across time and culture, which Jung named *archetypes*. While we could imagine implications for any of Jung's twelve archetypes as we think about the identity of the Christian counselor-researcher, we connect most with his idea of the sage (also called "the wise old man") as we seek to follow our innate instinct toward knowledge and wisdom. We have asserted in this chapter that research is bigger than all of us, and we carry with us into the counseling room a deep and ancient wisdom that connects us to the Spirit and all who have come before us. It is wonderful to see how God's wisdom permeates secular ideas, and Jung's idea of the sage follows similar themes.

Jung explains, "The old man thus represents knowledge, reflection, insight, wisdom, cleverness, and intuition on the one hand, and on the other, moral qualities such as goodwill and readiness to help, which make his 'spiritual' character sufficiently plain."[b] We imagine many Christian readers will see characteristics of the triune God in this description, as well

---

[22]Stanton L. Jones, "An Integration View," in Johnson, *Psychology and Christianity*, 115.

as the biblical female personification of Wisdom we have referenced in this chapter. What if the Christian counselor-researcher identity, as we have been describing it, is one that both draws from a wisdom outside ourselves and seeks to become a source of that wisdom for others? What if we could move past the individualism of American research—perhaps seeking to gain tenure, publishing rights, or great renown—and instead become counselor-researchers with a collectivist framework? With this view, we would rely on this collective unconscious—this spiritual wisdom—to do our work well, and we would also view our research process as one for the common good.

Richard Rohr highlights this idea for the spiritual life when he writes, "When you live [as the True Self] you are somehow 'shared' and participating in Something Larger. You are not doing it; it is being done to you."[c] Rohr goes on to describe the spiritual liberation that comes from simply enjoying life, and in this case the research process, without its needing to contribute to individual advancement. When we give ourselves fully to it, this is the freeing of the self that the research process can offer to us.

What is your view of the Christian counselor-researcher identity? How would you pull together the themes of spiritual formation, compassion, acquisition and application of knowledge, and wisdom? As we explored in chapter one, what would it be like for you to operate as the true self whom Rohr describes? How might you bring the unconscious into the conscious to connect with ancient and God-given wisdom with intentionality and purpose? Our hope for this book is that, rather than providing answers, we present you with ideas that raise more questions for personal and professional exploration and growth. The Holy Spirit and the sage will guide you on your research journey, as they have for us.

[a]Carl Gustav Jung, *The Archetypes and the Collective Unconscious* (Princeton University Press, 1969), 42.
[b]Jung, *Archetypes and the Collective Unconscious*, 222.
[c]Richard Rohr, *The Naked Now: Learning to See as the Mystics See* (Crossroad, 2009), 78.

EXAMPLES OF EVIDENCE-BASED INTEGRATIVE PRACTICE

So, practically speaking, what does applying research in clinical practice look like? We have referred many times to "evidence-based practices," and this is certainly a common term in the counseling field. There are several ways to think about the application of research in clinical practice, and we will provide specific examples in turn. First, we can begin with the Christian tradition and allow our curiosity from this lens to lead us to develop psychologies and counseling approaches. Thus, we would have foundationally Christian evidence-based practices that have been tested via research.

This first way of thinking has been captured by those who hold a "Christian psychology" view, such as Robert C. Roberts and P. J. Watson.[23] A second way of engaging in a Christian integrative process in the application of research to clinical practice is to weave Christian ideas into evidence-based practices for Christian counseling and psychotherapy, including many examples of both ways of thinking.[24] Everett L. Worthington Jr., Eric L. Johnson, and Joshua N. Hook describe several "Christian-accommodative" approaches using CBT or trauma therapies, as well as couples therapy treatments, that were built on Christian foundations of grace and forgiveness. A third approach is to simply use the best research-based strategies without a specific Christian-integrative element, and this is the wisest course of action when working in secular environments, as we uphold the ethical principle to avoid imposing our Christian beliefs on our clients. Finally, we may find that there are many effective clinical strategies that have not yet earned the badge of "evidence-based practice" due to challenges in testing them

---

[23]Robert C. Roberts and P. J. Watson, "A Christian Psychology View," in Johnson, *Psychology and Christianity*, 149-78.
[24]Everett L. Worthington Jr., Eric L. Johnson, and Joshua N. Hook, and Jamie D. Aten, eds., *Evidence-Based Practices for Christian Counseling and Psychotherapy* (IVP Academic, 2013).

via research studies. Some therapeutic approaches, such as CBT, are easy to manualize and research. Other theoretical frameworks, like psychodynamic, person centered, narrative, or existential therapies, may not be as easy to condense into an eight-week study with a formulaic methodology. There is room for wise application of well-established counseling theories, using regular assessment as a means of determining their effectiveness for a particular client. Let's look at some examples in each of these four categories.

Evidence-based practices from Christian psychology. Christian psychology seeks to develop evidence-based counseling interventions that begin from the foundation of the Christian tradition. One excellent example of this comes from Joshua Knabb and colleagues, who developed and evaluated a trauma intervention using the lectio divina approach to meditation on Scripture.[25] In their study, they offered a two-week online trauma-treatment program that used these Christian meditative practices. It is important to note that prior to the development of this intervention, the authors examined the relationships between Christian contentment, Christian gratitude, negative affect, and trauma symptoms. They found that negative affect (measured by the twenty-item Positive and Negative Affect Schedule) mediated the relationship between Christian contentment and trauma symptoms. The study did not find this mediating relationship via Christian gratitude.

Given that finding, Knabb and his team created a meditative intervention focused on increasing spiritual contentment using the lectio divina process with Psalm 34 as a Scripture reading. The study also provided a comparison treatment group, who engaged in a lovingkindness meditation that was not connected to Scripture or Christian tradition. With their Christian sample (about

---

[25]Joshua J. Knabb et al., "Lectio Divina for Trauma Symptoms: A Two-Part Study," *Spirituality in Clinical Practice* 9, no. 4 (2022): 232-52, https://doi.org/10.1037/scp0000303.

two-thirds Protestant and one-third Catholic), these researchers found that trauma symptoms improved significantly with the use of the lectio divina scripturally based meditation, while the loving-kindness meditation group did not have significant improvement of symptoms. They theorized that the difference in improvement related to attachment constructs, namely that Christians would have a strong attachment to God and thus be more helped by a meditation rooted in Christian tradition and Scripture. As with any study, we would not seek to generalize this finding to populations that were not studied (i.e., a Christian-based meditation would be likely to help Christians, but it may not be an evidence-based practice for secular clients or clients of other faiths).

A second example of Christian-derived evidence-based practice comes from the work of Everett Worthington over many decades. He developed and studied the REACH Forgiveness intervention, which outlines a process of Recalling the hurt, Empathizing with the other, Altruistic connection to forgiveness as a gift, Commitment to forgiveness, and Holding onto forgiveness.[26] While this intervention has been adapted for secular settings, the REACH intervention is built on Christian principles and has been tested among various populations. In 2020, Worthington served on a research team led by Loren Toussaint that implemented the intervention with Christian college students (N = 99).[27] This study compared three groups: the REACH forgiveness intervention, the Forgive for Good intervention (a secular approach developed by Fred Luskin), and a control group (no intervention). Both treatment conditions resulted in significant

---

[26]Brian McNeill, "After Four Decades, Everett Worthington, Leading Expert on Forgiveness, Set to Retire from VCU's Department of Psychology," VCU News, April 24, 2017, https://news.vcu.edu/article/after_four_decades_everett_worthington_leading_expert_on_forgiveness.

[27]Loren L. Toussaint, Brandon J. Griffin, Everett L. Worthington, Mitchell Zoelzer, and Frederic Luskin, "Promoting Forgiveness at a Christian College: A Comparison of the REACH Forgiveness and Forgive for Good Methods," *Journal of Psychology & Theology* 48, no. 2 (2020): 154-65, https://doi.org/10.1177/0091647120911109.

decreases in unforgiveness and significant increases in forgiveness (on both forgiveness scales used). The REACH Forgiveness intervention was significantly different from the Forgive for Good intervention only in the area of "emotional forgiveness" at the two-month follow-up measurement. Overall, both interventions were more effective than nonintervention in the control group. In 2024, Worthington and colleagues again demonstrated the effectiveness of the intervention with a much larger sample of 4,598 in five countries outside the United States, and the body of research on this forgiveness intervention continues to grow.[28]

We wish we could say that there are myriad studies such as these that provide evidence for uniquely Christian interventions, but there are not. Some biblical counseling models, particularly nouthetic counseling, have generally resisted engagement in the research process and thus do not have an evidence base for their effectiveness. For example, an EBSCO search for "outcomes biblical counseling" with years ranging from 2009 to 2024 produced zero results. Journals that may contain some studies on biblical counseling models are also frequently not indexed (and thus not present in EBSCO search results and difficult for the average researcher to obtain).

A similar search for "Christian counseling interventions" produced thirty-seven results, with only a handful providing outcomes research for specific treatment interventions. Many of these were coming from researchers in South Korea and the Philippines, which may offer a model for Christian clinicians in the United States to follow. Most often, searches for Christian evidence-based practices lead to established interventions (such as Cognitive Behavioral Therapy or Acceptance and Commitment Therapy) that

---

[28]Man Yee Ho et al., "International REACH Forgiveness Intervention: A Multisite Randomised Controlled Trial," *BMJ Public Health* 2, no. 1 (2024): e000072, https://doi.org/10.1136/bmjph-2023-000072.

have been tested with an integration of Christian ideas. We will continue our exploration of these examples next.

Evidence-based practices with Christian integration. Since the 1950s, Christian psychologists and counselors have been seeking to learn from the breadth of psychology research and integrate the Christian faith in both theoretical and practical ways. There are quite a few examples of Christian-integrated practices that are foundationally similar to the secular versions of the same. We will highlight two such studies in this section, with an encouragement to the reader to search for additional studies like these in the *Journal of Psychology and Christianity, Journal of Psychology and Theology, Journal of Spiritual Formation and Soul Care*, and others. Many laborers have spent their lives devoted to the work of the integration of psychology and Christianity, and we certainly owe them a great debt as we seek to engage in both evidence-based and faith-based work with our clients.

CBT is arguably one of the most researched counseling approaches, with many offshoots that continue to spring up in our modern third-wave era. Christians have formally and informally applied Christian ideas into CBT techniques, a relatively easy idea given the connection between replacing negative thinking and being "transformed by the renewal of your mind" (Rom 12:2). Kristy Ford and Fernando Garzon provide an example of a study that examined the effectiveness of a Christian-accommodative mindfulness technique rooted in third-wave CBT.[29] Note the word *accommodative*, which is frequently used when describing ways that Christian counselors have modified evidence-based treatments for use with Christian populations.

---

[29]Kristy Ford and Fernando Garzon, "Research Note: A Randomized Investigation of Evangelical Christian Accommodative Mindfulness," *Spirituality in Clinical Practice* 4, no. 2 (2017): 92-99, https://doi.org/10.1037/scp0000137.

In their study, Ford and Garzon had two treatment groups: one using CBT mindfulness techniques with Christian adaptation, and the other using only CBT mindfulness techniques. Their sample of Christians (college students, staff, and faculty with a mean age of twenty-seven) participated in three weeks of group treatment in addition to guided exercises at home. These researchers found that the Christian mindfulness intervention significantly improved depression symptoms, while the nonreligious mindfulness did not. Additionally, they noted that the participants in the Christian-accommodative mindfulness group had significantly better treatment adherence than those in the nonreligious treatment group.

Another example of adapting an evidence-based practice for a Christian population was presented by Jennifer Ripley and colleagues.[30] These authors built on the foundation of strategic couples therapy, an approach developed and studied by Jay Haley and others. Incorporating Christian themes of forgiveness, sanctification, prayer, and virtues, Ripley and her team established protocols for hope-focused couples therapy. In this study, they evaluated the effectiveness of their approach by conducting their intervention with couples over six to twelve sessions (mean of 8.79 sessions). Couples could choose to engage in a Christian-based version of the couples therapy or a secular version.

Unlike in prior studies, in which Ripley and others had not found differences (i.e., equally positive outcomes) between the Christian and secular versions of the treatment, this study showed that the couples who chose the Christian approach did not fare quite as well as their secular counterparts.[31] The authors noted that the Christian

---

[30]Jennifer Ripley, Lindsay Solfelt, Anna Ord, Rachel C. Garthe, Everett L. Worthington Jr., and Tiffany Channing, "Short- and Long-Term Outcomes of Hope Focused Couple Therapy," *Spirituality in Clinical Practice* 10, no. 4 (2023): 271-88, https://doi.org/10.1037/scp0000286.

[31]Jennifer S. Ripley and Everett L. Worthington Jr., *Couple Therapy: A New Hope-Focused Approach* (InterVarsity Press, 2014).

clients sometimes displayed an "idealized religious self," meaning that they were trying to manage the perceptions of the counselor and present themselves as good Christians. This observation, discussed in the research team's supervision groups, aligns with the common finding that Christian populations tend to have an elevated Lie Scale on the MMPI-2.[32] We highlight this study to provide you with one of the many complexities in conducting research on Christian populations and Christian evidence-based practices: Sometimes religious behavior can get in the way of treatment.

The studies we have chosen to highlight here provided interesting insights that we felt would be a useful introduction. Note the names throughout the citations in this chapter, as they have been the Christian pioneers leading the way in these lines of research. Worthington, Ripley, Hook, Johnson, McMinn, Jones, Coe, Hall, Knabb, Garzon, and many others have created a pathway for those of us newer to Christian research. Staying connected to the journals we mentioned earlier and attending the annual conference of the Christian Association for Psychological Studies (CAPS) are excellent ways to follow the continued progress of Christian integration research. Some of these authors have also served as personal mentors to us, and for that we acknowledge our thanks.

Evidence-based practices for any setting. We turn now to a few studies that provide an evidence base for counseling interventions that can be used in any setting. Before we dive in, we remind you to always consider the population represented in the research sample prior to applying these strategies to your clients. Too often, clinicians tout "evidence-based practices" as if such a label meant that the treatment approach had a permanent and

---

[32]Keith Marlett, Lee A. Wetherbee, and Anthony Donofrio, "Normative MMPI-2 Profiles of Christian Counseling Students: An Investigation of Subculture in Standardized Testing," *Pastoral Psychology* 61, no. 1 (2012): 71-83, https://doi.org/10.1007/s11089-011-0373-4.

extensive reach with few limits. Even in the realm of evidence-based interventions, we always need to examine which populations have been studied along with understanding the exact protocols of the intervention. Unfortunately, we have also encountered clinicians who claim to use evidence-based practices such as dialectical behavior therapy (DBT), CBT, or ACT but do little more than basic talk therapy with an occasional exercise or worksheet. We would encourage you to follow these interventions in the ways they have been studied with the types of clients for whom they have proven effective. Where there is a need for additional research, we encourage you to use your career to add to our body of knowledge with underrepresented populations and innovative counseling strategies.

We begin this section with a study comparing the effectiveness of CBT and emotion-focused therapy (EFT) in helping clients with emotional expression among those with mild to moderate depression.[33] These authors used treatment protocols from Aaron Beck and Ruth Greenberg, who each developed these approaches, respectively. This study supported the findings of many earlier studies that both of these evidence-based treatments were effective with this primarily female, Portuguese population. Their participants (twenty-six in the CBT group and twenty-four in the EFT group) all increased in their engagement with emotional processing and decreased their depression symptoms, while the outcomes between the groups did not significantly differ. We'd like to point out that sometimes in research, a nonsignificant result is actually a positive sign. In this case, as with many others, a treatment approach that is not significantly different from CBT

---

[33]Patrícia Pinheiro, Miguel M. Gonçalves, Inês Sousa, and João Salgado, "What Is the Effect of Emotional Processing on Depression? A Longitudinal Study," *Psychotherapy Research* 31, no. 4 (2021): 507-19. https://doi.org/10.1080/10503307.2020.1781951.

shows excellent promise given the well-substantiated effectiveness of CBT. In this study, not only do we see the general effectiveness of the treatments, but we have an additional population (Portuguese women) for whom these have been shown to be useful.

Another study evaluated the effectiveness of DBT with adolescents in a partial hospitalization program (PHP).[34] Data were collected between 2019 and 2022 on teens who participated in the PHP, and out of 205 clients served the researchers were able to use 146 for their sample. The PHP consisted of multiple groups per day, all based on the principles of DBT (i.e., mindfulness, distress tolerance, emotion regulation, and interpersonal effectiveness). The researchers measured outcomes using the Depression, Anxiety, and Stress Scale (DASS-21) along with additional scales rating suicidality, coping skills, and mindfulness. The teen population showed significant improvement on every measure after twenty days of DBT group interventions. This study adds to the literature demonstrating the effectiveness of DBT with a variety of clinical populations.

Finally, exposure and response prevention (ERP) is highly regarded as the gold standard of evidence-based treatment for obsessive-compulsive disorder (OCD).[35] As new technologies emerge, clinicians and researchers are testing innovative adaptations for this intervention. One such study from a group of Iranian researchers examined the effectiveness of using virtual reality to simulate exposure therapy as compared with the standard in vivo approach.[36] Using an adult population with a clinical diagnosis of

---

[34] Esther S. Tung, Kristen L. Batejan, Caroline Johnson, Peggy M. Worden, and Alan E. Fruzzetti, "Effectiveness of DBT Partial Hospitalization Program for Adolescents and Young Adults," *Counseling Outcome Research & Evaluation* 15, no. 2 (2024): 123-42, https://doi.org/10.1080/2150 1378.2024.2342590.

[35] Dianne M. Hezel and H. Blair Simpson, "Exposure and Response Prevention for Obsessive-Compulsive Disorder: A Review and New Directions," *Indian Journal of Psychiatry* 61, suppl. 1 (January 2019): S85-92, https://doi.org/10.4103/psychiatry.IndianJPsychiatry_516_18.

[36] Razieh Javaherirenani, Seyede Salehe Mortazavi, Mohammadreza Shalbafan, Ahmad Ashouri, and Abbas Ramezani Farani, "Virtual Reality Exposure and Response Prevention in the

OCD, the researchers randomly assigned the twenty-nine participants to one of the two groups. The intervention protocols for the two groups were similar, except for the use of virtual reality to present "contaminated environment" scenarios. The control group participated in the usual in vivo exposures within a real-world environment.

These researchers found significant differences in the improvement of OCD symptoms, with the virtual reality group outperforming the in vivo group. They theorized that the immersive nature of virtual reality created a more effective strategy for working through distressing exposures in a hierarchy over time. Certainly, there are many more studies to come on how innovative uses of technology can improve on the success of evidence-based treatments.

Theoretical approaches to use with regular assessment. There are many effective counseling strategies that are being used daily by clinicians, yet they have not made their way into the research literature. While we support the use of evidence-based techniques, we do not believe that research fully represents every useful approach to counseling. Notice in the prior sections how many of the studies tested interventions that were in some way built on the concepts of CBT. This does not necessarily mean that CBT is the most effective treatment modality, but it is widely researched due to the ease of creating treatment protocols within this theoretical framework. For psychodynamic, humanistic, or existential treatments, that is not the case. In this final section highlighting outcomes-focused research, we will discuss studies that demonstrate promising clinical strategies yet lack a treatment manual or protocol that can be easily tested. These studies have a strong

---

Treatment of Obsessive-Compulsive Disorder in Patients with Contamination Subtype in Comparison with in Vivo Exposure Therapy: A Randomized Clinical Controlled Trial," *BMC Psychiatry* 22, no. 1 (2022): 1-16, https://doi.org/10.1186/s12888-022-04402-3.

foundation in psychological theories that have long been examined by research, even if they did not provide a specific within-subjects or between-groups analysis. We have already encouraged you to use regular assessment as a normal part of your clinical practice to determine for yourself the effectiveness of your strategies with your clients. With that in mind, let's explore some research on nonmanualized counseling treatments.

A systematic review of narrative counseling offers a wide-angle view of studies that have been done on this treatment modality. In this case, the population of the authors' focus is those with eating disorders.[37] In the title of their paper, Janet Conti and colleagues highlight the exact issue we are describing in this section: There is evidence-based practice and "practice-based evidence." Counselors using this treatment approach know that it works, but the evidence has not yet run through the scientific rigor of the peer-reviewed research process. Here the authors conclude from the thirty-three identified studies in the meta-review that narrative therapy has shown promise in its efficacy for treating eating disorders. However, they also conclude that more research is needed to truly place this approach into the category of evidence-based practice. Most of the studies in their search relied on participant descriptions rather than outcomes-driven data. This lack of outcomes research is true for many populations and many counseling interventions, and as counselor-researchers we can heed this call in the literature and work to add more outcomes studies to the body of knowledge.

---

[37] Janet Conti, Lauren Heywood, Phillipa Hay, Rebecca Makaju Shrestha, and Tania Perich, "Paper 2: A Systematic Review of Narrative Therapy Treatment Outcomes for Eating Disorders—Bridging the Divide Between Practice-Based Evidence and Evidence-Based Practice," *Journal of Eating Disorders* 10, no. 1 (2022): 1-9, https://doi.org/10.1186/s40337-022-00636-4.

A second example of promising research on theoretically based interventions comes from a research team in Italy who studied the use of psychodynamic therapy with children and adolescents.[38] Psychodynamic counseling approaches have been very hard to include in evidence-based research with any population due to the challenges of creating specific protocols to conduct a therapy that is inherently built on a dynamic process. However, these researchers provide an example of outcomes research using psychodynamic principles and comparing two groups: individual therapy versus therapy with added family support.

The study presents a couple of challenges that make it difficult to generalize. First, other than a one-sentence description of the aims of brief psychodynamic therapy on page 4, the article does not provide a way for future researchers to replicate their methods. They write, "This psychotherapeutic model is based on some key principles: (a) attention to the client-therapist relationship; (b) the therapist has an active role during treatment; (c) identification of a specific problem; (d) therapies have a time-limit and a fixed number of sessions." How would we continue to test the effectiveness of psychodynamic therapy with such a limited definition? Second, their two groups had statistically significant differences at baseline, making it impossible to compare their outcomes. Both groups had significant improvement, whether receiving therapy with or without parental involvement. Thus, the study helps us understand that the treatment was effective for each group, yet leaves us wondering more about their methodology.

---

[38] Michela Gatta, Marina Miscioscia, Lorenza Svanellini, Andrea Spoto, Manuela Difronzo, Maxim de Sauma, and Emilia Ferruzza, "Effectiveness of Brief Psychodynamic Therapy with Children and Adolescents: An Outcome Study," *Frontiers in Pediatrics* 7 (December 2019): 501, https://doi.org/10.3389/fped.2019.00501.

We will conclude our exploration of evidence-based practice with a final theoretical article regarding the concept of "existential empathy."[39] Existential therapy is an excellent example of a difficult-to-define (and therefore difficult to research) treatment modality. Likewise, empathy as a construct is challenging to quantify and measure. The author here discusses these concepts broadly within both existential and humanistic frameworks. The idea of the therapist simply "being" with the client—how do we conduct outcomes research on such an intervention? By what methods would we truly determine whether each clinician had done the "being" correctly? Similarly, how do we measure outcomes of improvement when clients come to therapy with existential concerns? Would we assess a resolution to the concern, or a decrease in a specific symptom, or increases in certain spiritual formation processes?

The author points to several qualitative studies in which the clients are able to freely name points of existential concern that improved for them. While they were not provided with Irvin Yalom's core existential questions, they were able to identify areas of improvement that directly aligned with his ideas. Siebrecht Vanhooren provides some description for clinicians who wish to practice—or research—existential empathy:

> Existential empathy opens the possibility for the client to experience and explore their existential concerns in a safe therapeutic relationship. Through existential empathy, the therapist helps the client to be with their most intimate concerns that are at the same time the deepest struggles of humankind. The therapist helps the client to stay with this concern, to fully sense it, and to find words or other symbols that express how the client experiences their existential struggles in the here-and-now.[40]

---

[39]Siebrecht Vanhooren, "Existential Empathy: The Challenge of 'Being' in Therapy and Counseling," *Religions* 13, no. 8 (2022): 1-11, https://doi.org/10.3390/rel13080752.
[40]Vanhooren, "Existential Empathy," 5.

While this is certainly not as airtight as a manualized treatment, it is possible to build a research protocol around such a definition and conduct outcomes research to determine the effects of existential empathy. Indeed, many have studied the broader elements of therapy that make it effective regardless of the intervention (often known as *common factors*). Regardless of our theoretical frameworks or specific treatment modalities, the body of literature points to the effectiveness of counseling on the whole. For this reason, we caution the exclusive use of evidence-based practices in the counseling room but encourage the Christian counselor-researcher to maintain an objective eye when doing their work with clients. Remaining rooted and grounded in research helps both when you are following the protocols of a specific evidence-based practice and when you are employing theoretically based strategies that have been more broadly developed in research.

LIFELONG HABITS FOR RESEARCH-BASED CLINICAL PRACTICE

As we have advocated throughout this book, we believe that when a counselor remains consistently connected to research, they support their effectiveness, act strategically, and grow in wisdom. For most master's-level counselors, this looks like being a regular consumer of research, applying what you learn from research in the ways we described in the previous section, and engaging in ongoing assessment of your clients. One effective way to stay connected is to join one or two professional organizations that provide a published academic journal at least quarterly. Most likely, you will receive each issue digitally, as fewer organizations continue to print paper copies without additional cost to you. It is important for you to develop a personal strategy for how you can read and integrate the information from the digital journals. We suggest finding a device that you use frequently, such as your phone, tablet, or computer, and creating a file specifically for these digital issues. If you want to digest the information slowly, set a reminder on your phone or schedule a time in your monthly calendar when you will read one to two articles at a time. When you read the articles, take notes and ask yourself, What else does this make me curious about? Challenge yourself to look up one or two of the more recent references to expand your knowledge on the topic even further. You might not do that for every article, but choose one to two per year that spark your curiosity and take you deeper.

In addition to reading articles, you will also need to engage in continuing education if you have any type of professional license. Seek out opportunities that train you on evidence-based practices and specific research-based counseling skills. Some of these trainings also offer certifications that can be useful to you in communicating your skills to clients. Of course, both consuming research and engaging in clinical training on evidence-based practices can be done in a community of peers who spur you on. Remain curious and connected to colleagues with whom you can talk about your observations with your clients and their progress. Read articles together and discuss them, or attend continuing education training, workshops, and conferences together. Wonder aloud together, innovate, and challenge yourselves to remain in the mindset and characteristics of a Christian counselor-researcher.

EMDR: A Story of Counselor-Researcher Innovation

You never know what might happen when a counselor goes for a walk. According to the EMDR Institute, this very common form of exercise sparked an idea for Francine Shapiro in 1987.[a] As she walked in a park, Shapiro began to notice that her unpleasant feelings about distressing memories decreased with physical activity. That led her to wonder whether movement or stimulation on both sides of the body would help clients process traumatic memories more successfully. Her researcher hat went on, and she tested her theory, ultimately noting that stimulation by itself was not enough to improve symptoms. Over the next few years, Shapiro added additional cognitive therapy components to the treatment approach and named it Eye Movement Desensitization (EMD). She published a case study and later a controlled trial in 1989 that demonstrated the effectiveness of one to five sessions of the treatment.

Shortly after, other researchers began to run experiments with EMD and other forms of treatment, finding that the intervention was as effective as other established counseling methods. The advantage, however, was in the short length of EMD treatment versus other treatments that may need sixteen or more sessions on average. By 1990, Shapiro was beginning to train other mental health clinicians and present her research findings at conferences. The next year, EMD was renamed EMDR, adding the idea of reprocessing memories as a key component of the treatment.

By 1992, Shapiro established the EMDR Institute and held the first EMDR conference. Throughout the mid-nineties, Shapiro and others continued to conduct and publish randomized clinical trials using EMDR protocols. She also wrote a textbook, which she later updated in 2001. These research studies examined the effectiveness of EMDR in veteran populations as well as civilian populations with trauma symptoms. By 2004, the American Psychiatric Association deemed EMDR as an "effective treatment" for trauma. Shapiro has received numerous awards for her work, and EMDR has been adopted worldwide as a gold standard of treatment for PTSD. Just before her passing in 2019, Shapiro published a third edition of her textbook. The EMDR Institute carries on her work to this day.

Shapiro's life is an inspiration for counselor-researchers as we think about the intersection of our everyday lives, our clinical work, and research. As we discussed in chapter one, research stems from the things we wonder about. Innovative treatments can develop from our observations of ourselves and our clients as we go about our daily lives. Imagine if Shapiro had simply gone home and never taken action on her spark of an idea. Or perhaps she could have tried out her ideas on a handful of clients and found that it helped them. She could have even just published one study and felt proud of her accomplishment. Instead, Shapiro chased this idea and caught the attention of others who were able to study her method as well. She diligently wrote, presented at conferences, established training, and devoted her life to the idea. For nearly thirty-five years she labored as both a clinician and a researcher, and her impact on the counseling field has been profound. Perhaps few of us will be as wide reaching as Francine Shapiro, but her story illustrates the possibilities when we lean into curiosity.

[a]"History of EMDR," EMDR Institute, January 3, 2024, www.emdr.com/history-of-emdr/#timeline.

Some of you will continue on to doctoral studies and become producers of research. Within a doctoral program you will begin this pursuit, and we hope you continue to contribute to the body of literature through research in an ongoing way throughout your career. I (Kristen) recall a mentor of mine telling me while I was in my doctoral program that I would have to find my own balance of teaching, clinical work, and research. She said, "I find that you can't really do all of those roles at once. You have to choose." I did not want to hear that at the time, and in the first few years of my career as a professor I tried to maintain a clinical practice and a research agenda on top of my full-time teaching job. However, as my career has advanced and I have taken on a program director role in addition to leading the university's Institutional Review Board, I have had to significantly cut back on working with clients. This decision has not been easy, and in part I struggle with the idea that I have so much more knowledge now with less ability to apply it in the clinical setting.

For many of us, it is a balancing act to determine which roles will be larger or smaller at various phases of our lives. It is often true that we cannot serve in every role. We use wisdom and seek God's leading to best use all our gifts in different ways for his work at all stages of our careers. Again, we remind you and ourselves that we are each just one small part of a much larger whole. Regardless of the distribution of our work responsibilities at any given time, we can allow the Spirit to transform us and shape us as we play our part in producing, consuming, teaching, or applying research in the counseling field.

CONCLUSION

As we come to the end of this book, we encourage you to pause once again and sit with God and with yourself. Ask yourself the questions we asked at the beginning of chapter one: Who is God, and who are we as humans? How might our relationship with God influence our approach to research? What is God's intention for you even in this first step of your research path? We hope that some of your thoughts have become more fully fleshed out as you have read this volume. We hope that you have felt inspired to engage in the research process with your whole self, and have learned more about what that might mean for you on your spiritual journey. We invite you now to pray a final prayer with us as you continue to keep the ideas in this book alive in your soul.

> O God! Who enlightens every person that comes into this world, we ask You to enlighten our hearts and minds with the splendour of your grace: that all our thoughts and works may be worthy and pleasing to Your Majesty and that we may love You truly and serve You faithfully.[41]

DISCUSSION QUESTIONS

1. Share your insights from this chapter and from this book as a whole. What has most stood out to you as you have read? How have your thoughts changed and developed throughout your reading?

---

[41]Evelyn Underhill, *Evelyn Underhill's Prayer Book* (SPCK, 2018), 70.

2. Do you personally identify with the title "Christian counselor-researcher"? Why or why not?
3. Which of the Christian counselor-researcher traits do you most fully embody? Which one is a growth area for you? What is one step you could take to foster growth?
4. What were your reactions to the idea of building on biblical wisdom through applying research? If you are familiar with the five views, which resonate most with you?
5. Which of the four types of evidence-based practices do you intend to use most in your clinical work? What specific techniques would you like to study more directly?
6. What is one specific habit you want to establish and maintain throughout your career to stay connected to research?

LEARNING ACTIVITIES

1. In groups of three to four, identify at least three professional organizations to which you might choose to belong. Write down which ones offer a scholarly journal and answer the following questions about each:
    a. What is the name of the journal?
    b. What types of articles are published?
    c. How often is a new issue released?
    d. In what formats is it available?
    e. Which devices are best for downloading and/or viewing the articles?
    f. Does the organization offer a student rate? (If so, now is the time to join!)
2. Individually or in small groups, find one original research study from the past ten years not mentioned in this book that

provides evidence of the effectiveness of a clinical strategy. After reading the entire article, answer the following questions:

a. What were the characteristics of the population in the study? To whom could this clinical intervention be applied?
b. What theoretical framework serves as the foundation for the clinical intervention?
c. What were the strengths and weaknesses of the research design and methodology?
d. What types of analyses were used in the study, and do you believe they were robust enough? Was the sample size adequate?
e. Could you replicate the study's intervention in your own clinical practice? If not, what additional information would you need to apply the findings of the study?

Index

action research, 195-97
ANOVA, 137-38
    F-tests, 138
assimilation, 37-39
assumptions, 56-60
attachment, 17, 21, 54-55, 91-92
attunement, 171-72
authenticity, 168-69
biopsychosocial-spiritual, 100-102
bracketing, 89-90
care, caring, 76, 80-81, 98, 103
    See also values
case study, 193-95
central limit theorem, 116
coding, 177
cognitive-behavioral therapy, 141
collective unconscious, 223-24
compassion, 169-71
constructivist, constructivism, 62-65, 69
correlation, 129
critical realism, 64-65
culture, 85-89, 106, 109, 111
curiosity, 9-13, 33-34, 38-40, 100, 105, 206-8
descriptive statistics, 118, 122
discernment, 72
diversity, 78-82, 84, 96-100
emic, 165
epistemology, 51, 61-62
ethical, 78, 121
ethics, 81, 84, 103, 138
ethnocentrism, 86-87
ethnography, 186-89
evidence-based, 110
experimental design, 137
factor analysis, 132, 148
family, 91
flourishing, 13-27
formation, 103, 148, 154
    spiritual, 204-6, 219
generalizations, 64
gratitude, 136-37
grounded theory, 190-93

humility, 39, 72, 104-5, 109, 134-36
hypothesis, 62-63, 67
imaginary, 43-48, 52-59, 65, 71-72, 82, 85, 96, 164-66
    social, 43, 100, 103
    See also story
instruments, 108-9
interpretation, 111, 161, 165
interventions, 110-11
Jesus (as model), 22, 27, 31-32, 44-46, 166-97, 200, 210
learning, 38
levels of explanation, 56-57
mainstreaming, 87-88, 106
meaning-making, 177-78, 200-202
member checking, 111
methodology, 53-54, 61
mixed methods, 65, 107
multicultural competence, 107-8
narrative, 179-82
normal distribution, 116
norming, 108, 110
objective measure, 67
ontology, 49, 51
participant, 109
parts of self, 27-30, 35
peer review, 134
persuasive pattern of truth, 67, 71
phenomenology, 182-86
Piaget, Jean, 39
positivist, positivism, 61-62, 65-67
power, 107
qualitative, 65-66, 69-71, 107, 160-62, 164, 199-200
    methods, 178
quantitative, 65-68, 71, 107, 115
    methods, 137
questions, 163, 167-68, 172-74, 176-77
redemptive, 45-6
regression, 149
    logistic, 152
relativism, 49-50, 52

reliability, 68
research agenda, 19, 34, 42, 57, 107, 149, 166
research data, 111
research design, 141
research method, 107
research question, 76
responding, 174-76
schema, 38-39, 72
secular naturalism, 49-50, 59
shalom, 4, 13
sin, 83, 92
statistical analysis, 67
story, 44, 82, 96, 100, 159-60
    Christian, 45-46, 81-85, 107
synthesis, 177-78
Taylor, Charles, 43
theistic naturalism, 51-52

trustworthiness, 71
truth, 48
t-test, 138, 147
type I error, 145
type II error, 142
validity, 68
values, 76, 80-81, 83, 88, 165
values conflict, 89
variables, 105
    predictor, 151
variance, 67
virtue, 19-22
Vygotsky, Lev, 40
Watson, Paul, 57-58
wisdom, 107, 130, 132, 144-45, 151, 166, 185, 204-5, 209, 219-23
within-subjects, 143

*An Association for Christian Psychologists,
Therapists, Counselors and Academicians*

CAPS is a vibrant Christian organization with a rich tradition. Founded in 1956 by a small group of Christian mental health professionals, chaplains and pastors, CAPS has grown to more than 2,100 members in the U.S., Canada and more than 25 other countries.

CAPS encourages in-depth consideration of therapeutic, research, theoretical and theological issues. The association is a forum for creative new ideas. In fact, their publications and conferences are the birthplace for many of the formative concepts in our field today.

CAPS members represent a variety of denominations, professional groups and theoretical orientations; yet all are united in their commitment to Christ and to professional excellence.

CAPS is a non-profit, member-supported organization. It is led by a fully functioning board of directors, and the membership has a voice in the direction of CAPS.

CAPS is more than a professional association. It is a fellowship, and in addition to national and international activities, the organization strongly encourages regional, local and area activities which provide networking and fellowship opportunities as well as professional enrichment.

To learn more about CAPS, visit www.caps.net.

The joint publishing venture between IVP Academic and CAPS aims to promote the understanding of the relationship between Christianity and the behavioral sciences at both the clinical/counseling and the theoretical/research levels. These books will be of particular value for students and practitioners, teachers and researchers.

For more information about CAPS Books, visit InterVarsity Press's website at www.ivpress.com/christian-association-for-psychological-studies-books-set.

Finding the Textbook You Need

The IVP Academic Textbook Selector
is an online tool for instantly finding the IVP books
suitable for over 250 courses across 24 disciplines.

ivpacademic.com